Creative Development

Also by Robert Kelly

Educating for Creativity: A Global Conversation (2012)

*Creative Expression, Creative Education: Creativity as a
Primary Rationale for Education* (co-edited with Carl Leggo, 2008)

Creative Development

Transforming Education through Design
Thinking, Innovation, and Invention

ROBERT KELLY

Brush Education Inc.
www.brusheducation.ca
contact@brusheducation.ca

Editorial: Laurie Thomas, Nicholle Carrière

Cover and Interior Design: Carol Dragich, Dragich Design; Cover images: paint can: Sergey Nivens, iStock; yellow background: andipantz, iStock

Research: Erin Quinn, Stephanie Bartlett

Graphics, illustrations, and photos: Robert Kelly, Melina Cusano, Erin Quinn, Stephanie Bartlett, Danny Cooper, Keith Christensen, Ashley Pannakkal, Mary Ann Reyes, Deeter Schurig, Carla-Jayne Samuelson, Jasmine Johal, Design for Change, The Etude Group

Library and Archives Canada Cataloguing in Publication

Creative development : transforming education though design thinking, innovation, and invention / edited by Robert Kelly.

Includes bibliographical references.

Issued in print and electronic formats.
ISBN 978-1-55059-668-7 (paperback).—ISBN 978-1-55059-669-4 (pdf).
ISBN 978-1-55059-670-0 (mobi).—ISBN 978-1-55059-671-7 (epub).

1. Creative ability—Study and teaching. 2. Creative thinking—Study and teaching. 3. Creative teaching. 4. Effective teaching. 5. Learning. I. Kelly, Robert W., author, editor

LB1590.5.C74 2016   370.15'7   C2016–903483–6
                                      C2016–903484–4

We acknowledge the support of the Government of Canada
Nous reconnaissons l'appui du gouvernement du Canada | Canadä

Contents

Acknowledgements

We acknowledge and appreciate the support of Alberta Education for funding the research, development, and production of this volume through a conditional grant.

We would like to thank all of the contributors to this book who gave freely of their time despite busy schedules and deadlines to share their passion for creativity in educational practice and the transformation of education.

We would also like to thank the professional educators who are also graduate students in education at the University of Calgary and the University of Manitoba who participated in both the Creative Development and Design Thinking for Innovation prototype programs and courses as creative co-designers and co-adventurers and who made this volume possible.

INTRODUCTION

The Concept of Creative Development

ROBERT KELLY

Education as Creative Practice, Not Consumptive Practice

Let's begin on the waters of Loch Long in Scotland. British conceptual artist Simon Starling is staging an event on the loch entitled *Autoxylopyrocycloboros* (2006). The work takes the form of a voyage in a twenty-foot-long wooden boat called *Dignity* that had been previously recovered from the bottom of Loch Long and completely refurbished. Starling fitted the boat with a single-cylinder marine steam engine. The artist, accompanied by a collaborator, embarks on a voyage in this small, steam-powered vessel, using wood from the boat itself as fuel. They feed wooden pieces and planks pried from the boat one bit at a time into the engine's boiler until the *Dignity* is no longer seaworthy, reaching a point where it sinks and returns to the bottom of the loch. Not to worry—both boat occupants are wearing life jackets!

Autoxylopyrocycloboros can be interpreted metaphorically in many ways. A self-destructive preoccupation with consumption seems to stand out. This is an apt metaphor for traditional mainstream educational practice and its preoccupation with the consumption of curricular content and the assessment of a student's capacity to restate or retell this content as measures of successful educational practice. Despite the best efforts of many involved in present-day, industrial/factory-informed school structures to engage students to learn, the inertia of this highly consumptive-intense educational model skews many well-intended, new, innovative educational initiatives into servants of the consumption juggernaut. Green (as cited in Cheek, 2015) argues that this inertia has a way of gobbling up innovations and stripping them of their most transformative elements, leaving these systems intact—impervious to deep and lasting change. Cheek adds that these educational structures have remained relatively stable while large-scale societal changes have significantly altered learning needs. Waks (2014) and Leadbeater (2008) argue that this model, taken for granted by many as what education is supposed to be, has outlived its usefulness. They further argue that the time has passed for attempting to retrofit new tools to old educational processes. The time has come to open the floodgates to collaborative, creative work accessible through the Internet and innumerable networking and interactive channels with implications for new ways of educational practice. The current educational structures, which are predominantly consumption intense, are not sustainable against the backdrop of significant social and cultural change.

Creative Development: Transforming Education through Design Thinking, Innovation, and Invention presents educational practice as a creativity-intense practice as opposed to a consumption-intense practice. Implicit here is an educational imperative that educational design has to enable collaborative, creative environments that go well beyond equipping learners and educators with discipline competency. Educational design must shift toward a learner and educator disposition that emphasizes creative design practice characterized by learning through engagement in original research, production, and action. A disposition speaks to the tendency to act in a certain manner under given circumstances, or when something is dispositional in nature that there is an increased likelihood that effective actions will be taken when confronted with problematic situations (Costa & Kallick, 2014). This would apply to problems that are both extrinsically and intrinsically generated. What is the educational sense of equipping both learners and educators with discipline content knowledge without a corresponding disposition that enables the initiation of new learning through problem setting and ultimately innovation and invention?

If we practise something often enough, we will eventually do that action or sequence of actions well, whether it is a positive or a detrimental action. In sports, it is common to engrain bad technique through inappropriate practice. In education, if we engage educators and learners for the majority of time in the consumption and demonstration of any type of memorization or internalization of discipline content, we can get good at doing just that. However, we cannot assume that this type of practice implies that someone will automatically be proficient at engaging in creative practice for innovation and invention. We cannot assume that this type of practice leads to the development of intrinsically motivated creative problem setters and problem solvers. To develop competency in creative practice, educational design must encompass systematic, longitudinal creative development that ultimately enables student-initiated innovation and invention to be practised on a continual basis. This has profound implications for the role of the teacher and teacher education as educators move from more traditional teacher-centric roles to teacher-as-designer roles. As designers, educators create and facilitate learning experiences and learning environments for students engaged in diverse creative practice in an interconnected global culture (Kalantzis & Cope, 2010).

Original Research, Production, and Action

Let's now move to Iceland. I recently visited the newly created LungA School, an innovative school of arts and creativity for applicants 18 years and over from around the globe. During a driving, mid-September rainstorm, I arrived in Egilsstadir, a major administrative center in eastern Iceland. As I got out of the aircraft and approached the tiny terminal my excitement grew as I could see the smiling face of Jonatan Speljborg, one of the creators of the new LungA School in the tiny village of Seydisfjördur at the end of a long fjord, about a 30-minute drive from Egilsstadir.

I had met with Jonatan two and a half years earlier in my office at my home university in Calgary in western Canada. Jonatan had been at the Banff Centre and had been directed to me by a mutual colleague to discuss a school he was planning to start that had a focus on creativity. The concept of his proposed LungA School was fascinating for me at the time because of its central focus on creativity in educational practice. It was even more exciting to be actually visiting the school, now up and running with secured government funding, after following it through its developmental stages from concept to form.

However, what was most intriguing to me about the first visit with Jonatan was the context in which this initiative came about. At the time Jonatan was in his third year at the Kaospilot, a private university of enterprise and design in Aarhus, Denmark. Jonatan is also from Denmark. The LungA school initiative was a third-year culminating project created by Jonatan and two of his Kaospilot colleagues. Here was a third-year university student collaborating to create a new school in another country! I immediately reflected on what typical third-year university students in North America would be doing in their normal course of studies. Engaging in original research and production at this level is not the norm, with the focus typically on engaging discipline complexity development.

A question arises: "Where in K to postsecondary education is educational design and practice conducive to innovation through student-initiated original research and corresponding original action and production?" In Kelly (2012), Adam Royalty of Stanford's d.school contends that almost all of what students do is work on problems that have already been solved. The need for discipline understanding is certainly essential in engaging in creative practice. However, he goes on to question why we don't trust learners to come up with original problem-solving solutions and why we typically wait in formal education until someone reaches graduate school or has lived a substantial portion of their lives before we engage in original research and production.

Let's now move to Bhutan in the eastern Himalayas, a country bordering China and India. Kiran Sethi's global Design for Change initiative out of Ahmedabad, India, empowers learners as young as eight years old to originate school- and community-based problems and to engage in actions to solve these problems. The children at Ragatung Primary School in the Chukha area of Bhutan had a major safety issue along their walk to and from their school. Their daily journey was an hour and a half each way and took the children along topography that had potentially dangerous steep drop-offs alongside the pathway. This daily route to school also had some potentially dangerous obstructions. Through the Design for Change lens, a group of students at this school engaged the community and recruited the necessary expertise to construct a lengthy bamboo fence along the pathway to ensure the safety of the students on their daily trek. They cleaned up and reduced many of the pathway obstructions to effect change for the benefit of everyone. This is only one example from a vast sea of Design for Change young learner initiatives from around the globe. These learners apply design thinking to a wide range of problems, including environmental concerns and human rights issues. The Design for Change method and more examples are featured in Creating Development 4—Design Thinking for Change.

Creative Development: Transforming Education through Design Thinking, Innovation, and Invention is designed to equip educators with theory, strategies, and tactics that enable the creation of educational spaces that are conducive to student-instigated original research and production at any level of education and across the discipline spectrum. These educational environments are characterized by a focus on systematic creative development, enabling learners and educators to engage in increasingly more complex levels of creative practice over time.

A Global Perspective

Now that we have a foundation from which to understand creativity-intense education, let's look at challenges that lie ahead, from a global perspective, to issues that will require an incredible amount of innovation and invention. The United Nations' (2015) Resolution 70/1 *Transforming Our World: The 2030 Agenda for Sustainable Development* put forward the following goals outlined in Table 1.

TABLE 1: U.N. AGENDA FOR SUSTAINABLE DEVELOPMENT GOALS

Goal 1	End poverty in all its forms everywhere
Goal 2	End hunger, achieve food security and improved nutrition and promote sustainable agriculture
Goal 3	Ensure healthy lives and promote well-being for all at all ages
Goal 4	Ensure inclusive and equitable quality education and promote lifelong learning opportunities for all
Goal 5	Achieve gender equality and empower all women and girls
Goal 6	Ensure availability and sustainable management of water and sanitation for all
Goal 7	Ensure access to affordable, reliable, sustainable and modern energy for all
Goal 8	Promote sustained, inclusive and sustainable economic growth, full and productive employment and decent work for all
Goal 9	Build resilient infrastructure, promote inclusive and sustainable industrialization and foster innovation
Goal 10	Reduce inequality within and among countries
Goal 11	Make cities and human settlements inclusive, safe, resilient and sustainable
Goal 12	Ensure sustainable consumption and production patterns
Goal 13	Take urgent action to combat climate change and its impacts
Goal 14	Conserve and sustainably use the oceans, seas and marine resources for sustainable development
Goal 15	Protect, restore and promote sustainable use of terrestrial ecosystems, sustainably manage forests, combat desertification, and halt and reverse land degradation and halt biodiversity loss
Goal 16	Promote peaceful and inclusive societies for sustainable development, provide access to justice for all and build effective, accountable and inclusive institutions at all levels
Goal 17	Strengthen the means of implementation and revitalize the global partnership for sustainable development

Implicit in these comprehensive goals is the need for educational design and practice that enables the development of a disposition of creative design. That disposition is required to initiate original research and production that will lead to innovation and invention. Costa and Kallick (2014) contend that, going forward, this will necessitate the transformation of educational design and practice from a content-oriented, subject-centred, test-driven framework to a view of education being dispositional in nature. They recognize that students will likely have to invent or reimagine their vocation more often than the previous generation. Further, they espouse that in the context of twenty-first-century learning, the way ahead depends on development of capacities for creativity, collaboration, communication, and critical thinking. Kalantzis and Cope (2010) add that "building the knowledge capital of a society, the creative capacities for innovation as well as the sensibilities to navigate ambiguity and complexity—is now fundamental" (p. 202).

Operationalizing Creative Development

It is one thing to call for educational design that is conducive to creative development through continual creative practice leading to innovation and invention, it is yet another thing to make it happen in educational practice. It is a call we all experience from many directions whether it is an inspirational TED talk, the burgeoning proliferation of Maker Faire events, or a call for more economic innovation from government. However, operationalizing this shift within the fabric of daily educational practice is the challenge we all face. This goes well beyond bringing in yet another new trend or way of doing into existing traditional educational organizational structure and practice. *Creative Development: Transforming Education through Design Thinking, Innovation, and Invention* is about systematically operationalizing educational practice through the concept of creative development, which means enabling the growth in the level of complexity in which one can engage in creative practice over time. Creative development is viewed as essential in education for enabling educators and learners to engage in meaningful original research, production, and action, which leads to innovation and invention. As a result, creative development is viewed as being equally important as more traditional developmental strands such as literacy and numeracy.

This volume begins with an examination of the vocabulary in the field of creativity relative to general educational practice, and then provides a detailed description of the eight interwoven, developmental strands that comprise longitudinal creative development. This is followed by a discussion of the characteristics of an educational culture conducive to collaborative creativity, which is essential for enabling creative development to flourish. The journey continues with a detailed description of what systematic engagement in creative practice entails through the lenses of ideation and design thinking and practice over time. We then go right to the shop floor for a detailed examination of learning experience design and assessment as creative development through the lens of teacher as designer, facilitator, collaborator, and mentor. This volume finishes with a look at implications for teacher education and thoughts on the way forward for transforming educational practice to incorporate the concept of creative development. Throughout this book, voices and examples from the field are highlighted in the Creative Development features to further develop understanding of, and insight into, the concept of creative development and how it can be educationally enabled. *Creative Development: Transforming Education through Design Thinking, Innovation, and Invention* is an invitation for educators and learners to embark on a journey of lifelong creative development to enable an engaging educational culture and life journey of hope, imagination, exploration, experimentation, and invention.

REFERENCES

Autoxylopyrocycloboros. (2006). In Our Artists—Commissions: Simon Starling. Retrieved from http://covepark.org/commissions/simon-starling

Cheek, D. W. (2015). A panoramic view of the future of learning and the role of design(ers). In B. Hokanson, G. Clinto, & M. W. Tracey (Eds.), *The design of learning experience: Creating the future of educational technology* (p. 5). Dordrecht: Springer. http://dx.doi.org/10.1007/978-3-319-16504-2_2

Costa, A. L., & Kallick, B. (2014). *Dispositions: Reframing teaching and learning.* Thousand Oaks: Corwin Press.

Kalantzis, M., & Cope, B. (2010). The teacher as designer: Pedagogy in the new media age. *E-Learning and Digital Media, 7*(3), 200. Retrieved from http://dx.doi.org/10.2304/elea.2010.7.3.200

Kelly, R. (2012). *Educating for creativity: A global conversation.* Edmonton: Brush Education.

Leadbeater, C. (2008). *We-think: The power of mass creativity.* London: Profile Books.

United Nations (2015). Transforming our world: The 2030 agenda for sustainable development. In *Sustainable Development Goals.* Retrieved from www.un.org/sustainabledevelopment

Waks, L.J. (2014). *Education 2.0: The learning web revolution and the transformation of the school.* Boulder: Paradigm Books.

1

Understanding Creativity, Creative Capacity, and Creative Development

ROBERT KELLY

The Core Concepts of Creativity, Creative Capacity, and Creative Development

To begin to develop an understanding of the concept of creative development we must first examine the nature and meaning of the core concept of creativity. *Creativity* can mean so many different things to so many different people in so many different contexts. This poses a problem when building educational practice around the concept of creativity, as the set of assumptions that we make about this concept will inform how it manifests itself in application to teaching practice. Diverse interpretations of the concept of creativity can have profound implications for the nature and extent of enabled potentials. It is important to arrive at an operating definition of the concept of creativity that lends itself to the growth and development of engagement in creative practice over time.

Defining creativity

Piirto (2004) describes the word *creativity* as having its roots in Latin and meaning "to make or produce" or "to grow." She goes on to describe the concept of creativity or the practice of being creative as being originative. She describes the word *originative* as implying the making of something new; therefore, to be creative is to make something new or novel. The concepts of originality and creativity are inextricably linked in this description of creativity.

Sawyer (2012) describes two definitions of creativity rooted in an individualist approach and a sociocultural approach. He describes the individualist definition as "Creativity is a new mental combination that is expressed in the world" (p. 7). He further elaborates that, in this context, creative combinations of thought and production may not be new to the world, but as long as they are new to the person's mind they would fit into an individualist definition. He likens this to Csikszentmihalyi's (1996) little-c creativity, which encompasses creative acts carried out on an everyday basis. Improvising while cooking or thinking of ways to prevent the family dog from escaping out of the backyard are examples of this everyday creativity. Sawyer (2012) describes the sociocultural definition as "Creativity is the generation of a product that is judged to be novel, and also to be appropriate, useful, or valuable by a suitably knowledgeable social group." This is likened to Csikszentmihalyi's (1996) Big-C creativity, where creative production is recognized as novel and important in a field or domain.

These two definitional strands are complementary and are very useful when applied to the concept of creative development in an educational setting. They potentially represent a developmental continuum—the level of sophistication of engagement in creative practice by a learner evolves from being novel, relative to their own developmental history, to having significance within a broader social group in a domain or field.

Perhaps one of the most educationally useful definitions of creativity that can be applied to both contexts is Lubart's (2000) "a sequence of thoughts and actions that leads to novel, adaptive production." Creativity ultimately involves bringing ideas or thoughts into some kind of form that can be shared in a currency or medium of the field where it occurs. The level of complexity or sophistication at which an individual engages in creative practice at a point in time is referred to as creative capacity. The growth in creative capacity over time is referred to as creative development. This developmental evolution begins with an understanding that human beings, by nature, are an adaptive species. Human beings from their earliest days to their senior years engage in Csikszentmihalyi's (1996) small-c creativity in everyday living that shares an affinity with Sawyer's (2012) individualistic creativity. This intuitive/adaptive creativity is part of the innate human disposition. The educational imperative is to enable the longitudinal growth and development of a learner's creative capacity to grow from innate intuitive/adaptive creativity to the ability to engage in sustained creative practice through original research and production that takes on increasing levels of sociocultural importance.

Understanding originality

Being creative implies being originative (Piirto, 2004). The concept of original work as a result of creative production has to be taken into consideration here as well. If the desired outcome of a collaborative educational culture of creativity is to enable learners to ultimately engage in original research and production, then the context of the application of the word *original* must be carefully examined. Guilford (1962) described the concept of originality as a response that is unusual, far-fetched, or remote representing something that is statistically infrequent among a common group. When interpreting the degree of originality of a given response, it is important to use a dual-tracked definition in educational application. It is educationally inappropriate and unrealistic to compare a young learner to creative practitioners at the top of their respective fields to assess whether the learner's response is original or not (Kelly, 2012). When facilitating creative development, it is more useful and productive to assess a learner's response for its degree of originality relative to the past creative production outcomes of the learner (Starko, 2010). This creates developmental space for reachable, realistic goals for creative development over time without the onerous constant comparisons to mature, creative producers who have developed work through intense research and experimentation over considerable periods or even lifetimes.

In an educational context, it is important to apply a sliding or evolving definition to the concepts of creativity and originality to enable the operationalization of systematic and continuous creative development over a learner's educational and life journey. This respects the diverse developmental paces in creative growth of individual learners by assessing creative development relative to the individual's previous creative production. The ultimate educational goal is to have each learner engage over time in increasingly more complex creative practice that has increasing sociocultural value.

The vocabulary of creative processes

The concepts of creativity, creative capacity, and creative development have many associated terms and vocabulary that need to be clarified to enable greater precision in the application of tactics and strategies for the creative development of learners in educational practice. A definition of terms also advances the understanding of creative processes. Terms such as *imagination, innovation,* and *invention* are often used interchangeably with the concept of creativity and require closer examination for more precise application. Terms such as *divergent thinking, flexible thinking, elaborative thinking,* and *ideational fluency* need to be understood in relation to creative development or they can be easily be taken out of context in educational practice and be perceived as teaching creativity without any sense of their relation to comprehensive creative development. How do the terms *entrepreneurship, enterprise,* and *design thinking* relate to the concepts of creativity and creative development? A clear understanding of these interrelated and often overlapping concepts will enhance their application to teaching and learning.

Wallas (1926) described a stage theory of creative process that informed many variations of descriptions of creative processes that followed. He broke the creative process down into four discernable stages (shown in Table 1.1).

TABLE 1.1 WALLAS'S STAGES OF THE CREATIVE PROCESS

Stage 1	Preparation refers to setting the problem to start the process in motion.
Stage 2	Incubation refers to the active subconscious stage where ideas are elaborated upon and redefined.
Stage 3	Illumination is the idea that emerges as a potential solution to the original problem.
Stage 4	Verification points to testing out the idea in the currency of the discipline or field where the problem is located to see if it is a viable solution.

Over time, many variations of the stage theory of creative process emerged. As these variations unfolded, a shift occurred from a belief that the creative process was largely a subconscious process to a belief that it was a process that could be mediated and influenced. Osborn (1963), one of the originators of brainstorming, added ideation, a dynamic stage of deliberate idea generation, to the mix as testimony to this transition.

There are many characteristics that are associated with creative behaviour. Guilford (1959) described several of these traits of creative individuals, including those outlined in Table 1.2.

Guilford goes on to add capacities for convergent and divergent thinking to this list. Convergent thinking refers to thinking toward a solution or problem resolution by sorting through possible alternatives. Divergent thinking speaks to open-ended thinking and the generation of numerous potential problem-resolution alternatives. The application of convergent and divergent thinking is discussed in more detail in chapter 3 (Engaging in Creative Practice).

TABLE 1.2 TRAITS OF CREATIVE INDIVIDUALS

TRAIT	DESCRIPTION
Fluency of thinking	The ability to think effortlessly, especially in ideation
Flexibility in thinking	The capacity to readily abandon old ideas and accept new ones
Originality	The capacity to come up with unusual ideas that are remote from previous concepts
Redefinition	The capacity to give up old interpretations of concepts or objects and replace them with new ones
Elaboration	The capacity to fill in details or to add details to a general scheme
Tolerance of ambiguity	The willingness to accept some uncertainty, precluding rigidity in thinking

Imagination

Many of these characteristics of creative behaviour involve active engagement of the imagination. Imaginative thinking is closely associated with the dynamic of generating new ideas or the process of ideation. Singer (1999) describes imagination as "a special feature or form of human thought characterized by the ability of an individual to reproduce images or concepts originally derived from basic senses but now reflected . . . as memories, fantasies or future plans" (p. 13). Imagination is an integral part of the creative process but not a synonym for the concept of creativity. In the creative process, an idea or set of ideas has to manifest itself in a field or discipline area as some sort of shared form, often through continued ideation and experimentation over time. There is the implication here of moving from thought to form. Imaginative thinking can be viewed as a synonym for the oft-used term creative thinking because imaginative thinking is the fuel and vision that drives the creative process.

Innovation and invention

Innovation and invention are the contextual results of creative practice. Each of these terms derives its meaning from the specific context in which it occurs. Innovation represents the application of creative thinking (Runco, 2014) and can be defined as the process of implementing new ideas to create value for an organization. This may mean creating a new service, product, system, or process, or enhancing existing ones. The term *innovation* is often associated with business and industry where there is a specific context and audience for the application of creative practice. Runco (2014) contends that the results of specific innovation have a larger accountability in usefulness to their intended audience or market, not necessarily pushing the limits of originality compared to other manifestations of creative practice. Amabile (1988) describes innovation as creative practice applied within an organization. Sawyer and Bunderson (2013) point to a differentiation of creativity and innovation through the context of the application of creative practice. Creativity can be seen as being associated with the creative production of individuals, while innovation is often associated with the application of creative practice in organizations.

Grasty (2012) describes invention as creating a product or process for the first time and innovation as placing the product or process into a new context. He uses Apple's iPod as an example of innovation. The iPod wasn't the first music device or the first music-sharing system invented. The innovation was that the iPod combined design and accessibility into a comprehensive music ecosystem that irrevocably changed the music industry. With this example, it is clear that invention and innovation are two terms that are very closely related. Inventions are not created out of a vacuum of knowledge and discovery. They most often evolve out of previous experimentation and research. For example, Christopher Cockerell was credited with the invention of the hovercraft, an air-cushion vehicle capable of travelling over land, water, mud, or ice. There were several inventors along the way to the invention of the hovercraft who attempted various manifestations of air-cushion or airfoil-type vehicles, but all required forward motion to lift the vehicle. Cockerell's breakthrough came in being the first to perfect successful technology for maintaining an air cushion under the craft, resulting in a practical vehicle that could engage in continual use.

When applying the terms *innovation* and *invention* to educational practice, it is important to employ a sliding interpretation of both concepts to the production of a young learner, as is the case with the concepts of creativity and originality. The creative production of a learner can be perceived as inventive or innovative when compared to their previous production, whether the work has been produced elsewhere or not. As the learner increases creative capacity over time, and their corresponding creative production gains greater sociocultural relevance, their work can be compared to creative production in the broader field or domain and be perceived as inventive or innovative in that wider context.

Entrepreneurship

Eisenmann (2013) describes the concept of entrepreneurship at Harvard's Business School as the pursuit of opportunity beyond resources controlled. Entrepreneurship is most often associated with the business field. For many, it conjures up a vision of someone with high risk tolerance and a unique idea that grows into a highly profitable enterprise. However, the entrepreneurial disposition is not limited to the business field or purely to profiting in a market economy. It can be applied to social innovation, the development of nonprofit organizations, or the development of any number or combination of educational, cultural, or commercial initiatives.

The term *entrepreneur* speaks to a disposition that embodies attributes such as risk taking, seeking and visualizing new ideas, and a capacity to mobilize resources to help implement ideas (Runco, 2014). Entrepreneurship is often associated with innovation as it can involve the visualization, creation, and implementation of novel ideas. This has considerable implications for educational practice. A consumption-intense educational culture does not necessarily breed the entrepreneurial disposition, as it is fundamentally risk averse and vision averse. It is adverse to risk and vision because most learning is focused on predisposed outcomes and the measurement thereof. A creativity-intense educational culture on the other hand enables the development of the entrepreneurial disposition as the self-motivated vision of novel ideas, and the corresponding experimentation and recruitment of resources to implement those ideas are valued and encouraged. The entrepreneurial disposition and resulting innovative enterprise through problem seeking and problem solving are essential for dealing with the complexities of existing and emerging communal, regional, and global challenges across commerce, culture, and education.

Design, design thinking, and design practice

For many, design, design thinking, and design practice are the accessible lenses for the application of creative practice leading to growth in creative development. If creativity is the mother ship of thoughts and actions that lead to novel, adaptive production, design represents concrete, contextual, creative problem solving in which creative processes are applied to specific situations.

Just as the word *creativity* can be interpreted in many ways, Berger (2009) describes the word *design* as a term needing its own dictionary.

He describes numerous definitions of design from many in the field as encompassing an aspiration to create, a passion to help humankind, a strategy to affect change, and the desire to impact the world. Some related examples of the definition of design (Berger, 2009, p. 29) include the following:

- "The art of making something better beautifully." Joe Duffy
- "The act of giving form to an idea with an intended goal: to inspire, to delight, to change perception and behaviour." Clement Mok
- "A plan to make something, for a specific purpose, with a specific audience or user in mind." Michael Beirut
- "The human capacity to plan and produce desired outcomes." Bruce Mau
- "Moving from an existing condition to a preferred one." Milton Glaser
- "The art of planning." Paula Scher
- "The soul of a man-made creation." Steve Jobs

Both Berger (2009) and Brown (2009) describe how the application of design practice has evolved historically from a focus on product design to a much broader application to transformational design and the design of experience. Bruce Mau's (2004) *Massive Change* calls for a much broader application of design to include built environments, transportation technologies, revolutionary materials, energy and information systems, and living organisms. As such, design practice is seen as being applicable to almost every creative problem-solving situation faced in everyday living.

IDEO's (2016) *Design Thinking for Educators Toolkit* is an accessible resource for educators that describes the design process through five progressive stages:

1. Discovery: Preparing research and approach to a challenge
2. Interpretation: Searching for meaning and framing opportunities
3. Ideation: Generating and refining ideas
4. Experimentation: Making prototypes and getting feedback
5. Evolve: Developing the concept further

There is a definite affinity between IDEO's five design stages and classic stage theories of creativity dating back to Wallas in 1926 and Osborn's (1963) introduction of the stage of ideation.

Framing design thinking and its application in this contextual, concrete nature makes design much more accessible to educators and the general public as it is seen as having practical application. Many, when confronted with the word *creativity*, are often overwhelmed with the breadth and depth of this term and its abstract associations or they default to a perception that creativity is only an arts thing or a product thing (Runco, 2014). This often leaves educators agreeing that the whole "creativity-in-education" concept is nice and that it has potential positive implications for educational practice, but it also leaves them wondering how to implement this and where to start, or thinking that it really isn't practical in the daily routine. The application of design thinking and design practice in educational practice is a great practical entry point for many educators to begin to transform educational culture into a creative culture, leading to longitudinal creative development of learners. The proliferation of makerspaces in public education is testimony to the accessibility of design practice, which has the potential to lead to a much broader comprehensive creative culture. The educational challenge will be to grow this culture in a meaningful and sustainable manner and for it not to be yet another new trend that gets gobbled up by a consumption-intense system that strips it of its most transformative elements. The educational imperative is to transform general educational practice to a creativity-intense practice conducive to the creative development of educators and learners over time.

The Eight Interwoven Strands of Creative Development

Creative development is defined as the growth in creative capacity (of an individual or organization) over time. *Creativity capacity* refers to the level of complexity at which one can engage in creative practice at a point in time. Creative development is seen as the growth from the natural human disposition of intuitive/adaptive creativity to the development of capacities to engage in increasingly more complex, sustained creative practice characterized by original research and production that has greater sociocultural relevance and importance. Sustained original research and production is characterized by imaginative vision that leads to recurrent iterations of idea generation and prototyping over time.

In applying the concept of creative development to the long-term educational growth and development of a learner, we can easily get bogged down in the numerous dimensions and complexities of the concept of creativity when it comes to educational application and implementation. Do we focus on Guilford's (1959) characteristics of creativity, building instructional design around enhancing specific attributes such as flexible thinking and divergent thinking? If we focus on establishing design-intense makerspaces in a school setting, is that furthering creative development? If our educational institution is an inquiry-based school or a school that focuses on project-based learning, does that constitute creating an environment that is conducive to long-term creative development? The answers to all of these questions could be yes or no, or all points in between, depending on the contexts in which they are played out and whether they are part of a larger educational ecology whose overall focus is creative development.

Beghetto, Kaufman, and Baer (2015) and Drapeau (2014) demonstrate interesting and diverse strategies and tactics for enhancing creative practice and understanding in typical consumption-intense educational environments. However, the inevitable educational question arises: "Can we teach creativity?" In a traditional sense, in most educational settings, attributes of creative practice could certainly be enhanced and a discipline-based understanding of creativity theory and practice could be taught. There is a major educational difference in approaching creativity as an enhancement for traditional educational practice and as a discipline area, as opposed to a focus on dispositional growth through comprehensive creative development. More pertinent questions specific to creativity in education would be "How can we create educational environments conducive to creative development?" and "How can we continually increase the creative capacity of educators, learners, and all involved in the educational environment?"

The eight interwoven strands for creative development take into account the need for a comprehensive, interrelated structure that speaks to the interrelated ecology of the factors that contribute to creative development. They are not meant to be perceived in isolation, but rather are meant to be viewed and used collectively for dispositional growth and development over time. The eight developmental strands are

- collaborative development,
- research/investigative development,
- self-instigative development,
- generative development,
- experimentational development,
- discipline complexity development,
- critical/analytical thinking development, and
- creative sustain development.

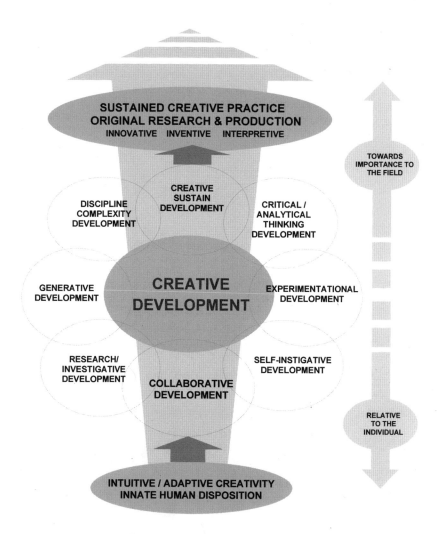

Figure 1.1 Creative development

Collaborative development

Collaborative development is a foundational developmental strand in the ecology of creative development. Chapter 2 (The Educational Culture of Collaborative Creativity) is devoted to understanding the foundational principles upon which this culture is built. Traditional consumption-intense educational practice fosters behavioural patterns and dispositions that are counterintuitive to collaborative creativity. Learning environments must be created in which all ideas are valued and all participants can engage in collective innovation and invention without fear, anxiety, and corresponding resultant dissociation. Collaboration exponentially enables creative growth and development through each of the interrelated developmental strands. We are social beings. It is sad to see students in classes at any level of education go through a school year or semester without any meaningful communication or collaboration with someone else in the room. The greatest creative resources, available to any learner or educator, are the hundreds of readily available peers and colleagues in their immediate educational environment and beyond. Effective mobilization and utilization of this tremendous resource through collaborative development has immense creative potential.

Charles Leadbeater (2008) contends, "Greater individual participation will not on its own add up to much unless it is matched by a capacity to share and combine our ideas" (p. 5). He elaborates that new generations will be defined by what they share, not by what they own. Leadbeater goes on to say that:

> *Creativity has always been a highly collaborative, cumulative, and social activity in which people with different skills, points of view, and insight share and develop ideas together. At root, most creativity is collaborative; it is not usually the product of a lone individual's flash of insight. (p. 6)*

Collaboration is often confused with the terms *cooperation* and *compliance*. Randy Nelson of Pixar in Edutopia (2008) describes cooperation as "that thing that is a definition of a protocol that allows you not to get in each other's way." Cooperation often entails a group initiative in which group members each contribute to a finished product or project. The sum of all of the parts equals a finished product in an assembly-line sense. We have all had the experience as educators and learners where we have been part of group project, each contributing a piece to the final form. In a related context, administrators and educators have often used the word *collaboration* to acknowledge widespread organizational compliance to a master initiative. Being complicit to organizational initiatives is viewed as collaboration, whether one had anything to do with the initiative or not. True collaboration goes much deeper than cooperation or compliance in these contexts, however. Pixar's Nelson elaborates on the meaning of the concept of collaboration:

> *Collaboration has to mean something different. It can't be a synonym for cooperation. Collaboration for Pixar means amplification. The amplification you get by connecting up a bunch of human beings who are listening to each other, interested in each other, bring separate depth to the problem, bring breadth that gives them interest in the entire solution, allows them to*

> *communicate on multiple different levels, verbally, in writing, in feeling,*
> *in acting, in pictures; and in all of those ways, finding the most articulate*
> *way to get a high fidelity notion across to a broad range of people so they*
> *can each pull on the right lever.*

Collaborative development characterized by sensitive, effective communication and social interaction supported in a broader educational culture conducive to collaborative creativity is the gateway to longitudinal creative development.

Self-instigative development

Self-instigative development refers to a pivotal developmental strand in the broader ecology of creative development focused on developing a learner and educator disposition of sustainable intrinsic motivation with greater learner autonomy. This typically involves transitioning from an extrinsic-motivation educational orientation to intrinsic motivation where learners are able to initiate learning in a supportive environment of collaborative creativity. This entails growing the capacity to initiate increasingly more complex creative explorations that are of intellectual and emotional relevance to the learner (Kelly, 2012).

To be motivated means to be moved to do something. Deci and Ryan (2000) describe intrinsic motivation as "the doing of an activity for its inherent satisfaction rather than for some separable consequence" (p. 56). They describe extrinsic motivation as "a construct that pertains whenever an activity is done in order to attain some separable outcome" (p. 60). They further contend that, after early childhood, opportunities for intrinsically motivating experiences are increasingly limited, as social and occupational demands require participants to engage in tasks that are primarily not intrinsically motivated. Traditional educational practice is not spared from this phenomenon. A hyperfocus on discipline complexity development, and its corresponding assessment and measurement, takes precedence over everything else in the educational spectrum, especially as learners approach grade-point-average standards for postsecondary admissions. Deci and Ryan (2008) evolved their interpretation of motivational contexts to the terms *autonomous* and *controlled motivation.* "Autonomous motivation involves behaving with a full sense of volition and choice . . . whereas controlled motivation involves behaving with the experience of pressure and demand toward specific outcomes that comes from forces perceived to be external to the self" (p. 14). Autonomy in this context does not imply isolation, but rather independence in a broader interdependent, collaborative, creative culture (Pink, 2009).

Self-instigative development characterized by intrinsic motivation and autonomous orientation enable authentic, meaningful engagement when it is part of comprehensive creative development. Pink further expands on research that reflects that individuals who are autonomous and intrinsically motivated have "higher self-esteem, better interpersonal relationships, and greater general well-being than those extrinsically motivated" (p. 80). Thomas (2009) connects intrinsic motivation with the emotional connection that energizes and reinforces continued engagement. He explains that through the lenses of opportunity and accomplishment, the sense of choice, meaningfulness, competence, and progress collectively give intrinsically motivated participants the feeling that they are actually accomplishing work that is significant and worthwhile. Resultant validation along with personal and collaborative empowerment enable sustained creative development.

Research/investigative development

Creative practice through original research and production requires constant fuel. Mature creative producers in any discipline surround themselves with stimuli-rich environments. They have learned to set problems, ask questions, and develop an investigative disposition where any experience or conversation—active or passive—is stimulus for potential creative production. They actively seek stimuli for creative production on a continual basis.

We come into the world with this disposition as natural-born researchers and investigators. We spend much of our preschool days investigating, gathering information intentionally, and sometimes unintentionally, through endless exploration, interaction, and experimentation with the world around us. The Reggio Emilia approach to preschool and primary education inherently values this disposition and is designed around growing it in a supportive educational environment (Gandini et al., 2015). We would assume that learners entering formal education with this disposition would be well positioned to develop into engaging in increasingly more sophisticated forms of research throughout their formal education journey. However, in consumption-intense educational environments, this natural curiosity that goes hand in hand with natural intuitive/adaptive creativity quickly evolves into much more limited research practice, characterized by finding and reporting of curricular content. Gardner (1984) comments on a U-shaped development path where the creative practice of preschoolers shares a lot in common with mature, creative producers (the top of each side of the U), but only after resurfacing after years of schooling during which these practices are minimized (the bottom of the U). Much effort in these educational environments is spent on trying to restore this innate curiosity through inquiry-based learning and many other initiatives, so students will engage with curriculum content with the investigative enthusiasm of a preschooler. The inertia of researching for reporting, assessment-driven teaching practice and the perceived relevance of extrinsically driven curricular content limit these initiatives in achieving their ideals.

Comprehensive creative development characterized by self-instigative development, where there is a growing sense of ownership, purpose, and meaning, is conducive to investigative development. A supportive, collaborative environment is a rich, immediate source of investigative fuel. In this context, students have authentic reasons for their intrinsically driven curiosities to grow into questions, problem setting, experimentation, and, ultimately, innovation and invention. With this process of investigative research, learners constantly seek fuel for creative production, which becomes personally relevant. Research/investigative development is optimized in the broader ecology of the interrelated creative development strands.

Generative and experimentational development
Generative development involves developing the capacity to create alternatives for creative production. This is associated with divergent thinking—one of Guilford's (1959) characteristics of creative individuals—where the focus is on generating numerous potential problem-resolution alternatives. Experimentational development involves bringing ideas into form, where they are prototyped for further analysis and refinement. This is associated with convergent thinking, in which the focus is on thinking toward a solution or problem resolution by sorting through and selecting possible alternatives.

Smith (1998) sees idea generation as the indispensible core of creativity. The dynamic of idea generation is described in detail in chapter 3 (Engaging in Creative Practice). Sustained creative practice requires a great deal of fuel. Artist's block, writer's block, and general creative block are usually the result of a lack of stimuli—a lack of ideas. Sweeney (2004) stresses the importance of quantity in idea generation when it comes to fueling the creative dynamic. Increased quantity of ideas through divergent thinking exponentially increases the probability of a novel or innovative outcome as exposure to more and more ideas leads to increasingly more diverse idea combinations.

Many educators have worked with learners who are very fluent in ideation but have difficulty in converging all of their thoughts to a prototyping stage in the currency or medium where the creative exploration is taking place. These learners have plenty of ideas but do not know what to write or make. Experimentational development becomes important here, as creative practice involves bringing ideas that can be tested and refined into form. This process involves a capacity to engage in convergent thinking. In fact, it involves a learner not just thinking about what they want to make, but also converging thoughts to engaging in an actual medium or materials of what is being created. Experimentation through prototyping is generative as well. Feedback from testing of prototypes informs further ideation that informs further prototyping and refinements.

Generative and experimentational development are closely intertwined but distinctly different. We can only live in the thoughtful world of imagination for so long before bringing a concept into a form that can be shared and tested. Generative and experimentational development are the main drivers of inventive momentum once the creative dynamic is set in motion.

Critical/analytical thinking development and discipline complexity development

The creative process involves a continual input of stimuli along with the constant generation of problem-resolution alternatives in thought and form. All of this incoming information has to be assessed for its quality, usefulness, and relevance for the set problem at hand. All generated alternatives must be assessed through comparative analysis to converge on an appropriate problem resolution.

Warnick and Inch (1994) define critical thinking as "involving the ability to explore a problem, question, or situation; integrate all the available information about it; arrive a solution or hypothesis; and justify one's position" (p. 11). Scriven and Paul in Padget (2013) define critical thinking as "the intellectually disciplined process of actively and skillfully conceptualizing, applying, analyzing, synthesizing, and/or evaluating information gathered from, or generated by, observation, experience, reflection, reasoning, or communication, as a guide to belief and action" (p. 7). Critical/analytical thinking development is closely interrelated with discipline complexity development as each discipline has its own unique nuances with respect to analysis and understanding of its content and processes, whether it is an artistic context, a scientific context, or otherwise.

Discipline complexity development refers to the growing learner understanding of the knowledge content, processes, and techniques of a discipline area or field(s) of study. Traditional educational practice is typically very discipline-understanding intense. Advancing discipline understanding through discipline complexity development and critical/analytical thinking development across the discipline spectrum is essential for fueling creative practice as creative initiatives occur within and across discernable fields of study. Creative practice does not occur in a vacuum. However, the broader ecology of creative development does not solely exist to serve discipline complexity development. It is precisely the opposite: contemporary educational design should configure discipline complexity development and critical/analytical thinking development as an integral part of the collective interwoven developmental strands that serve comprehensive creative development within a supportive collaborative culture.

Creative sustain development

As learners gain creative confidence, creative capacity begins to grow (Kelley and Kelley, 2013). This growth entails engagement in more sophisticated creative practices. This is the developmental spine of the concept of creative development involving the growth in creative capacity from natural intuitive/adaptive creativity to sustained creative practice. Creative sustain development refers to developing the capacity to sustain recurrent iterations of idea generation and experimentation through prototyping over time against a backdrop of greater discipline complexity in the initiation and engagement of original research and production. Complex creative initiatives require rigour and perseverance to maintain and sustain. They require complex, collaborative supportive structures to fuel and sustain momentum whether developing a new technology or engaging in social innovation. The level of sophistication of creative sustain that a learner exhibits is a good indicator of creative capacity and creative development trajectory. As we can see, the concept of creative sustain among the eight developmental strands of creative development is very hard to discuss without consideration of the other strands and how they collectively enable each other through this ecological dynamic that facilitates longitudinal creative development.

Factors Limiting Creative Development

Establishing an educational culture of creativity requires a substantial, concerted effort to cultivate an educational environment that is conducive to sustained creative growth and development. Identifying factors that limit creative development, along with the corresponding tactics and strategies to counter these underlying negative forces, is essential in establishing an educational culture conducive to creative development. If left unattended, these factors develop into skew effects that inhibit any kind of change or cultural transformation and leave well-meaning educators wondering why, after considerable time and effort, their initiatives bore very little transformational fruit.

Extrinsic motivation, early closure, outcomes known, and dissociation

Educators trying to engage students in content-laden, extrinsically driven learning environments expend incredible amounts of time and energy maintaining learning momentum. Whether it is developing ways to inspire and motivate students to learn about the Mbuti, one of several indigenous pygmy groups in the Congo region of Africa, or to deal with a mathematical abstraction, teachers are constantly faced with the challenge of making remote concepts relevant to learners in attempts to advance discipline understanding. This is the primary challenge of educational practice that is so single-mindedly focused on discipline complexity development as the center of the educational universe. These educational environments rely heavily on measurements of content understanding and on compliant and cooperative behaviour from learners to be deemed successful. It does not take learners in this environment very long to figure out that the majority of the work they are doing is not originative, but rather characterized by outcomes that are known. In other words, most of the work they produce is intended to exhibit a standard or meet an outcome that is already known by educators. "Is this what you wanted?" or "What is she looking for on her tests?" are common student questions that expose this preoccupation with outcomes that are already known. These questions also reveal emotional and intellectual distancing by learners. These environments rely heavily on extrinsic motivation to sustain engagement. Such environments are not sustainable when it comes to maintaining educational relevance to learners. Nor do they sustainably empower learners to engage in self-instigated innovation and invention. They are counterintuitive to creative development.

Learners in this context who demonstrate content understanding and who are also compliant and cooperative are most likely perceived to be good students. In contrast, students who do not demonstrate discipline understanding through traditional assessment regimens and/or are not compliant or cooperative are perceived as having deficits or as being a management issue, or both. An extraordinary amount of instruction in teacher education programs is devoted to dealing with deficit-based instruction along with numerous management issues. These strategies can be educationally very useful in specific learning needs contexts. However, one of the by-products of immersing learners in content-laden, consumption-intense, extrinsically driven educational environments is that an extraordinary number of learners, each with incredible potential, disengage because they feel disempowered and invalidated. They become emotionally and intellectually detached from this educational environment and dissociate from it.

Another by-product of this type of educational environment is early closure when it comes to idea generation. Educational practice focused on known outcomes fosters a "right-answer" culture among the students, who have virtually no incentive to generate ideas or to experiment with their own thoughts and aspirations through divergent thinking. They are rewarded almost completely based upon their demonstration of convergent thinking; specifically, how closely they can approximate an outcome that is already known. When an opportunity arises to invite the exploration of ideas for creating, many educators in this setting become frustrated with students who close on idea growth early and whose first idea is often their last as students become conditioned to play it safe in order to avoid mistakes. Learners default to what they know because it is safe and secure. J. K. Rowling (2008) describes playing it safe as failure by default. This tendency poses considerable limitations on developing any hint of inventive momentum as the generative engine of creative practice is shut off.

The machine organization, standardization, and hyperconsumption

Daniel Pink (2009) asks the question "When we enter the world are we wired to be passive and inert? Or are we wired to be active and engaged?" (p. 89). He reflects that traditional organizational and management practice tends to default to the perception that we are all passive and inert:

> ... *certain assumptions about the basic natures of those being managed. It presumes that to take action or move forward, we need a prod—that absent a reward or punishment we would remain happily and inertly in place. It also presumes that once people do get moving, they need direction—that without a firm, reliable guide, they'd wander. (p. 88)*

This reflects the default management and administrative attributes that Mintzberg (1989) would associate with machine organizations characterized by top-down control, detailed planning, and formalization of procedures. This type of organization relies almost exclusively on extrinsic motivation for perceived success. It is a type of organization that is also typically built around standardization. Educational jurisdictions, educational organizational structures, and corresponding policies reflect these attributes despite embracing creativity and innovation as one of the pillars of twenty-first-century learning. It creates a situation that is counterintuitive to the development of an educational culture of intrinsically motivated learners engaged in innovation and invention. I have never met an educational administrator who does not in some way, shape, or form value the benefits of creativity and innovation. However, the inertia of educational practice informed by varying degrees of machine organization attributes precludes sustained creative development as central to the fabric of education. The Common Core State Standards Initiative and its corresponding assessments in the United States are testimony to this stunted creative development. Educators are left to valiantly wedge in creative practice despite the inertia of a system that is primarily informed by standardization and machine-organization characteristics. There are great examples of enabled creativity, innovation, and invention in pockets in public education and private and charter schools throughout North America, but they are the exception and not the norm.

Vertical comparisons, social isolation, mistrust, and permissions

Yet another by-product of assessment-intense, content-laden educational environments that limit creative development is the development of vertical comparison hierarchies. Students are ranked compared to each other. The highest achievers are at the top of the pyramid. A high grade-point average is of the highest educational value. We expend considerable effort in education, at the school level and system-wide, on strategies and tactics designed to help students get higher grades that equate to higher levels of achievement and overall school or system success. Knowing the level of discipline complexity development of any learner is not a bad thing. It is certainly useful in informing learning experience design for student understanding and development. The problem occurs when it is the only thing guiding learning experience design. It is a question of imbalance and the relationship of discipline complexity development to a broader educational context. These traditional practices seldom support the comprehensive creative development of learners or make substantial educational space for increasing the creative capacity of learners' creative practice. Discipline complexity development is viewed as the epicenter of educational development instead of part of more comprehensive interrelated developmental components for increasing creative capacity. Students immersed in this system come to view their educational identities not from the broader perspective of their creative accomplishments and creative potentials (through collaborative engagement in real-world problems for real-world audiences), but rather through their vertical comparison ranking in the narrow world of discipline complexity development measurement.

This approach is dated and fundamentally invalidating for students who are not at the top of the measurement pyramid, and it is misleading for those who are at the top. Students will often define their educational identities through their deficits or their vertical hierarchy status, and not through their creative practice accomplishments and potentials. This invalidation, accompanied by hypercompetition for grades, leads to social isolation and an inherent mistrust of others. Both of these factors are counterintuitive to developing the supportive, highly interactive, collaborative culture necessary for comprehensive creative growth and development.

This educational identity perception is carried into adulthood and can be incredibly limiting when it comes to engaging in creative practice. Learners of any age lack the confidence to engage, as they perceive themselves as incapable of competently doing something. They are afraid to make mistakes, something that is fundamental to experimentation and creative practice. And most importantly, they are reluctant to give themselves permission to engage in a personally relevant creative exploration without knowing the initial outcomes because they have rarely, if ever, been given this permission in their years of schooling.

Teachers do not deliberately set out to invalidate students. They are in the practice of education because they care about the growth and development of students. However, the system in which most educators are placed is implicitly invalidating, which leads to an incredible amount of white noise and discordance being carried around by educators and students. They know there is something more educationally; something beyond existing practices that enables validating growth and creative development. Chapter 6 (Creative Development in Teacher Education, the Field, and Beyond) addresses some of the issues in teacher education that need to be addressed as part of a much larger transformation of educational culture if comprehensive creative development is to be enabled.

Creative engagement factors: blocking ideas, fear, and anxiety

Collectively, the factors that limit creative development become trajectory-changing skew effects when educators attempt to engage students in substantial student-owned and initiated creative initiatives. On the surface, these creative journeys have all of the right attributes and great appeal, as they are very much well-intended, student-centered initiatives with plenty of student choice. However, the collective impact of the limiting skew effects creates considerable inertia that hinders or blocks creative engagement and sustain.

Change anxiety among learners surfaces early when shifting from extrinsic motivation to student-initiated creative production. Learners become conditioned to being explicitly told what to do inside a very clear structure of expectations. Moving into a more fluid social environment of creative production, where initial outcomes are unknown and learning is more open ended causes considerable stress and anxiety for many. Once they come to trust the processes of collaborative creativity through experience and learn that these processes can potentially bear incredibly innovative fruit, these anxieties dissipate. However, if change anxiety is not recognized or dealt with at the onset of creative exploration, it will undermine any momentum from the very beginning.

As learners engage in creative practice, they become immersed in idea generation. Divergent thinking and the generation of alternatives are essential for fueling the creative process. Often when students are presented with many choices from research/investigation and collaborative interaction, they become overwhelmed and flounder because they do not know where to converge toward problem resolution. This paradox of choice can impede creative progress and is largely the result of a need for convergent thinking refinement. Closely associated with paradox-of-choice issues is the notion of thought-to-form anxiety. This anxiety occurs when learners have generated many viable ideas as possible problem resolutions but experience difficulty or anxiety in engaging in any medium for prototyping. They end up in an ideational circling pattern. This pattern is also the result of a need for convergent thinking refinement, as well as a need to overcome the fear of failure with engagement of media in the currency of the problem whether it is familiar or unfamiliar. The divergent-convergent dynamic of ideation is discussed in more detail in chapter 3 (Engaging in Creative Practice).

In the context of enabling student-initiated original research and production, the door is opened for big ideas. Writing a book, starting a business, or initiating real-world social innovation are just a few examples of where learners and educators can go. Sustained creative practice requires rigour through recurrent iterations of idea generation and prototyping over time. This is intuitively different from short-term, right-answer educational culture in which the creative sustain in any learning experience is limited compared to what is required for sustained creative practice. In sustained creative practice, this discrepancy can result in end-product anxiety. Learners who have not gained the experience to trust that sustained, collaborative, creative practice can lead to the positive resolution of more complex, larger-scale initiatives become overwhelmed with the task at hand. Instead of trusting and focusing on the incremental creative processes and actions to get to final problem resolution, learners succumb to the anxiety of disproportionate end-product expectation. They have trouble visualizing a potential innovative problem resolution. This is partially the result of immersion in product-intense learning cultures. The educational culture of collaborative creativity is a very rich, process-intense educational environment. Immersion is this environment builds social trust, process trust, and creative trust through collaborative empowerment, all of which leads to creative production.

REFERENCES

Amabile, T. M. (1988). From individual creativity to organizational innovation. In K. Gronhaug & G. Kaufmann (Eds.), *Innovation: A cross-disciplinary perspective* (pp. 139–166). Oslo: Norwegian University Press.

Beghetto, R. A., Kaufman, J. C., & Baer, J. (2015). *Teaching for creativity in the common core classroom*. New York: Teachers College Press.

Berger, W. (2009). *Glimmer*. Toronto: Random House.

Brown, T. (2009). *Change by design*. New York: HarperCollins.

Csikszentmihalyi, M. (1996). *Creativity: Flow and the psychology of discovery and invention*. New York: Harper Collins.

Deci, E. L., & Ryan, R. M. (2008). Facilitation optimal motivation and psychological well-being across life's domains. *Canadian Psychology, 49*(1), 14–23. http://dx.doi.org/10.1037/0708-5591.49.1.14

Deci, E. L., & Ryan, R. M. (2000). Intrinsic and extrinsic motivations: Classic definitions and new directions. *Contemporary Educational Psychology, 25*(1), 54–67. http://dx.doi.org/10.1006/ceps.1999.1020

Drapeau, P. (2014). *Sparking student creativity: Practical ways to promote innovative thinking and problem solving*. Alexandra: ASCD.

Edutopia. (2008). Randy Nelson on learning and working in the collaborative age. Retrieved from edutopia.org.

Eisenmann, Thomas R. (2013). Entrepreneurship: A working definition. Harvard Business Review. Retrieved from hbr.org.

Gandini, L., Hill, L., Cadwell, L., & Schwal, C. (Eds.). (2015). *In the spirit of the studio: Learning from the atelier of Reggio Emilia*. New York: Teachers College Press.

Gardner, H. (1984). *Art, mind, and brain: A cognitive approach to creativity*. New York: Basic Books.

Grasty, T. (2012). *The difference between innovation and invention*. In Huffpost Tech. Retrieved from huffingtonpost.com.

Guilford, J. P. (1962). Creativity: Its measurement and development. In S. J. Parnes & H. F. Harding (Eds.), *A source book for creative thinking* (pp. 151–168). New York: Charles Schribner and Sons.

Guilford, J.P. (1959). Traits of creativity. In H. H. Anderson (Ed.), *Creativity and its cultivation* (pp. 142–161). New York: Harper.

IDEO. (2016) Design thinking for educators toolkit. Retrieved from designthinkingforeducators. com

Kelley, T., & Kelley, D. (2013). *Creative confidence: Unleashing the creative confidence within us all*. New York: Crown Business.

Kelly, R. (2012). *Educating for creativity: A global conversation*. Edmonton: Brush Education.

Leadbeater, C. (2008). *We-think: The power of mass creativity*. London: Profile Books.

Lubart, Todd I. (2000). Models of creative process: Past, present and future. Creativity Research Journal, 13(3–4), 295–308.

Mau, B. (2004). *Massive change*. London: Phaidon Press.

Mintzberg, H. (1989). *Mintzberg on management*. New York: The Free Press.

Osborn, A. (1963). *Applied imagination*. New York: Charles Scribner.

Padget, S. (Ed.). (2013). *Creativity and critical thinking*. New York: Routledge.

Piirto, J. (2004). *Understanding creativity*. Scottsdale: Great Potential Press.

Pink, D. H. (2009). *Drive: The surprising truth about what motivates us*. New York: Riverhead Books.

Rowling, J. K. (2008). *The fringe benefits of failure, and the importance of imagination*. Speech. Retrieved January 25, 2016, from news.harvard.edu

Runco, M. A. (2014). *Creativity: theories and themes: Research, development and practice* (2nd ed.). San Diego: Academic Press.

Sawyer, R. Keith, and Bunderson, Stuart. (2013). Innovation: A review of research in organizational behavior. In *Innovation and growth*: pp. 13–55. http://dx.doi. org/10.1142/9789814343558_0002

Sawyer, R. K. (2012). *Explaining creativity: The science of innovation*. New York: Oxford University Press.

Singer, J. L. (1999). Imagination. In M. A. Runco & S. R. Pritzker (Eds.), *Encyclopedia of creativity* (Vol. 2, p. 13). San Diego: Academic Press.

Smith, G. (1998). Idea-generation techniques: A formulary of active ingredients. *Journal of Creative Behavior, 32*(2), 107–134. http://dx.doi.org/10.1002/j.2162-6057.1998.tb00810.x

Starko, A. J. (2010). *Creativity in the classroom* (4th ed.). New York: Routledge. (Original work published 1995)

Sweeney, J. (2004). *Innovation at the speed of laughter*. Minneapolis: Aerialist Press.

Thomas, K. W. (2009). *Intrinsic motivation at work*. San Francisco: Berrett-Koehler Publishing.

Wallas, G. (1926). *The art of thought*. New York: Harcourt Brace.

Warnick, B., & Inch, E. (1994). *Critical thinking and communication* (2nd ed.). New York: MacMillan.

CREATING DEVELOPMENT 1

A Journey into Connectivity, Creativity, Imagination, and Perception

A CONVERSATION WITH JOHN J. CIMINO JR., EDITED BY ROBERT KELLY

John J. Cimino Jr. is president and CEO of Creative Leaps International, The Learning Arts, and Associated Solo Artists. Educated with a background in music and voice (Manhattan and Juilliard Schools of Music), biology and physics (Rensselaer Polytechnic Institute), and learning theory (State University of New York at Albany). Cimino holds a uniquely interdisciplinary perspective dedicated to learning and human development. He is also an award-winning operatic singer, concert performer, and composer.

My Journey into Creative Development

If I reflect on what has shaped my view of creativity, I have to acknowledge that I come from passionate love affairs with three fields of endeavour, three disciplines. My first love was probably the sciences. I pursued advanced studies in biology and physics for several years. But a second love that grew to be at least as powerful for me was music. At first it was simply listening to music—to classical music in particular—and initially and very particularly to the piano preludes of Frederick Chopin. At age twelve, when I first heard these pieces, it was transformative for me. I had never really listened to classical music before, but once I heard those initial sounds, it was a language that went straight to my heart. It went straight to my fragile adolescent heart and seemed to be empathetic with my inner life, such as it was back then in all its shyness, wildness, and unknowing. I gravitated to those preludes like a moth to flame and in the thousands of hours I spent listening to them, that music literally formed the architecture of my emotions and imaginative life. It became my deepest truth, my sense of self.

It didn't take long for me to think that I could double the voltage of that experience by bringing Chopin's music together with my reading of a book by Albert Einstein and Leopold Infeld called *The Evolution of Physics*. I would literally lie on my bed, put Chopin's music on the turntable and pick up this book, this incredible narrative by Albert Einstein, and the two experiences together would bring me to a place of mystery, exuberance, adventure, and to quiet, spacious moments of wonder and comprehension. It was the first time I can recall consciously experiencing a world view, that is, a sense of how the world was working, or at least how my inner world was working, and that I needed both these extraordinary voices—the explanatory theoretical voice coming from the sciences and then this wordless inspirational, exploratory voice that came from music. Together, their power seemed infinite to me. So right from the start, although I could not have verbalized it back then, I was thoroughly into this dual channelling of disciplines, an interdisciplinary exploration or however we might chose to describe it.

As I moved toward my twenties, I became more conscious of my dual love affair with art and science and began to think of it as a somewhat mischievous slipping across boundaries. I had read the C. P. Snow book on the great divide of the disciplines, and I thought to myself "Yes, okay, I see how history has created this divide. But I'm not feeling it, I'm not living in it, I'm living in something different where science and art are intriguingly juxtaposed and playful with one another, and I'm hungry for more of it." Very soon it became clear that this fascination to explore art and science together was compelling me into yet another field, a third field common to both that has remained with me all my life. And that is the study of perception, thought processes, how we think and learn. And so I studied curriculum and instruction and the philosophy and psychology of learning, and best of all, I had the opportunity early in my twenties when hired straight out of RPI as a science teacher at a private school, to try out all sorts of things. Amazingly, I was given carte blanche to invent curriculum in the sciences and ultimately create courses reaching clear across the academic spectrum. I developed a course called "Thinking and Perceiving" because I thought it was important for adolescents to become more aware of their own mental and perceptual processes, so they wouldn't be oblivious to their capacities and simply pushed around by status quo forces. I wanted them to know and to respect the fact that they have a mind of incredible potential, that they have a heart capable of generosity, kindness, and love, that they are complete beings capable of moving and working in any and all directions.

So these three fields, the perception-thinking-and-learning piece plus the music and the sciences, became for me the three strands that all my adult life have been pulsing in some kind of triple-helix relationship, informing virtually everything I have done. If I reflect on my world view today and my sense of the inner world from which I operate, I don't believe I'm especially conscious of the disciplinary boundaries traditionally impressed on the problems and challenges I wrestle with. On the inside, it's all one piece. The landscape is continuous, varied, and reflexive, but ultimately one uninterrupted expanse. I take this as given. I simply come to each task before me with these three aspects as part of the equation. That's the foundational piece.

SEEDING DESIRE FOR A LIFE FILLED WITH LEARNING AND LIVING THROUGH CREATIVITY

If I look to my own experience and endeavour to extrapolate from that and the scholarship of many years, for me the ultimate fundamental is desire. We need to plant seeds of desire in our students. And right alongside desire, or within that seed of desire, are the love of play and the joy of curiosity. These things come to life through engagement with one's interior world and through collaboration with the friends and colleagues around us. It's an interior and exterior sense of engagement that manifests through play and exploration powered by direct access to desire and curiosity.

If that engine is primed and running on all cylinders within a young person, then that young person's learning is unfettered and unstoppable. But priming a young person's desire can sometimes be difficult to do. We live in a world of structures and rules and pre-formed paths, and we have felt the need to impress these things on young learners. This becomes a series of filters and constraints that in all too many instances crushes and stifles desire and curiosity.

When I speak with teachers, I invite them with great compassion first and foremost to rediscover desire and curiosity in themselves, their own love affair with learning. What do they yearn to explore? Where are those impulses? They should be practised openly with a sense of ownership and delight, saying this is who I am and this is what I love to do. When a teacher can bring this positivity and desire into the classroom, he or she is modelling the love of learning we want to seed in our children. If students can perceive their teacher brilliant in her delight of creativity, exploration, and learning, they too will seek that brilliance and feel empowered to explore their curiosities, their desires for a life filled with learning.

THE POWERFUL CONNECTION BETWEEN CREATIVITY AND CONNECTIVITY

I want to juxtapose this beautiful and powerful word "creativity" with another word equally beautiful and powerful, "connectivity." Both words can be linked to a sense of play, to exploration and desire. For me, they have always formed the yin and yang of our learning experience. Creativity and connectivity—each informs and empowers the other. To energize and release creativity in students, we need to build around them an environment so rich in sensory experience and ripe with the curiosities of the wider world that every step they take, by virtue of their own desire to explore, meets up with possibilities for personal discovery and connection. Connectivity needs to be embedded in the fabric of the resources they are reading, the concepts they are exploring, and the educational environments they are learning to navigate.

If we would grow creativity, we need to create an environment of connectivity. We also need to help students to sense that seeing connections among ideas is important, but seeing connections in the living world around them as we do in the ecology of nature is even more important. To see, to perceive, and to understand that connectivity is in the nature of Nature itself, with a capital N. That, that's what makes the living world living. From the point of view of my physics training, one could point just as well to the inorganic world, to the physical world of subatomic particles, fields and waves—all interconnected.

"It's all a matter of relationships." Gregory Bateson used to say this quite a lot, that the essence of things is not so much what they appear to be in themselves (e.g., their definitions and properties as individual entities). What is crucial are the relationships of those entities to one another that gives them their true identities. Each thing is only something in relation to something else. So, we want to be able see this connectivity as a character- istic of our world, from the subatomic into the organic world, the micro and macro systems. That's the way the world works. I carry with me this belief system that connectivity is everywhere, and if, as a student, I actually enjoy connecting the things I see about me in my world, well, I'm just doing what comes naturally to human beings. It should flow as easily as that.

This beautiful word "connectivity" and its complement "creativity" have tremendous power in the realm of our human interactions as well. My dear friend, philosopher of education Maxine Greene, was fond of saying again and again that "imagination makes empathy possible." She wanted us to know that our gifts for imagination and creativity are more than tools for gaining us innovative advantage, but are the basis of our humanness, our sense of family with other human beings and other life forms. Empathy is our social connectivity.

These are such huge concepts—creativity and connectivity—and they manifest themselves on so many levels in a lifetime. They need to be funda- mental to what happens in our educational environments.

RESCUING PERCEPTION FROM BELIEF: IMAGINATION, CREATIVITY, AND THE INNER WORK OF ART

Throughout this entire realm of educating for creative development, grow- ing young minds and young human beings, I've been fascinated, as I men- tioned earlier, by the centrality of our processes of perception. Think for a moment, probably the most frequently paired word with *perception,* as we commonly think of it, is *illusion;* that is, perceptions that lead to wrong con- clusions or what we call *misperceptions.* But these misperceptions and illu- sions are not just the result of flaws in the biomechanics of our eyes. It's far trickier than that. If we go back to the wonderfully insightful English poet William Blake, we learn that he referred to these limited and limiting percep- tions as the direct consequence of our "mind-forged manacles." "As a Man is, so he Sees." In other words, he was saying that our beliefs inform our percep- tions. Our beliefs can limit, bias, or liberate our perceptions. So, perception really is a trickster process, governed in part by biological mechanism and in part by our quality of mind. "As the Eye is formed, such are its Powers." I feel that educators are in the business of forming "the Eye." Not just the visual anatomic eye, but the eye that is the mind. And, let's change the spelling now, the "I" which is the self, that too. That's what's really at stake here. So we must be deeply invested in the formation of the eye, that eye of imagination that sees possibility, that sees beyond appearances, that expands the vision of the biological eye and, in so doing, participates intimately and powerfully in the formation of the self.

I like to play with a phrase that came to me some years ago that captures some of the riddle of perception as it applies to our experience of art. It's simply this: "the inner work of art." Think about that for a moment—the inner work of art. First, there's the inner work that is compelled by the very experience of art. Whether we are observing it, swimming in it, or making it, there's inner work aplenty going on, sharpening our senses, perspectives, skills, and lots of exploring and reflecting. Good, solid inner work. But ultimately, all that inner work has a catalytic effect on you yourself, such that the inner work of art is now engaged in the formation of the self. Now "the work of art" is you, your self. Not just a verb process of doing inner work. Yes, that's important. But the result of doing inner work is that you have created and continue to create change in your self; you are forming your self, self-authoring—the inner work of art is the self.

If the experience of art can be enlivened to the degree of catalyzing interior processes that expand our capacities and the acuity of the senses and the curiosity that we have for making connections and understandings, we are forming a self that is unstoppable. This is what we want our young people to experience. We want to help them to form themselves so their inner eye is powerful, so that the self that they author is powerful. That's the connection between perception and belief I was talking about earlier that has fascinated me all these years.

Neuroscience, by the way, has revealed so much about how we think and learn, including the fact that our biological processes engaged in the act of perception, activating particular components of our neuroanatomy, are virtually identical and in many ways indistinguishable from the biological mechanisms engaged by imagined experience. So *imagined experience*, which we might think of as experience generated from the inside and projected outward via our sensory channels (e.g., interior vision, interior sound, and so on) is the mirror image of *perceived experience*, which uses the same sensory channels to bring the outside world inside. The anatomic realities of both processes are virtually identical. In this light, imagination is not some nebulous, disembodied process. Imagination is as anatomically and physically embodied as the simple—not so simple—act of perception.

2

The Educational Culture of Collaborative Creativity

PART 1—THE FOUNDATIONS OF AN EDUCATIONAL CULTURE OF COLLABORATIVE CREATIVITY

ROBERT KELLY

Collaboration as Natural Practice and Innovation Imperative

An educational culture that is conducive to collaboration is absolutely essential to enable a broader educational culture of creativity. This entails inherent educational design without its built-in skew effects that limit creative development.

What is culture? Merriam-Webster's (2016) simple definition describes culture as "a way of thinking, behaving, or working that exists in a place or organization." The Center for Advanced Research on Language Acquisition at the University of Minnesota (2016) defines culture as "the shared patterns of behaviors and interactions, cognitive constructs, and affective understanding that are learned through a process of socialization. These shared patterns identify the members of a culture group while also distinguishing the members of another group." Lederach (1995) defines culture as "the shared knowledge and schemes created by a set of people for perceiving, interpreting, expressing, and responding to the social realities around them" (p. 9).

We are social beings. We acquire behavioural patterns and understandings of rules and ways of being in a group quite readily and at a very early age. We pick up on patterns very quickly and internalize them as normal ways of doing within a group. In formal education, learners acquire patterns and expected ways of knowing and doing quite easily.

I can remember when my then six-year-old son came home from his first day of school in grade one with a craft that resembled a spider. It was made from half an egg carton with pipe-cleaner legs and other decorations. I asked him, "Did you make that in art today?" and his answer was, "Ya, we did spiders this year." I was hung up on the fact that he added "this year" to his response. It was only the first day of his second year in formal schooling. I asked him, "What do you mean, this year?" and he replied, "We made caterpillars last year out of the same materials. We just used the whole egg carton instead of half of one." He was already on to pattern and predictability of education.

This is in stark contrast to an experience I had with six- and seven-year-olds at an earlier visit to experience the learning culture of Brightworks, a private school in San Francisco that I describe in Kelly (2012). Gever Tulley, the school's founder (also founder of the Tinkering School), instructed me on my first day to go along with the six- and seven-year-old group to a small lake in Golden Gate Park to launch the boats they had designed and built. I assumed they were model boats. However, once we started loading everything for the trip, I quickly realized that these were actual boats the learners had designed and constructed. The boats had been tested in a makeshift pool in one corner of the school. The field testing of the actual boats by the students at Stow Lake was an adventure but very rich in learning and feedback about refining prototypes for further testing. This was an educational culture built around collaborative design and invention.

Andy Smallman, co-founder of Puget Sound Community School, a private school for grades six to twelve in Seattle, reflects on the nature of a collaborative educational culture and how it is constructed:

> The imperative of a collaborative educational culture is that if you do not have a space in which people feel safe, secure and supported then students will not be enabled to collaborate. The ongoing development of this environment is something that has to be constantly attended to. Students have to feel respected and safe enough to step out to connect and collaborate. Collaboration within this environment is just natural to human beings. If you are in a space where you feel safe and secure and supported, you will want to start engaging with other people. A starting point is to remove any barriers that are in the way. I think many educational settings are inadvertently creating obstacles and barriers that prevent students from collaborating with other students or even students collaborating with adults. These environments are individually based. They are characterized by inherent structures that reduce educational practice down to simply

telling all the students that they have to do this particular thing and
they get to do it with these people for a certain amount of time and then
they have to compete with these people in order to get that high grade or
whatever represents achievement. That's the antithesis to collaboration.
Collaboration is natural practice and behavior in a safe and supporting
environment. You don't necessarily have to create the space, you have to
eliminate what we've done a lot in education and then it just happens.
(A. Smallman, personal communication, January 16, 2016)

Human beings have an innate disposition for intuitive/adaptive creativity that enables us to improvise our way through any number of challenges that are part of everyday living. In supportive, collaborative environments, this capacity can be grown to enable engagement in more complex and sustained creative initiatives. Sawyer (2007) talks about how "children are readily able to improvise if left on their own" (p. 31). He characterizes successful improvisational and collaborative teams as those where "members play off against one another, each person's contributions providing the spark for the rest. Together, the improvisational team creates a novel emergent product, one that's more responsive to the changing environment and better than anyone could have created alone" (p. 14). This resonates with Nelson's notion of amplifying the ideas of those in one's collaborative environment (Edutopia, 2008). This also speaks to the exponential increase in the power and potential of a collaborative group versus someone working alone. This is becoming increasingly more apparent in a growing interconnected world. Leadbeater (2008) believes that new generations will be defined by what they share, not by what they own. The sharing of ideas is a central value of the rapidly growing Maker Movement (Hatch, 2014). Waks (2014) further adds that " in this new culture of making and connecting, learners increasingly expect to connect and will turn increasingly away from learning environments that constrain collaboration" (p. 89).

One of the principle barriers toward the development of a collaborative culture is the notion that ideas are the personal property of individuals (and thus must be guarded from any potential competition). This privatization of ideas is connected to this and other inherited values of the broader market economy culture. Lakhani (cited in Elbaek, 2006) sees ideas and knowledge in this context as being viewed as privately owned commodities that are bought and sold. Trade and economy are further viewed as being about the monetary value of things instead of natural interrelated human activity. Lakhani contends that the preoccupation with the commodification of knowledge and ideas, and its accompanying hypercompetition and inherent privacy, has led to endemic alienation and a lack of community—the antithesis of a truly compassionate, empathetic, collaborative culture. Tom and David Kelley (2013) of the design firm IDEO maintain that in order for any collaborative innovative team to work, "people have to buy into the mindset of working together toward a shared solution" (p. 186). They further explain that in this collaborative context, "No one person is responsible for the final outcome. It is the result of everyone's contribution. Instead of individuals protecting 'my idea,' colleagues become comfortable with group ownership" (p. 186).

Infinite Potentials, Interrelatedness, and Perpetual Change

At the very core of an educational culture of collaborative creativity is individual and collective empowerment in any number of communities. Empowerment begins with hope—the optimistic belief that positive outcomes are attainable in the future. Learners and educators have to be equipped with the appropriate tools to grow a hopeful disposition. This is difficult to achieve without being part of a supportive, collaborative culture. Comprehensive creative development within a supportive, collaborative environment empowers each participant with the capacity and tools to act to fulfill aspirations borne out of hopefulness. It inherently breeds a collaborative, creative culture characterized by a disposition of hope, imagination, exploration, experimentation, and invention. I like to frame this educational culture of collaborative creativity as being built upon three foundational principles:

- the principle of infinite potentials;
- the principle of interrelatedness, and
- the principle of perpetual change.

These three foundational principles inform a balanced educational culture in which systematic creative development creates a catalytic educational environment where social/emotional development and cognitive development can grow and flourish.

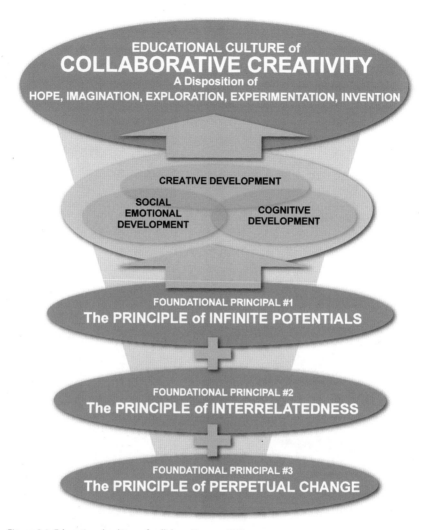

Figure 2.1: Educational culture of collaborative creativity

The principle of infinite potentials

The principle of infinite potentials refers to a belief that any idea has the potential to grow into an infinite number of combinations of new ideas, which leads to adaptive, novel production through collaborative, creative practice. This principle is rooted in a corresponding belief that any human being as the generator of ideas has the potential to produce an infinite number of adaptive, novel productions through their engagement in collaborative, sustained creative practice. Ideas for creative production that are planted in high-stimuli collaborative environments have unlimited potential for cross-pollination and hybridizing into new entities. The dynamic of idea generation is discussed in detail in chapter 3 (Engaging in Creative Practice). To carry the seed metaphor further, a seed for potential creative production that is planted in infertile ground has limited potential for growth. If the educational environment is not designed around creative development, how will learners or educators ever come to know or realize their creative potentials and the empowerment that comes with them?

Educational systems that measure learner success solely through discipline complexity development are only attending to one of many factors that work interdependently to enable creative development. Learners ascending through a system in which their potential and achievement valuation is based solely on discipline complexity achievement and corresponding vertical comparisons develop their self-perception of their personal potential through these valuations. The result is the endemic under-enabling of learners and educators that is inherent in these systems, which ultimately results in widespread under-empowerment. More importantly, participants in these consumption-intense educational cultures often internalize a belief that they are limited in their creative capabilities—a belief that is carried into adulthood. We become very good at consuming but not very good at acting and creating through empowerment. The unfortunate part about this perception of disempowerment is that the very opposite is true; many carry on in everyday life without ever realizing their unlimited creative potential or even becoming aware that they had any potential at all. This does not imply that everyone will eventually become a Picasso or a T. S. Eliot, who are well known by many across their respective fields. However, any generated idea can mathematically continually morph exponentially into new iterations. The potential of this idea becomes a microcosm for the potential of anyone's creative life journey. Waking up every morning to infinite possibilities with the capacity to realize them is far more hopeful than seeing oneself as a B or a D student. The principle of infinite potentials informs a broader educational culture of collaborative creativity in which the infinite potentials of all participants are assumed and enabled through comprehensive creative development.

The principle of interrelatedness

The principle of interrelatedness refers to a belief that every organic and inorganic entity is connected. As social beings, every human action has an impact on other human beings and the world around us. An understanding of the depth and breadth of the ecology of these inter-relationships is essential to mobilizing the inherent power of creating collaboratively and understanding its impact. Developing a capacity for empathy is at the core of mobilizing the potential of collaborative creativity. Empathy can be described as the ability to see and feel things through the eyes of others, characterized by sensitive communication through the sharing of thought and feeling (Cooper, 2011). It is part of broader social/emotional development. Cooper (2011) adds that "the immediate conditions in which people are able to interact, and the emotional capacity of the individuals both facilitate and constrain the development of empathy" (p. 8).

Goleman (1995), in explaining the concept of emotional intelligence, describes how empathy is central to the social skills needed to manage the impact of one's thoughts and emotions on others while understanding the thoughts and emotions of others. Bell (2014) adds that empathy is essential for effective team building to maximize productivity. Sawyer's (2007) description of the characteristics of effective creative teams stresses the importance of engaging in deep listening and building on the ideas of others to enable collaborative creativity. This is best accomplished through sensitive communication and compassionate interrelationships. In this process, all participants are validated and all ideas are accepted and built upon with sensitivity to the impact of the resultant actions on everyone and everything. Creative development will not occur in educational environments that inadvertently foster alienation, fragmentation, and lack of community. Leadbeater (2008) further adds that "Greater individual participation will not, on its own, add up to much unless it is matched by a capacity to share and then combine our ideas" (p. 5). The development of interrelationship sensitivity, understanding, and functionality enables an educational culture of collaborative creativity.

The principle of perpetual change

This principle refers to the belief that educational design should enable participants to adapt to perpetual change and to create positive, perpetual change through original research, production, and action. The pace of change is rapid whether due to technological innovation, macro-economics changes, environmental changes, population growth, or social/cultural changes. It is very difficult for organizational structures to catch up to change and adapt because of the inertia of resistance from

professional culture and other stakeholders who are used to predictability and stability. Organizational transformation requires the development of not only a capacity to manage change, but also a capacity to
embrace and initiate positive change. Borgen and Windeløv-Lidzélius
(2013) describe change competency as the ability to think in new terms,
to learn and unlearn, and to manage ambiguity, complexity, and turbu-
lence. This change competency is accompanied by action competency.
Action competency is defined as the ability to show initiative, set goals,
prioritize, make decisions, and get things done. Adapting to change and
initiating positive change in an educational context requires addressing,
engaging, and acting upon real-world problems for real-world audiences
(Richardson, 2012). This requires the support and potential power of a
collaborative, creative culture.

Machine-organization educational structures continually resist fundamental change. Waks (2014) corroborates this reality, noting that
"the impulse for change has been contained by the dominant paradigm"
(p. 31). Further to this belief, he states that "Policy makers have continually tolerated variations in the surface elements of schools so long as the
deep structural elements of the hierarchical school—the pre-determined
curriculum sequences, distinct subject matters, and standardized tests—
remain in place" (p. 31).

An educational culture of collaborative creativity requires fundamental organizational change. It has to reinvent to become inventive to
reflect cultural and societal change in a networked world. Mintzberg's
(1989) innovation organization built on the adhocracy organizational
structure is designed around enabling invention and certainly points the
way to the future shape and form of educational practice. It is characterized by its fluid, dynamic, flattened structure working in shifting multidisciplinary and transdisciplinary teams to enable innovation. Experts
come and go as needed depending on the inventive task at hand. These
structures are typically technologically intense. They value and enable
entrepreneurship and intrapreneurship (entrepreneurship within an
organization).

Innovative organizations can exist on their own or as innovative/
adhocratic sub-organizations within a larger organization. This is a
possible path to incremental transformation of traditional educational
practice. The positive educational energy of an educational culture that
assumes its participants have infinite creative potentials is innately validating for its members. An educational culture built on compassionate,
sensitive communication and heightened interrelationship awareness is
nurturing and fertile ground for invention. An educational culture that

is designed to enable the creation of positive change through innovation and invention is exciting—and hopeful.

REFERENCES

Bell, J. (2014). *Emotional intelligence: A practical guide to mastering emotions.* (Kindle). B00K3ZVILW.

Borgen, O., & Windeløv-Lidzélius, C. (2013). Change competence. In *Mastery in the making.* Retrieved from Kaospilot.dk.

Center for Advanced Research on Language Acquisition, University of Minnesota. *What is culture?* Retrieved from Carla.umn.edu.

Cooper, B. (2011). *Empathy in education: Engagement, values and achievement.* London: Bloomsbury Academic.

Edutopia. (2008). Randy Nelson on learning and working in the collaborative age. Retrieved from edutopia.org.

Elbaek, U. (2006). *Kaospilot A-Z.* Aarhus: KaosCommunication.

Goleman, D. (1995). *Emotional intelligence.* New York: Bantam Books.

Hatch, M. (2014). *The maker movement manifesto.* New York: McGraw-Hill.

Kelly, R. (2012). *Educating for creativity: A global conversation.* Edmonton: Brush Education.

Kelley, D., & Kelley, T. (2013). *Creative confidence.* New York: Crown Business.

Leadbeater, C. (2008). *We-think: The power of mass creativity.* London: Profile Books.

Lederach, J.P. (1995). *Preparing for peace: Conflict transformation across cultures.* Syracuse: Syracuse University Press.

Merriam-Webster Dictionary and Thesaurus. Definition of "culture." Retrieved on January 26, 2016 from Merriam-Webster.com.

Mintzberg, H. (1989). *Mintzberg on management.* New York: The Free Press.

Richardson, W. (2012). *Why school?* New York: TED Books.

Sawyer, R.K. (2007). *Group genius: The creative power of collaboration.* New York: Basic Books.

Waks, L. (2014). *Education 2.0.* Boulder: Paradigm Publishers.

PART 2—CREATING CONDITIONS FOR A CULTURE OF COLLABORATIVE CREATIVITY

PAULINE BRODERICK, ELIZABETH COFFMAN, AND BERYL PETERS

Pauline Broderick is veteran teacher, arts educator, and curriculum developer with a special interest in the arts and social change. She teaches in the Faculty of Education at the University of Manitoba and has worked professionally as an actor, writer, and producer.

Elizabeth Coffman is an instructor in art and drama in the Faculty of Education at the University of Manitoba. She is a founding member of the Alliance for Arts Education in the province of Manitoba. She has recently published a volume entitled *Dramatic Play in the Early Years*.

Beryl Peters, PhD, has taught art and music in schools and universities from Texas to the Yukon. She is an arts education consultant with the province of Manitoba, where she develops and writes arts curricula and resources.

The Need for Collaboration

The collaborative process begins with a positive—a yes, a willingness to begin. It assumes a position of trust that when given an invitation, participants are eager to step up and contribute to endeavours bigger than themselves. When creative collaboration works, it is generative and sustaining. When it doesn't work? Well . . . can you remember group experiences where the groups and topics were assigned? Where time limits and roles were imposed and we were asked to cooperate and come to a consensus? Creative collaboration? Sometimes it happened, but other times, individuals dominated the conversation and persuaded group members to go along with them. Those who disagreed became silent and, in the end, a brave soul took over and wrote it all down. Some of us carry the legacy of these early experiences with us as we consider what collaboration means in today's world.

In the twenty-first century, creative collaboration must go beyond the old notion of group work. Look at the world around us. Technology is extending us in ways that were science fiction to the previous generation, yet many of our approaches to teaching and learning remain rooted in the last century's transmission models. Today, we are able to connect and create in ever-changing ways. We can communicate with each other across the globe instantaneously; we cross boundaries of time and space, culture, and discipline. Never before in the lifespan of the species have we simultaneously been so connected and so isolated, "so informed and so unaware . . . so free in thought and so bound by what bombards us" (Redekopp, 2015). We are educating in paradoxical times. Present circumstances demand a relevant reframing of what collaboration means for the current generation.

Considerations for collaboration

Collaboration is a process and a practice that unites two or more points of view in relationship and common purpose (Slater & Ravid, 2010). It is a community of care that starts with one, then one in relation to another and the larger group. Fels and Belliveau (2008) refer to it as a "generative space of possibility" (p. 26). Creative collaboration is a culture of involved individuals who willingly contribute their thinking and energy toward an agreed upon expression of ideas.

Unpacking the nature of the collaborative process can provide insights into an educational space that balances the needs and contributions of the individual within the ecology of the group. This is an educational space that invites individual agency while also inviting and enticing collective creation. This depiction of collaboration is more complex than simple protocol can capture. Recognizing this complexity, we offer a description of the conditions that enable a culture of creative collaboration. It is a field guide if you will; a loosely drawn map that orients the reader to the lay of the land as we understand it. It is offered to those whose adventurous spirits will take them there. These conditions are happening all at once, but putting them in the form of directions helps to answer the question: "What can an educator do to support a culture of collaborative creation?"

RECOGNIZE THAT THE LEARNING CONTEXT ALWAYS IMPACTS COLLABORATIVE EFFORTS AND PROCESS.

The individuals involved, the community attitudes, the tools and technologies used, and the physical space all interact dynamically to shape the context of the creative, collaborative process. Individuals bring the sum of who they are into the educational place. Being responsive to specific contexts requires that we recognize the existing circumstances as places of beginning. Without judgement, we start with where the group is and work to invite them in to a shared creative practice. Read the group. Consider the interactions of individuals and the energy they bring to the moment. Renowned drama educator, Dorothy Heathcote (1984) would encourage everyone to accept and celebrate all of these conditions.

BE PREPARED TO SLOW DOWN.

From the onset, there are no shortcuts to creating an environment in which people feel safe to share their thinking and are willing to take creative risks. An investment of time is necessary. We need to consider how we make time, take time, and shape time to support a culture of collaborative creation. Time spent thinking and working on community relations is essential to the creative, collaborative process. Our thinking shifts to value the pause, silence, daydreaming, wondering, experimentation, failure, and the many iterations necessary for idea development. This can be a challenge to the "cult of efficiency" where expeditiously arriving at a predetermined goal is the primary concern (Gross Stein, 2002).

UNDERSTAND THAT LEADERSHIP ROLES IN THE COLLABORATIVE PROCESS ARE NOT STATIC.

At different points we may be a facilitator, mentor, coach, cheerleader, collaborator, connoisseur, critic, or an audience member. Once we step beyond the transmission model that has dominated the educational landscape, we can consider how we choose to position ourselves in relation to student learning. Consider what role to play and when. It changes according to individual needs, the nature of the group, and the shifting and emerging contexts. Flexibility is key and it can be learned.

ACKNOWLEDGE THAT EVERYONE IN THE GROUP HAS SOMETHING TO CONTRIBUTE.

This sounds simple, but it requires the creation of an environment in which individuals feel safe to authentically invest themselves in the process. The facilitator works to surface different experiences, while at the same time encouraging sufficient interaction among diverse orientations to enable new ideas to emerge. Too often the goal is to homogenize perspectives rather than invite multiple, diverse points of view that will enrich the collaborative process. Fenwick (2012) affirms that we do better when we actively recognize our "respective diversity and languages, rather than seeking to immediately find commonality—not just recognizing but learning to be explicit about one's own expertise and explicitly engaging others' diverse expertise were critical processes for enabling emergence" (p. 142).

Learners and educators are more likely to engage in a collaborative process when they feel their contributions are recognized and that all voices are valued. This in itself takes time and will require an equalization of power relations in the group. In a creative, collaborative culture, we work to decentralize control and eliminate hierarchy. We let go of our own fixed agenda to build on what is present within the group and support what is yet to emerge. Participation is always an invitation to be supported in finding meaningful ways to contribute to the process.

ESTABLISH COMMON PURPOSE.

Although there is no expectation of homogenous outcome, creative collaboration has purpose, intention, and focus. We ask ourselves "What do we want to do? What is the task at hand? What are the individual and group questions? What do we want to know? What is important and what is meaningful to us?" Probing questions can help to establish direction for action. Start with the nub of an idea. Ripples go out and bump into things. We can't predict where an idea is going to go as the process is emergent and co-evolving. Keep questions open-ended and don't worry if there are no answers—yet! Ideas are banked and recorded in what may be termed an artifact trail to encourage recursive engagement. You never know when an idea generated in week one can be re-energized and brought back into action. We work to keep ideas in play and available to inform and enrich direction. Not every idea is used but ideas belong to everyone and they all shape the process.

ENABLE A COLLABORATIVE, CREATIVE ENVIRONMENT.

If we enter the process with a fixed idea of what will occur, we eliminate the opportunity for other voices to emerge. We quash the possibilities of the serendipitous, the surprise, and ultimately the possibility of innovation. We all bring with us an inherent desire to connect. Once connection is made, we find links to each other and ideas begin to generate.

Start with baby steps. What is the smallest thing we can do together? In the process of generating ideas, we tease out points of connection that let all participants see their contributions as part of a whole. In a collaborative, creative environment, we work to support multiple avenues of exploration and expression—multiple windows into whatever is the focus of our collective attention. We invite different perspectives to contribute to our collective process and emerging understanding. For example, we may wonder, "If we were looking at this from the perspective of a dancer, what would we see? A scientist? A business lens? A historical lens? A cultural lens?" We may also consider "What language shapes our thinking?" Recognize and value diversity as an asset and a catalyst for continued exploration and new connections. Individual contributions are valued and serve to establish an idea-rich environment, and they also help to articulate the parameters of a locally constructed understanding of an issue. As we make explicit our partial perspective, our creative collaboration becomes an expression of who and what we are in the moment.

There are numerous strategies out there that can be employed to scaffold a gentle introduction to collective engagement. In our experience, the arts can be especially fruitful here. Dance, music, visual arts, and drama can be infused in any learning environment. They invite us to focus our collective attention and to get out of our chairs and move together. They sensitize our perceptions and remind us of the power of story. They remind us what play is and let us practise low-risk inter-actions where mistakes are teaching moments. They encourage us to imagine together.

THE TASK AT HAND MUST HAVE SIGNIFICANCE AND MEANING FOR THE GROUP.

No one wants to invest energy in a trivial pursuit. The task has to be worth our efforts. The facilitator works to illuminate the significance of the task, drawing on input from the group. The collaboration must be seen as desirable and doable, and it can't be imposed. However, it can be negotiated and it can be shaped. A plan of action will emerge from rich and recursive interactions between people and materials. Idea gen-eration and incubation are actively sought and supported as part of the convergent/divergent pulse of ideation within the creative process (Kelly & Leggo, 2008).

EXPECT STRUGGLE.

Often we work to minimize or eliminate struggle in the collaborative process. It is not a neat and tidy procedure, and struggle is a necessary element that draws out the critical impulse. Lean in to places of resis-tance because they can offer insights and deepen our thinking. We work to create spaces that shape learning but also allow players to actively struggle, which ultimately leads to new insights. Always be open to "the game changer," the moment when a new idea bursts into the process and we recognize it to be innovation. We can't tell you what it looks like in advance of it happening, but we know it when we see it.

A Threshold of Promise

As we embody a collaborative stance and embrace our creative potential, we step onto a new threshold of promise, one that engages us in a range of possibilities for what education might mean for our learners. In the electric surround, performative environment we now inhabit, new stories need to be told. These stories are yet to be written and when they are, we will want them to be creative collaborations, won't we?

REFERENCES

Fels Elliott, M., Fels, L., & Belliveau, G. (2008). *Exploring curriculum: Performative inquiry, role drama and learning.* Vancouver, British Columbia: Pacific Educational Press.

Fenwick, T. (2012). Complexity science and professional learning for collaboration: A critical reconsideration of possibilities and limitations. *Journal of Education and Work, 25*(1), 141–162. http://dx.doi.org/10.1080/13639080.2012.644911

Gross Stein, J., & CBC. (2002). The cult of efficiency. CBC Massey lectures. Toronto: Anansi Press.

Heathcote, D., Johnson, L., & O'Neill, C. (1984). *Dorothy Heathcote: Collected writings on education and drama.* London: Hutchinson.

Kelly, R., & Leggo, K. (2008). *Creative expression, creative education: Creativity as a primary rationale for education.* Calgary, Alberta: Brush Education.

Redekopp, R. (2015) "Where is the wisdom?" poem retrieved December 2015 from http://rredekopp.blogspot.ca/2015/12/facts-to-thoughts-to-wisdom.html

Slater, J. J., & Ravid, R. (2010). *Collaboration in education.* New York: Taylor & Francis.

CREATING DEVELOPMENT 2

Building Trust and Accepting Ideas

PAULINE BRODERICK, ELIZABETH COFFMAN, AND BERYL PETERS

The games and exercises described in this section offer opportunities to practise several qualities that support a culture of creative collaboration. Many of these activities have evolved from years of teaching practice and some have been around long enough to be part of common use. They are offered as a palette of possibility for gentle action. They are invitations to grow a culture that builds trust to enable acceptance of ideas from others in a truly collaborative setting. They are also invitations to invent your own activities to build trust among group members.

Who Are You?

In this activity, group members are seated in a circle. They introduce themselves by saying their name in a way that tells the group qualities about themselves or how they might be feeling at that particular time. For example, the first participant might wish to reveal that they are feeling tired and so they might gesture downward and say their name in a quiet, sighing manner. If the next group member was feeling energetic, they might spring up, gesture upward, and say their feelings loudly and excitedly. Depending on the level of comfort of the group, the participants may echo each person's name in the same manner to share in their feelings and experience. Alternatively, after each participant has voiced her or his name, the entire group could say the participant's names together in turn as they were introduced, going around the circle.

A variation of this activity could be echoing names with rhythm and inflection. A participant begins the introductions by saying her or his name with a particular rhythm and inflection. The person beside them repeats the name in the same manner, and then adds her or his own name using a different inflection and rhythmic pattern. The next person repeats the name of the person sitting beside them, and then adds their own name in another inflection and pattern, and so on around the circle.

The Sound of a Name

In this expressive activity, the group stands in a circle and one person says their name with dynamic, expressive qualities. She or he uses melody and rhythm, with a corresponding movement, to communicate to other members in the circle. For example, one participant might walk into the circle and back out again while saying their name in rhythm loudly: [walk in] "Ann, Ann, Ann, Ann," [walk back] "Ann, Ann, Ann, Ann" [look at another participant across the circle]. The second participant, Karla, then repeats Ann's sound and movement and adds her own: [walk in] "Ann, Ann, Ann, Ann," [walk back] "Ann, Ann, Ann, Ann" [look at another participant across the circle], "Karla, Karla" [said with a low sound on "Kar," and a high sound accompanied by a jump on the syllable "la"]. Another participant then echoes Karla's sounds and movements before she or he adds her or his own name in sound and movement, and so the activity continues.

Find the Rhythm

This rhythm exercise begins as each group member claps a simple rhythm and then listens to the others so that the group can find one common rhythm that they can all clap together. When group members are all clapping the same beat, they then pat new rhythms until the group finds a common rhythm again. When the new rhythmic pattern becomes common, group members then snap new rhythms. The game can proceed through several different predetermined body percussion parts.

Rainstorm

To begin this activity, the group sits together in a circle and decides on a sequence of sounds to make a rainstorm.

1. The leader begins with the first sound; for example, a gentle rain sound created by rubbing her or his hands together, back and forth.
2. Next, the group member to the left of the leader, and then each subsequent group member, makes the leader's sound.
3. When the person to the right of the leader makes the original sound, the leader adds a new sound; for example finger snaps. The sound travels around the group in the same way as the first round, with each group member in turn making the sound.
4. After that sound and motion goes around the circle, foot stomps are added. Then the sounds are done in reverse order so the rainstorm is heard to die away, bit by bit.

Moving to the Drum Game

This game can be used to build trust with group members as they move through a room together without entering each other's personal space. It can also be used as scaffolding for the "Bubble Game."

1. One participant volunteers to play the drum.
2. Group members find a personal space or bubble where they cannot touch any other group member.
3. The group moves in response to the sound of the drum and can only move when the drum is heard. The participants make one movement every time they hear a drum sound.
4. Group members must work to ensure that, as they move, they do not enter any other group member's personal space or bubble. For example, if the drummer plays one sound and then stops, the participants make one motion and then freeze. If the drummer makes two sounds in a row, then participants make two different motions in response to the quality of sound. If the sound is short and sharp, then the motion must match. If the drum plays a steady, gentle beat, then the corresponding motion must also match.
5. Once the group has had a chance to become familiar with the sound of the drum, the drummer may make the game more challenging by speeding up or slowing down the drum beats, or by playing drum beats louder and softer, with the participants matching their movements to the sounds.

The Bubble Game

The purpose of this activity is to help and support group members and to create awareness of each other's personal space and the space in the room. The object of the activity is for the group to ensure that all participants make it safely from one side of the room to the other. Participants move in imaginary bubbles across a room to the sound of appropriate music (e.g., Saint-Saens, "The Aquarium"). Before beginning, group members co-construct or define the size of their bubbles. To begin, participants move their bubbles in various directions. For example, they may move up, down, or swirl around while maintaining awareness of other participants and avoiding entering their personal bubbles. If one participant enters another's bubble, then both participants must sit down at that place until another participant comes near them and blows their bubbles up again.

Be My Mirror

In this activity, group members work together to express mirrored patterns and movements.

1. To begin, the group stands together in a circle. One participant is chosen to be the leader and perform a particular rhythm and movement, such as hand clapping, and all group members mirror that rhythm and movement.
2. When the leader is ready, she or he silently communicates to another group member in the circle to take over as leader by locking eyes with that member. That member becomes the new leader and begins a new rhythmic pattern and movement, such as finger snapping, and the entire group again mirrors the new movement and sound.
3. The game continues for as long as desired.

Fill the Space

This interactive activity begins with the group walking around the room at a normal speed. Group members are encouraged to fill the entire space. Participants are coached to "change direction," "change level," and "change speed." At random moments, members are instructed to "FREEZE." At that point, participants must break freeze by making eye contact with the nearest group member and introducing themselves. For example, a group member may say, "Hello, my name is Vanda." As soon as introductions are finished, the group moves again. The intention is to connect with as many participants as possible while exploring a range of ways of moving in space. To add challenges, group members may be invited to move beyond eye contact and introductions to connect through body parts, perhaps by touching elbows, knees, toes, or fingers.

Self-Organization

To begin this activity, group members stand in a circle and one participant steps into the circle to identify who or what they are. For example, the first participant may say, " I am a park bench." Group members must then add to the scene by calling out who or what they are in relation to the first participant. For example, group members may say, "I am a tree," "I am a sidewalk," "I am a dog,""I am a building,""I am a bird."When everyone has contributed to the picture, the scene is done. The activity is repeated with as many scenes as group members can invent. With practice, relationships become more and more complex and nuanced.

The Sound Machine

To begin, clear a space and create enough room for the group to be together in one area. Group members will come together to make a musical instrument by using their bodies to create sounds and actions. The actions must be physical movements that correlate with the sounds that are made to create an ostinato (repeated sounds and actions). Inform the group that their chosen actions and sounds need to be easily repeated and that there is to be no speaking—the activity is built on trust.

A volunteer begins the sound machine by choosing a sound and a corresponding movement to be the centre of the machine. The remaining participants silently join in, when they are ready, to add onto the sound machine by connecting physically with one person to add variety in movement, levels, and sounds.

Participants should use a variety of levels, including sitting, standing, and lying down. They should also use a variety of body parts, such as hands, elbows, knees, and head. Movements should reinforce the sounds. For example, if the sound is high pitched, then the movement should be correspondingly high. If the vocalization is short, then the movement should be an abrupt and short motion.

When all participants are part of the sound machine, the leader allows the machine to work until a prearranged signal is given to halt. A final reflection on the successes and challenges of the activity will help group members consider what is needed to build a climate of trust and collaboration.

Things to Do in a Place

The group forms a circle to delineate a playing space to begin this activity. Invite the group to identify a series of locations where people may be said to "do things." Select one environment, such as a school, police station, hospital, or shopping mall. Invite volunteers to enter the circle and perform an action that would occur in the chosen location, without using words or sounds. Note how many actions the group can come up with in relation to a particular environment. The group reads the action and names it out loud. Once their action has been identified, the group member leaves the circle and another person enters. Group members continue acting out for as long as the group can come up with ideas for that location, then they move on to identify a new environment and perform actions for that location.

Joining In

In this activity, small groups create short rhythmic patterns and then play with other groups one by one until the entire group is playing together.

1. The large group is divided into smaller groups of approximately four in a group.

2. A leader is chosen, and she or he plays a favourite music selection or excerpt that all groups listen to together.

3. Each small group decides on a simple sequence of body percussion to perform to the beat of the music played by the leader. For example, one group might choose to alternate clapping and snapping fingers, another group might choose to walk forward and backward, and another group might choose to alternate patting thighs and clapping hands.

4. At this point, the leader plays the music. When the music is played, the groups perform their body percussion together as a group, but when the leader stops playing the music, the groups must stop.

5. A sequence of groups is chosen so that group 1 will begin, group 2 will join in, and so on. When the music begins, group 1 plays their body percussion. When the music stops, they stop. When the music begins again, group 2 joins group 1. When the music stops, they all stop. When the music begins again, three groups play together and stop together when the music stops. When the music is played for the final time, all groups will play and then stop together.

Word Songs I

In this game, group members collaborate together to create word songs.

1. The large group is divided into smaller groups of approximately four in a group.

2. Each small group, or individual members of the group, or the group together choose a word that they will use as a signal for a certain kind of sound. For example, the word "rain" could be used as the signal for hitting a triangle, jingling keys, rubbing hands together, or vocalizing "pitter patter."

3. Each small group then creates a first sentence using the suggested word. For example, the group might create the sentence "The rain fell gently on the ground." Instead of saying "rain," the word is played on the chosen instruments or with the selected vocalized sound. The sentence then sounds like "The (triangle) fell gently on the ground."

4. The group chooses a sequence of participants to add on to the first sentence, also using the cue word rain. For example, group members may say, "The rain fell gently on the ground." "The flowers loved to see the rain." "The rain made puddles everywhere." "The children played in all the rain." Each time the word "rain" is indicated, the chosen instrument is played instead of sounding the word.

5. Each group plays their word songs for the other groups.

Word Songs II

In this game, group members collaborate in a different way to create word songs.

1. The large group is divided into smaller groups of approximately four in a group.
2. Each small group chooses a topic they would like to explore (e.g., the theme of conflict).
3. Group members brainstorm individual sounds, gestures, or words associated with their theme. For example, for the theme of conflict, participants may suggest sounds such as hands loudly clapped together, or words such as "anger" or "disagree" shouted loudly.
4. One member of the group volunteers to be the conductor who points to each group member to make their sound or gesture, or to say their word. The conductor can use both hands to point to two people at once or hold a hand out to indicate that one member keeps sounding while other members are conducted to sound or stop. The conductor can also indicate volume of sound by making smaller or larger gestures and can change the tempo of the piece by speeding up or slowing down conducting gestures.

Body Percussion Rap

This activity involves group members using their bodies to create percussion music.

1. To begin, group members choose partners and take turns deciding what body percussion they will use to create a short rap. For example, partner one might decide to clap her hands twice. Partner two then adds on to the sequence by suggesting that they clap each other's hands twice. Then partner one might suggest that they touch each other's knees, first left and then right, and partner two adds that they should jump up and down twice.
2. Partners then find another set of partners to make a standing square of four. The same process of choosing percussion sounds is followed, but this time with four people.
3. The group of four then finds another group of four to revisit the process with eight people. Groups can then perform their percussion raps for each other.

Name Rap

In groups of four, participants in Name Rap create body percussion raps using each other's names.

1. In groups of four, participants introduce themselves to learn each other's names.

2. Group members work together to create a rhythm that matches the sound of each participant's name. For example, if "Joan" is said four times, it could be sounded with four repeated claps; "Eric, Eric, Eric Eric" could be eight snaps of alternating hands; "Sarah-Jo, Sarah-Jo, Sarah-Jo, Sarah-Jo" could be hands patting on thighs: left, right, left; "Peter Farraday, Peter Farraday, Peter Farraday, Peter Farraday" could be feet stomping in time to the sounds of the words.

3. The groups choose a sequence of names and perform the rhythms of the sequence using the chosen body percussion (or small percussion instruments if they are available).

4. Each group then extends the name rap by deciding on a short rhythmic section that can be played by all group members in between each rhythmic name pattern. For example, the extended name rap might take the form of four repeated claps, snap, clap, pat thighs, stomp; eight snaps with alternating hands; snap, clap, pat thighs, stomp; pat thighs left, right, left; snap, clap, pat thighs, stomp; feet stomp to Peter Farraday; finish with snap, clap, pat thighs, stomp.

Drawing Together

This activity can be conducted in small groups of three or four. On a large sheet of paper, one person draws an object, place ,or thing, or perhaps just a line or a shape. The sheet of paper is passed silently from one group member to the next, and each participant adds something that makes sense of the previous image. The group can continue to silently pass the paper around until the exercise is called to a halt. One individual in the group is given the task of creating a story from the collaborative image without comment from the rest of the group. As a point of discussion, group members may be asked to consider: "How difficult was it to draw on another person's idea?"

Same/Different

In this activity, groups of three or four are formed and each is given the same photocopied picture. The image may be a scene, a work of art, or a cartoon or illustration. Group members do not reveal their picture to the rest of their group. Without showing their image, each participant shares their impression of the picture without describing it or saying what they think it is about. For example, one group member might say, "My impression of this picture is that it is peaceful and calm." Another group member may say, "This picture is tense." Once all participants have shared their impressions, they reveal their images. Groups are encouraged to discuss their impressions and comments.

Feeling in Colour

In this artistic activity, each participant divides a piece of paper (any size) in two and is given an instrument for colouring. Although tempera paint is lovely to work with, any medium that involves colour is suitable for this activity.

1. Each group member privately chooses two contrasting emotions, such as joy/sorrow, gloomy/bright, pride/shame, relief/frustration, or hope/fear. Participants then use only lines, shapes, colours, and textures to express their chosen emotions and fill as much of one section of their paper as possible.

2. Participants place their work in a pile and group members take turns choosing pictures and talking about the work. While the speaker talks about another's work, the original artist simply listens without making comments.

3. Participants return the pictures to the pile and retrieve new pictures. The exercise continues with entirely new expressions to discuss. This time, both partners are welcome to interpret the creation they are looking at.

This activity challenges group members to let go of their own ideas and, without judgement, appreciate others and trust that they will appreciate their vision. As a point of discussion, group members may consider this question: "How difficult was it to draw on another person's idea?"

One Word Story Building

This simple activity begins with group members forming a circle. Together, group members will build a story one word at a time. A volunteer offers a word, and then each subsequent group member adds another word to the story until the narrative can no longer be sustained.

And Then

"And Then" begins with one group member starting a story. At any point in her or his narrative, the participant says "and then," and the story is passed on to the group member beside them. Together, the group builds a story, one section at a time, and continues as long as the group can sustain it. To add variation, the storyteller can step into the centre of the circle when speaking and pass the story to anyone in the circle.

3

Engaging in Creative Practice:
From Design Thinking to Design Doing

ROBERT KELLY

Design: The Accessible Gateway to Creative Development

Creative development is the systematic growth in creative capacity of an individual or group over time. Our creative capacity can only be increased by engaging in creative practice. In chapter 1 (Understanding Creativity, Creative Capacity, and Creative Development), we discussed how design practice represents concrete, contextual creative problem solving that applies creative processes to specific situations. As such, many perceive design practice as practical and accessible because the application of design thinking processes is highly contextual, thus giving immediate relevance to the task at hand for all participants. Design is also perceived as being discipline neutral in that it is applicable to virtually any context.

IDEO's (2016) *Design Thinking for Educators Toolkit* is perhaps one of the most accessible design-thinking resources available to education administrators, teachers, and parents. The authors describe the hopefulness of growing a disposition of design that embraces empathy, experimentation, and collaboration, noting that, "design thinking is the confidence that new, better things are possible and that you can make them happen" (p. 11). This hopefulness resonates with Clement Mok's description of design in Berger (2009) as "The act of giving form to an idea with an intended goal: to inspire, to delight, to change perception and behavior" (p. 29). There is an inherent optimism that comes from a belief that any number of educational, social, economic, or personal challenges we face on a daily basis have the potential to be resolved through design thinking and design doing. This belief is further enhanced when we realize that engagement in design practice enables the invention of completely new entities across a variety of fields as it makes our visions come to life.

Maker Movement, Tinkering, and Makerspaces

The current popularization and proliferation of the Maker Movement, makerspaces, and the corresponding learning by doing through tinkering in schools and communities is testimony to the broad accessibility of design thinking as the gateway to engagement in sustained creative practice. To many, the Maker Movement had its official beginning in 2005 with the launch of *Make* magazine and the subsequent staging of the first Maker Faire event in 2006 in San Mateo, California (Hatch, 2014). The staging of Maker Faire events has grown substantially since then across the United States and internationally. The Maker Movement phenomenon came about as a result of a perfect technological and cultural storm. That storm was particularly conducive to creative practice, as the Internet enabled interconnected innovation with information and subsequent technological developments amplified this potential for innovation to encompass rapid prototyping of ideas into form. Anderson (2012) elaborates: "Just as the Web democratized innovation in bits, a new class of 'rapid' prototyping technologies, from 3D printers to CNC machines and laser cutters, is democratizing innovation in atoms" (p. 7). As part of this movement, MIT's Center for Bits and Atoms (CBA) describes themselves as an interdisciplinary initiative exploring the boundary between computer science and physical science. CBA studies how to turn data into things and things into data. This capacity to turn data into things has increased dramatically because of ready access to powerful, easy-to-use tools, as well as easy access to knowledge and a desire to make something of high quality (Hatch, 2014). Anderson (2012) sees the Maker Movement with its inherent practice of rapid prototyping, invention, and entrepreneurship as a high-potential economic driver.

A makerspace is an interdisciplinary studio where any number of interdisciplinary initiatives can take place. In a community makerspace, it is not uncommon to see members who are designers, writers, scientists, or from any other walk of life working side by side. School makerspaces are also typically interdisciplinary design studios. They are often associated with the educational emphasis on innovation and invention in STEM (science, technology, engineering, and mathematics) education. The emergence of STEAM education with the addition of art and design speaks to a much broader relevance of makerspaces across the discipline spectrum and a recognition of design practice as the dynamic that greases innovation regardless of the discipline. The concept of a makerspace or an interdisciplinary design studio is not a new one.

Gandini, Hill, Cadwell and Schwal (2015) describe how Loris Malaguzzi, founder of Reggio Emilia preschools in Italy, established the *atelier* or interdisciplinary studio in preschools in 1965. This concept "evoked the idea of a laboratory for many types of transformations, constructions, and visual expressions" (p. 13). Who would have known then that technological advancement and cultural evolution would lead to a broader cultural and educational embracing of design practice in the interdisciplinary studio several decades later?

Malaguzzi (Gandini et al., 2015) contends that children are born with extraordinary potentials. Everyone maintains these potentials throughout their life journeys. Making and creating is a natural thing to do. People love working with their hands and making things. This natural instinct and its rewards are amplified in interactive, supportive, collaborative environments. Design thinking and design practice enable creative development in ways that resonate with our natural, human disposition.

The Design Process

The design process as the contextual application of creative practice is highly variable, but in instances where it is seen to flourish, it often moves through several stages. IDEO (2016) breaks down the design thinking process into five connected, progressive stages: discovery, interpretation, ideation, experimentation, and evolution.

Pre-invention to invention

Once the collaborative culture is established, developmental focus turns to self-instigative development and research/investigative development. It is important for learners to discover a creative challenge that they are passionate about, to engage the design process from an intrinsically motivated perspective. These developmental areas are necessary to engage in meaningful problem finding and problem setting to shape the development of a pre-inventive structure that is relevant and important to all of those invested in the design process.

A pre-inventive structure represents the broadly defined parameters of a creative exploration within a field or discipline that are wide enough to allow for exploration and experimentation but defined enough to prevent floundering from lack of focus (Finke, Ward, & Smith, 1992).

The pre-inventive structure points the group or individual learner in the right direction to bring research, refinement, and clarity to the challenge at hand. This framework leads to a much clearer understanding of the problem parameters, the intended audience, and the available resources for problem resolution through innovation or invention. If one is going to engage in design practice for the purpose of innovating or inventing, several questions have to be addressed. What is it that is going to be developed? How does one find something with enough motivational relevance to sustain a creative exploration? What does one need to know about the problem to shape the problem more specifically to proceed?

IDEO (2016) breaks down the design thinking process into five connected, progressive stages: discovery, interpretation, ideation, experimentation, and evolve. The stages of discovery and interpretation encompass pre-invention. In the discovery stage they state that "a clearly defined challenge will guide your questions and help you stay on track throughout the process. Spend time with your team to create a common understanding of what you are working toward" (p. 26). This is a very active research phase to find out as much about the challenge as possible to fuel informed constructive interaction among collaborators. It is active investigation. No research stone should be left unturned as conversations with experts or research from more traditional sources all provide fuel to shape and further define the challenge. Once a solid research foundation is established, then the gathered information has to be interpreted and shared to further refine, shape, and understand the challenge. IDEO's interpretive phase involves finding meaning and turning it into an actionable opportunity for design by "sorting and condensing thoughts until you've found a compelling point of view and clear direction for ideation" (p. 40). As the collaborative process proceeds to define the challenge, sensitive listening enables each participant to be part of a collective design process and to take ownership as an integral part of a group initiative. If everyone contributes to the sharing of research with the group, their DNA is automatically embedded within the whole design process.

Idea Generation

Once the design challenge has been clearly defined and we move from pre-invention to invention, the creative process requires large quantities of fuel in the form of ideas. Quantity is important to maximize the potential for an innovative outcome. Generative development through idea generation is a very active developmental strand that encompasses many of Guilford's (1959) characteristics of creativity, which includes the concepts of divergent and convergent thinking, fluency, flexibility, elaboration, redefinition, and originality.

A safe, trusting educational environment where all ideas are accepted is essential if idea generation development is to flourish. Sweeney's (2004) concept of a statusless environment avoids the creation of a potentially judgmental and intimidating vertical hierarchy where participants are reluctant to volunteer ideas for fear of rejection or invalidation. An educational "yes and" culture is much more conducive to idea generation development. In this culture, which is common in improvisational theatre circles, every participant learns to give and accept every offer of an idea. In Edutopia (2008), Nelson characterizes "yes and" practice as plussing, in which each participant adds to the ideas of others, in a sense amplifying everyone around them. In this scenario, no matter how far-fetched an idea may seem at the time of presentation, it is accepted, documented, and banked. Buzan's (2012) mind mapping is an example of how ideas can be visually banked to be shared with others and to track the journey of an idea as it combines with other stimuli.

It is essential that all generated ideas be given form to enable sharing, banking, and tracking. Relying on saturated memory for banking ideas risks forgetting ideas and instantly taking them out of play for any potential growth and development. Idea generation is recursive (McAdam & McClelland, 2002; Venuvinod, 2011). A banked idea that may have appeared to be irrelevant or far-fetched at the time of presentation can take on increasing relevance as ideas evolve and morph into new entities over time, and the idea may eventually become part of a new hybrid despite the initial perception of low potential.

This concept of idea potential speaks to a very important consideration specific to idea generation in design practice: at the onset of a creative exploration, a large quantity of ideas are necessary for any idea to grow and hybridize into new and wondrous innovative forms. Recurrent pulses of divergent idea generation are necessary throughout a sustained creative process as prototypes evolve through cycles of refinement and modification. A closer look at the dynamic of idea generation and the journey of ideas through sustained creative practice helps to enhance understanding of idea generation development.

The journey of an idea

As we have seen in chapter 1 (in Factors Limiting Creative Development), there are several dynamics at play that can potentially limit the growth and development of ideas in sustained creative practice. An idea can take several paths on its way to problem resolution depending on the characteristics of the educational environment where the generative effort is taking place. It is also dependent on the level of creative development of learners and educators in their capacity to engage in flexible thinking by being receptive to new ideas and able to elaborate on and redefine existing ideas.

IDEA LIMITATION.

Imagine a design challenge in which learners' initial ideas remain fundamentally the same as they are subject to early closure or any number of factors that limit creative development. The original ideas remain largely impervious to outside influence or modification. This can be a very frustrating situation for educators who expend considerable effort encouraging learners to explore and develop a range of alternatives before closing on a final resolution. This limitation can also be very frustrating for collaborating group members. Learners become very precious with their first responses to problems and resist any attempt to let go of an idea to explore other creative avenues. I often kid learners who will not let go of early ideas that they are very much like Gollum in *Lord of the Rings* who coveted the ring and referred to it as "my precious." A key strategy for encouraging learners to explore and develop alternative solutions is to have students record their ideas in some form that can be recalled or shared later. This will allow learners to let go of their original idea as it is banked and will always be there for them if they need it. In this context, ideas are like money in the bank. We deposit money in the bank with the knowledge that we can always withdraw it when it is needed. We trust that the money will be there and that we do not have to go to the bank every day to have them show us the actual money. Once learners learn to trust idea banking, it frees them to explore new possibilities that allow their initial ideas to grow and evolve.

IDEA PROLIFERATION.

Now imagine a very different scenario in which idea generation conditions are more favourable. In this context, learner-initiated ideas that are the start of the problem-setting sequences that potentially lead to exploration, discovery, and innovation over time can grow to combine and recombine with new ideas. The initial conceptualization can hybridize with ideas that are the result of social interaction, experiential or traditional research, and pertinent stimuli provided by educators or collaborating group members.

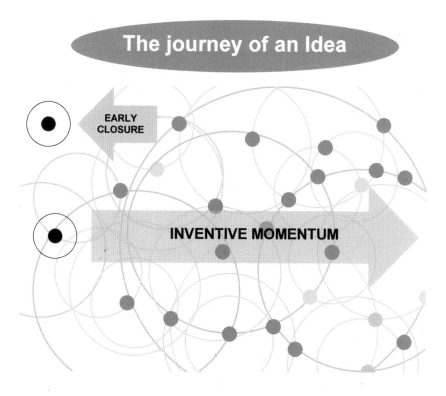

Figure 3.1 The journey of an idea

In *Educating for Creativity: A Global Conversation* (Kelly, 2012), I liken the journey of an idea to a potato cooking in a stewpot for a long period. The longer the raw potato is exposed to other flavours and influences in the cooking pot, the more the potato transforms in texture and flavour over time. In a day-old stew, one can still recognize the potato, but it has gone through considerable transformation of texture, flavour, and form. Ideas that are exposed to considerable external stimuli go through considerable transformation over time. The longer an idea is exposed to diverse stimuli, the greater the potential for the idea to evolve into something novel and innovative. The longer learners engage in this process, the greater the potential for a novel resolution to a design challenge resulting in innovation and invention.

The divergent-convergent pulse of ideation waves

If we were to map the journey of an idea through the creative exploration of a design challenge it would quickly become evident how much hybridization of the original idea takes place. As each idea radiates

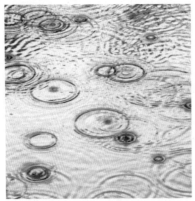

Figure 3.2 The radial pattern of rain droplets   Figure 3.3 The dendritic pattern of tree branches

IDEATION HYBRIDIZATION WAVES

1st 2nd 3rd 4th 5th 6th 7th

Figure 3.4 Ideation hybridization waves

outward, it intersects with other ideas to form new idea hybrids that are combinations of two or more ideas in varying proportions. This is akin to the pattern that rain droplets make as they strike a surface of water and each droplet creates an ever-expanding radial pattern that intersects with the expanding radial patterns of other droplets. The dendritic pattern of tree branches overlapping and intersecting with other branches is another way to characterize this phenomenon and is a popular mind-mapping strategy to demonstrate the journey and pathways of ideas (Buzan, 2012).

These hybrid ideas that are intersection points of existing ideas radiate outward to create even more hybrid idea intersections, which in turn radiate farther outward seeking more intersections with new ideas. This pattern repeats itself, growing the pool of alternative problem resolutions exponentially. Initial wave idea generation is characterized by minor idea development, where these ideas are often immediate, expedient problem

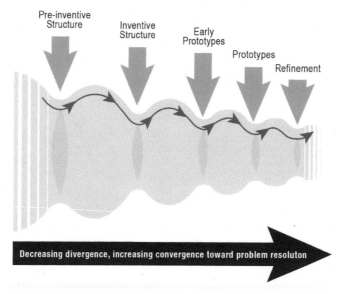

The DIVERGENT / CONVERGENT PULSE of IDEATION and PROTOTYPING

Pre-inventive Structure

Inventive Structure

Early Prototypes

Prototypes

Refinement

Decreasing divergence, increasing convergence toward problem resoluton

Figure 3.5 The divergent/convergent pulse of ideation and prototyping

resolutions that lack refinement. However, we do not know whether first-wave idea generation is the best alternative until several alternatives have been generated. Second-wave, third-wave, fourth-wave, fifth-wave idea generation, and so on, are identified by the number of hybridizations that inform the evolving ideas. Each successive wave of idea generation brings an increasingly more sophisticated combination of potential problem resolutions. This provides learners with a greater number of resolution alternatives and a much higher potential for an innovative response compared to the minimal potential of defaulting to one initial, precious idea.

Prototyping and Refinement

At a certain point in this dynamic, learners engaging in this creative exploration individually or as part of a group will have to decide when to converge on an alternative to bring it into form through prototyping and refinement. As learners progress through recurrent iterations of divergence and convergence, the divergent pulses become narrower.

In the initial stages of this extended ideational journey, the focus is on exploring the widest range of alternatives possible before deciding which one has the highest potential to propel the design challenge to an eventual prototype and then be subject to further refinement. This process can be viewed as deferring outcomes, as it precludes the often-engrained predisposition of early closure. These initial stages would be likened to planting as many new seeds as possible, to explore as many alternatives as possible. As this process proceeds through stages of divergence and convergence into prototyping, the divergence of ideas becomes more focused on refinement through the bracketing of more promising ideas that see variations of promising ideas generated through splicing, hybridizing, and the cross-pollination of ideas. Bracketing focuses on developing variations of an existing design element. As the design process continues toward resolution, bracketing increasingly addresses subtleties in design variations.

Bringing thoughts to form

IDEO's (2016) fourth design stage of experimentation focuses on prototyping, and the authors explain that "Prototypes enable you to share your idea with other people and discuss how to further refine it. You can prototype just about anything" (p. 58). They describe several forms of prototyping that can be created to initially test out ideas for feedback (see Table 3.1).

The prototyping stage represents an experimental stage in which thoughts are finally brought into form. This is the start of yet another generative journey as prototypes get tested, tried, or vetted by their intended audience for feedback, which informs redesign or refinement. Constantly attaining effective feedback is essential for design development throughout the design cycle. Giving ideas form and bringing them into a real context that they were designed for gives a constant stream of new information for refinement that could only have been discovered by trying something. For example, Hatch (2014) describes James Dyson, inventor of the bagless vacuum, as having gone through over five thousand design variations before settling on a final design.

Because the prototyping stage is still a generative stage, interesting feedback can occur that leads to unexpected discovery, causing the design process to go in a completely new direction. For example, O'Reilly (2016) describes how inventor Leonard Fish and chemist Robert Cox went from searching for a spray-on chemical composition to create an instant cast for a broken leg or arm to discovering something totally new. In testing prototypes of spray nozzles, they found that the smallest nozzle shot a string of resin over 9 metres (30 feet) across a room. This did not fit the criteria of the product they were trying to develop, but it

TABLE 3.1 FORMS OF PROTOTYPING

Mock-up	Build mock-ups of digital tools and websites with simple sketches of screens on paper. Paste the paper mock-up to an actual computer screen or mobile phone when demonstrating it.
Model	Put together simple three-dimensional representations of your idea. Use paper, cardboard, pipe cleaners, fabric, and whatever else you can find. Keep it rough and at a low fidelity to start, and evolve the resolution over time.
Storyboard	Visualize the complete experience of your idea over time through a series of images, sketches, cartoons, or even just text blocks. Stick figures are great—you don't need to be an artist. Use Post-it notes or individual sheets of paper to create the storyboard so you can rearrange their order.
Diagram	Map out the structure, network, journey, or process of your idea. Try different versions.
Story	Tell the story of your idea from the future. Describe what the experience would be like. Write a newspaper article about your idea. Write a job description. Create a letter to be sent to parents. Describe your idea as if it were published on the school website.
Advertisement	Create a fake advertisement that promotes the best parts of your idea. Have fun with it, and feel free to exaggerate shamelessly.
Role play	Act out the experience of your idea. Try on the roles of the people that are part of the situation and uncover questions they might ask.

Source: IDEO, 2016, p. 58

did make them laugh. After making their formula less sticky and adding colours, Fish and Cox had invented Silly String, a popular party favour for the toy market. O'Reilly adds that, interestingly, the military uses a version of Silly String to detect tripwires in rooms that may be rigged for explosives; it is easy to see the string hanging off previously invisible wires, and it is too light to set off explosives.

Always a Prototype—Perpetual Evolution

As the design process moves through the refinement stage, divergence becomes less pronounced as the design challenge becomes very specific to address subtle nuances of the design, typically through a bracketing strategy. This stage relies heavily on recurrent and effective feedback from resources from the environment for which the prototype was designed. Eventually resolution is arrived at and a final point of convergence is found. However, the design journey does not end there. Against the backdrop of perpetual change, everything that is produced, despite its finished and refined state, remains a prototype of sorts. Obsolescence sets in very quickly against a sea of constant technological and cultural change, and this creates the need for constant refinement, redesign, redefinition, and adaptation through design thinking and design doing. This continual engagement in the creative process leads to an increase in creative capacity and continual creative development.

REFERENCES

Anderson, C. (2012). *Makers: The new Industrial Revolution*. New York: Random House.

Berger, W. (2009). *Glimmer*. Toronto: Random House.

Buzan, T. (2012). *Modern mind mapping*. Cardiff: Proactive Press.

Edutopia. (2008). Randy Nelson on learning and working in the collaborative age. Retrieved from edutopia.org.

Finke, T. A., Ward, T. B., & Smith, S. M. (1992). *Creative cognition: Theory, research, and applications*. Cambridge: MIT Press.

Gandini, L., Hill, L., Cadwell, L., & Schwal, C. (Eds.). (2015). *In the spirit of the studio: Learning from the atelier of Reggio Emilia*. New York: Teachers College Press.

Guilford, J. P. (1959). Traits of creativity. In H. H. Anderson (Ed.), *Creativity and its cultivation* (pp. 142–161). New York: Harper.

Kelly, R. (2012). *Educating for creativity: A global conversation*. Edmonton: Brush Education.

Hatch, M. (2014). *The maker movement manifesto*. New York: McGraw Hill.

IDEO. (2016) Design thinking for educators toolkit. Retrieved January 19th, 2016, from designthinkingforeducators.com.

McAdam, R., & McClelland, J. (2002). Individual and team-based idea generation within innovation management: Organisational and research agendas. *European Journal of Innovation Management, 5*(2), 86–97. http://dx.doi.org/10.1108/14601060210428186

O'Reilly, T. (2016). Promise less, profit more. In *Under the influence*. Toronto: CBC Radio One. Retrieved from cbc.ca.

Sweeney, J. (2004). *Innovation at the speed of laughter*. Minneapolis: Aerialist Press.

Venuvinod, P. (2011). *Technology, innovation and entrepreneurship—Part III*. Dordrecht: Kluwer Academic Publishers.

Introducing Design Practice: The Idea Exchange, Mousetraps, and Elephants in the Room

ROBERT KELLY

Where Do We Start?

In Creating Development 2 (Building Trust and Accepting Ideas), we experienced activities that build toward transitioning from a culture of traditional educational practice to an educational culture that is focused on collaborative, creative production. As this collaborative culture slowly builds, the introduction of effective idea-generation methods and accessible design challenges promotes further collaborative development while developing understanding of the dynamic of design thinking and design doing.

When introducing design practice, it is important to start with a discipline-neutral challenge that is accessible to everyone. From this starting point, the challenge is not in the particular discipline realm of any of the participants, but rather in a statusless environment where anxiety is diminished and accessibility is maximized. There are many exercises that can be used to introduce design practice and support a collaborative, creative disposition.

Statusless Environments and Metaphorical Introductions

Sweeney (2004) talks about the benefits of creating statusless environments. A flattened, statusless culture enables trust and freer interaction. This is the opposite of being in a class or a group where there are established vertical hierarchies. Group members are less inclined to volunteer ideas, become vulnerable, or make mistakes in a setting that they feel may be judgmental or punitive. Developing a collaborative, creative culture starts the very moment group members are introduced to each other for the first time. These introductions are not based on group members' curriculum vitae (as that goes instantly to competitive vertical hierarchies). Strengths will eventually come out in collaborative work. Instead, it is important to choose an introduction strategy that celebrates the creativity and positivity of each group member, while precluding blatant competition based on accomplishments. There are many options for statusless introductions.

Once, I had the challenge of creating a statusless design environment among a group of highly credentialed professionals in an obvious organizational hierarchy. I chose to have everyone introduce themselves neither by name nor by organizational position or accomplishments, but rather by a verb that was a metaphor for something about them—a simple verb. Once they got over the initial "I think you are crazy!" moment, the verbs started to flow. After five rounds around the table of one-word verb introductions, it was amazing how much members of the group had discovered about each other. Those discoveries were made in a positive way that contributed to a flattened, statusless environment.

Flooding the room with hundreds of diverse, printed images that group members choose as personal introductory metaphors is another introduction alternative. Yet another alternative is for each group member to introduce themselves though simple personal objects that they show to the group as a metaphor for themselves. Regardless of the introductory strategy chosen, it is absolutely essential that group members introduce themselves in positive light. This positive tone enhances the group culture in the spirit of plussing ideas that follow and a creates fundamental belief in the principle of infinite potentials and that all group interaction is of a positive nature whether one is talking about themselves or someone's ideas.

The Idea Exchange

The creative process requires a lot of fuel in the form of ideas. This promotes divergent thinking, an essential practice to enable a concept to grow to its fullest inventive potential. Ideas can come from a variety of research sources. Perhaps the best idea sources in any creative exploration are the colleagues and peers in a learning group or classroom. It is amazing how learners can go through a whole semester or school year without really getting to know someone spending so much time in the same physical learning space as them. The idea exchange is a great way to generate a large number of ideas while creating a statusless environment. It is an ideal way to allow everyone to engage in genuine dialogue with the learning group, thereby breaking down the fears and any other barriers to communication that come with unfamiliarity. It sets the table for an interconnected classroom culture of collaborative creativity.

The idea exchange is set up in a way that may resemble speed dating. The group is divided in half and seated in two rows of facing chairs. In this setup, each learner faces another group member to create a discussion pair for idea generation. If you have twenty-two students you would have two rows of eleven chairs facing each other. Each pair gets five minutes to

Figure CD3.1: Educators engaging in an idea exchange for a design task

discuss and exchange ideas before moving to the seat to their right to begin a discussion with a new partner to grow even more ideas. The goal of the idea exchange is for each participant to grow the largest number of ideas possible through successive, rotating, one-on-one discussions with everyone in the group.

When the idea exchange begins, the rule of plussing applies. No one is allowed to criticize anyone else's ideas. The only thing group members are permitted to do during the idea exchange is to add to another member's idea by bracketing or suggesting a completely new idea to complement a member's suggestions. Cheerleading and hitchhiking are not considered plussing.

Each participant in the idea exchange must be able to make offers and accept offers. It is important before beginning the idea exchange that each participant generate their own personal list of preliminary ideas to bring to the idea exchange dynamic, otherwise they will have no offers to give and the verbally dominant in the conversation will take over any discussion. Ideas are the currency of this exchange. Participants need currency to begin participation.

The idea exchange can be used frequently throughout the duration of a design challenge at various stages of divergence and convergence to provide fuel and feedback as prototypes evolve and become increasingly refined. The frequent use of the idea exchange as a strategy for divergent thinking and idea generation allows everyone in the classroom to know what everyone else is doing. Everyone can be a constant source of new ideas for everyone else as research unfolds and ideas are uncovered that may be relevant to someone's creative exploration. The idea exchange can also fuel independent projects. In this context, independent work is highly collaborative. Once students become familiar with the idea exchange format, it becomes second nature to their daily regimen and a catalyst for developing a truly collaborative classroom culture.

Early Design Challenges

Another way to introduce design practice to a new group is to pick a fun activity that is discipline neutral to instantly create a statusless environment while allowing everyone to practice design-thinking fundamentals. Such activities reduce anxiety that may occur when group members feel overshadowed by the perceived experts in their group. These fun activities create a feeling that everyone is in the same boat and that the whole purpose is to have fun while learning basic design practice.

EXISTENTIAL TEA

To introduce design practice, create a simple challenge that everyone can buy into. For example, a design challenge that I like to use with groups that are new to design thinking is to redesign the common tea bag. Group members are challenged to create a tea bag that will not drip when it is removed from water and transferred to the compost or garbage. Everyone is familiar with this process, yet no one can be considered an expert.

The design challenge routine is very simple:

1. The design challenge is presented to the group, and each group member is given time to generate their own list of preliminary design solutions.
2. Preliminary solutions are then brought to an idea exchange where the goal is to grow as many idea alternatives as possible through plussing.
3. After the idea exchange, the whole group is divided into smaller working groups that now each have a large bank of ideas from which to draw for early prototyping.
4. After this point, groups go through recurrent rounds of divergence and convergence as time permits as they bring their concept into form.

The process can be stopped at any point in the sequence, as the goal is to demonstrate a basic way of engaging a design challenge in a collaborative setting. I'm often amazed at the range of diverse, imaginative design solutions that groups can produce in a short period in a fun design challenge. My favourite response was the creation of an existential tea for which the brewing and drinking were only imagined, and thus the dripping problem was solved.

MOUSETRAP POWER

After a warm-up activity, groups can graduate to a more time-intense activity that requires more concentrated idea generation, collaboration, and experimentation with demonstrated, tangible results. The mousetrap-powered design challenge is one of many that fit this bill. The goal is for each group to create a design that uses a mousetrap as the sole source of energy to break a balloon located at the opposite end of the room. Groups are given materials and preliminary rules to start the challenge.

Each group is given a bag of raw materials that contains the following: a mousetrap, a wooden paint stick, two metal eyelets, a short wooden dowel that fits through the eyelets, a Ping-Pong ball, some string, two CDs, some duct tape, balloons, and the plans to make a mousetrap-powered car (from Roberts (2011) or any number of other sources). The mousetrap-powered car plans may or may not provide a solution to the problem. The plans are merely a design starting point that each group has to assess for viability for potential design depending on how the rules for the design challenge are set up.

Each group is then given preliminary rules for the challenge. For example, groups must place the balloon on the floor on the opposite side of the room. Other possible rules include the following:

- The balloon is placed one metre off the floor on the opposite side of the room.
- The mousetrap has to be on the opposite side of the room from the balloon.
- The design sequence starts with the trap being sprung. That is the only physical contact allowed.
- Nothing can be attached to the balloon.
- Nothing can be above the level of the balloon.
- Whatever breaks the balloon has to somehow be attached to the mousetrap.
- No projectiles are allowed.
- Balloons may be used as a source of energy to complement the power of the mousetrap.
- Only the materials provided may be used in the challenge.

The level of difficulty for the challenge can be structured to suit the group. Note that this challenge works best in a room with a span of approximately twenty feet or six metres.

This activity follows the same design challenge routine as the tea bag challenge. Group members develop their own preliminary lists of ideas in response to the balloon-breaking design challenge. They bring these ideas into an idea exchange forum to grow their lists of alternatives. Working groups are not created until after the idea exchange. Once working groups are formed, they then go through the divergent/convergent sequences of prototyping and refinement.

Experiment with variations of this challenge. Use balloon power only. Allow the use of two mousetraps per group. Allow other materials. Keep it fun. Have students track their prototyping journey to document the design path and better understand the collaborative design process.

Figure CD3.2: Mousetrap-power design challenge materials

Figure CD3.3: A mousetrap-powered mechanism

THE ELEPHANT IN THE ROOM

Perhaps one of my favourite preliminary design challenges for any group new to design is the Elephant in the Room challenge. I got this activity from a former mentor, British sculptor Ray Arnatt. This design challenge is incredibly effective at establishing a collaborative culture of creativity while introducing participants to design practice.

The design challenge is simple. Build a life-size African elephant that is proportionally correct and has no flat surfaces. It can have one moving part if desired. Each group member is asked to bring in the following materials to conduct the challenge: five cardboard boxes, three newspapers, and one roll of string. No glue or tape is allowed. String and interlocking cardboard are the primary methods for joining and attaching objects. This design challenge at first seems quite daunting, but every group I have worked with has met the challenge and often surprised themselves in the process. The activity becomes a living example of the power of collaborative creativity.

Figure CD3.4: The elephant under construction

Figure CD3.5: The completed elephant

In this challenge, the same design procedure applies as per the previous activities. Each group member creates a personal preliminary list of ideas as to how to tackle the problem. These ideas are then brought to an idea exchange forum to expand the list of possible design alternatives. Groups of seven to ten members are then formed, and each begins the task of crafting an elephant. It is a good idea for each group to come up with a collaborative plan that will address group communication and inclusion of all group members in a meaningful way, as well as leadership issues.

Variations of the activity can be linked to the size of the final form. For example, a baby or a juvenile elephant can be crafted to make the activity easier. It is good to give the groups a shoulder-height benchmark to aim for in their planning and final design. In addition, with more than one elephant being built at one time, it is great to have groups help each other so the activity becomes a class initiative instead of a competition.

Creating a small herd of life-size elephants is a powerful symbol of what groups can accomplish if they apply design methods in a supportive, collaborative environment. After this point, they are ready to apply design thinking and design execution to any real-world problem for any real-world audience.

Oh, one last design challenge—what do you do with a herd of elephants once they are built? You can repurpose the materials that make up each elephant to respond to new design challenges that may have an architectural focus, an aesthetic sculptural focus, or may involve transforming the elephants into other life forms . . . or you could place them in the principal's office or a neighbour's classroom. Have fun with the elephants in the room.

REFERENCES

Roberts, D. (2011). *Making things move: DIY mechanisms for inventors, hobbyists, and artists.* New York: McGraw-Hill.

Sweeney, J. (2004). *Innovation at the speed of laughter.* Minneapolis: Aerialist Press.

Design Thinking for Change

AKANKSHA AGARWAL

Akanksha Agarwal has worked as a research catalyst with Design for Change, focusing on bridging theory and practice of school improvement and learning through design thinking. She has a master's degree in Development Studies from the Tata Institute of Social Sciences, Mumbai, and was a Gandhi Fellow.

The Design for Change Premise

Design for Change (DFC) builds twenty-first century skills in children through their engagement with the design thinking process. It gets educators to interact with their learners on topics drawn from their shared reality of school and the surrounding community. It offers an opportunity for educators and students to collaborate and learn from each other.

Children in schools today are being prepared for an uncertain future. Rapid technological advances have brought about dynamic changes in the world economy, and the nature of jobs and their required skills are constantly shifting. In this context, empathy and collaboration are gaining importance as diverse cultures interact with each other on economic and social terms.

Twenty-first century skills are therefore the key focus area of education across the world. DFC curriculum introduces design thinking to school children and provides them with an opportunity to apply their learning to a real-world context. Design thinking is a problem-solving process with the core values of empathy, collaboration, and optimism.

The Design for Change Process

Design for Change (DFC) started in 2009 at the Riverside School in Ahmedabad, India. Through collaboration with IDEO and Stanford's d.school, both pioneer institutions in design thinking, DFC created a four-step process—Feel, Imagine, Do, and Share (FIDS)–to simplify the design-thinking process for learners. Children go through these four steps to break down a problem into different parts and build an understanding of the multiple perspectives around an issue. The core focus of design thinking is on understanding a problem from the perspective of people involved in and affected by the problem. Learners move through the FIDS process to design and implement solutions, incorporating insights from their understanding of the needs of stakeholders.

FEEL

Through the DFC process, learners identify something that bothers them. This unique aspect distinguishes it from other design-thinking processes. It begins with a cartography exercise that gets learners to observe their own surroundings. Students draw a map of their school and home and mark the spots that either make them happy or sad. They are guided in this process by three lenses: social, emotional, and physical. They are asked to observe the tangible objects as well as the feelings of others around them and describe their observations to their classmates. The process of sharing and collectively voting on one problem gets learners and educators to interact and understand each others' thoughts and feelings. Also, when learners choose the problem themselves, they take ownership of it and this increases their engagement in the learning process.

IMAGINE

After choosing their hot spot and understanding its root cause, learners move to the next step of the process: imagine. They begin by visualizing a best-case scenario, which is a description of the goal they wish to achieve. Having an end picture in mind allows learners to brainstorm for solutions that are relevant to their identified opportunity for change. Together as a class, students vote for solutions they feel will have the maximum impact and would be appreciated by people who are affected by the problem.

DO

When learners have imagined their goal, they move onto the next step: do. This is the phase in which students initiate their process of change by prototyping their solution. This allows learners to get feedback on how their ideas translate into action. After a quick prototyping, students refine their ideas to incorporate feedback from stakeholders. Learners then move forward to prepare their plan of action and allocate responsibilities among themselves based on their abilities to implement their ideas. They create a timeline for their action steps and begin their transition into change makers.

Design thinking promotes a bias toward action, and similarly, DFC curriculum is based on the principle of learning by doing. Children's learning takes place when they act upon their thoughts, are able to see the outcome of their actions, and reflect on their learning by sharing it with others.

SHARE

Collaboration is another key principle of design thinking. Group activities are integral to each stage of FIDS. Learners come together as a class to collectively share their thoughts, vote for decision-making processes, and collaborate with each other to come up with innovative solutions. Therefore, implementation of DFC provides an opportunity to facilitate and showcase creative, collaborative learning in a classroom.

These creative and collaborative aspects of DFC offer the possibility of transforming the learning environment through an interactive pedagogy. Educators get to implement a student-centred learning process and experience the consequent shift in students' engagement in the classroom. Furthermore, the implementation of DFC allows educators to discover each learner's unique strengths as they showcase their skills of leadership, creativity, collaboration, empathy, and communication. This experience provides educators with a better perspective for understanding and believing in each learner's abilities.

THE CONSTRUCTIVIST APPROACH OF DFC

DFC offers a constructivist approach to learning as it creates a problem-based learning environment in the classroom. In Dewey's (1938) terms, it is the "problematic" that leads to, and is the organizer for, learning. The discussions among students during a DFC class are based on their initial observations about a problem. This creates a platform where a student's own knowledge about an issue is given value. The next process requires learners to understand multiple perspectives by interviewing others who are affected by their chosen problem. The perspectives of others can resonate with their own observations or even be contradictory. The learning process is therefore designed to get learners to examine their existing knowledge and create new learning based on it. This resonates with constructivist pedagogy and is a practical application of the theory.

The constructivist method of learning transforms a teacher's role into that of a facilitator as it is requires them to provide students with opportunities to observe, question, compare, and eventually generate their own understanding. The implementation of DFC creates opportunities for students and teachers to learn simultaneously. As such, it ties closely with Friere's conceptualization of "teacher as students and students as teachers," where both collaboratively work on a problem and contribute equally in the learning process. In this collaborative environment, DFC is implemented through a process of a dialogue between students and teachers wherein students act as critical co-investigators. For example, DFC activities lead to discussions in classrooms that are centred on real-world context. This allows educators to hear student's opinions and thoughts on their surroundings and the manner in which it affects them. These discussions remain open and informal and both educators and learners discover new things about each other. The freedom of expression is also helped by the premise that in DFC learning environments, students are not hindered by the fear of their answers being right or wrong. Rather, it is a space for them to bring forth their opinions and importance is given to independent and creative thinking.

The processes in DFC curriculum are designed to give emphasis to the student voices driving the learning journey. To achieve this emphasis, DFC curriculum is designed in a manner in which the content of the classes is co-created by students' understanding of a problem and their ideas for tackling that problem. To support this environment, educators enter DFC classes with uncertainty because, although they have prior knowledge of the process, they do not know the outcomes. This is markedly different from traditional educational practice in which educators often enter with pre-determined content and learning outcomes. Therefore, the methodology of applying DFC curriculum fosters a collaborative approach to learning in which students and teachers participate equally.

Samples of Design for Change Initiatives

Design for Change is guided by the belief that children have the potential to bring change and the FIDS process is a platform for unlocking their creative agency. The participation of children in the learning process empowers them and makes them more engaged and interested in learning. This participation is enhanced by a culture of openness and freedom that encourages authentic dialogue. The DFC project moves forward with collective brainstorming, and decision-making processes allow opportunities for each child to contribute. The following are four examples of Design for Change initiatives from around the globe.

COLOMBIA 2014: POWER OF LANGUAGE

Seventeen-year-old Jean and his friends were deeply troubled by the loss of their traditional Inga culture and language within their own school students at Etnoeducativa Bilingue Inga, Mocoa, in Colombia. In collaboration with their village elders, Jean and his friends designed and implemented a curriculum in their school to ensure that students would learn their traditional language and be aware of the knowledge within their own culture. They also conducted craft fairs and food festivals to introduce children to the richness of the Inga culture. As a result of their efforts, Jean and his friends made it possible for everyone in their school to speak the Inga language. Learn more about this story online: https://www.youtube.com/watch?v=BlLA_xHf lUY&index=10&list=PLOS7LSVwOyfKRlkAjEm27d0mrSuwQVFUv.

Figure CD4.1: A celebration of Inga culture and language

NAGALAND, INDIA, 2012: GARBAGE WARRIORS

Nagaland is a state in northeast India that borders Myanmar (formerly Burma) to the east.

Fifteen-year-old Rhilo and his friends from Dimapur, Nagaland, decided to tackle the problem of littering that was widespread in their school environment. They observed the students and interviewed them to understand their littering behaviour. They realized there was a lack of garbage receptacles in their school and also a lack of motivation on the part of the students to throw garbage away in a proper manner. Their design goal was to have all the students respect school property and take ownership of school spaces.

The children prototyped and designed new cone-shaped garbage receptacles, using bamboo sticks as the main material. They strategically placed these receptacles around their school campus, but they found that just designing and making more receptacles was not enough to solve the problem. The students designed an awareness initiative to promote the use of the new design and ultimately change behaviour. This initiative involved dressing up as "garbage warriors" to spread awareness of the new receptacles and proper disposal of garbage.

This initiative was quite transformative. Through their efforts, they managed to shift the behaviour of 700 students in their school to make it litter free. Learn more about this story online: https://www.youtube.com/watch?v=-bomxgG4rL4.

RAJASTHAN, INDIA, 2010: SAVING WATER FOR TOMORROW

Ten-year-old Renu and her friends were troubled by the lack of water in their village. They came together to think of different solutions and finally decided to dig water-harvesting wells with the help of their community elders.

The students mobilized their whole community by conducting rallies in which they shared their idea of rainwater-harvesting wells. The community then worked together to dig twenty wells to generate water for their village. The students managed to get everyone engaged in their idea, and together they solved the water crisis in their village. Learn more about this story online: https://www.youtube.com/watch?v=I2mWHrcmmc8.

DENMARK 2013: CROWD BIN

Oskar, Mark, and Andreas of Højer, Denmark, created a mobile app to solve their neighbourhood garbage problem. Their town lacked dustbins, and the students came up with the idea of crowd-sourced garbage bins. Their app allowed a crowd to come together to seamlessly maintain a garbage bin.

The students prototyped a lot of solutions in designing their bins and finally came up with the simple idea of placing a barcode on each bin. Any person walking by could take a picture of the bin's barcode, and the app would notify the community taking care of the garbage bin that it needed service. The students also set up an online platform to raise funds for their garbage app and were in conversation with the government to scale up their operations. Learn more about this story online: https://www.youtube.com/watch?v=HY-blAJIOokh.

Designing Educational Space for Creativity

DEETER SCHURIG

Deeter Schurig is an architect and multidisciplinary designer with an extensive background in theatre and scenographic design. As a project manager for the social enterprise cSPACE Projects, Deeter's current practice combines facility design for the arts and cultural sector with a placemaking approach to fostering vibrant, sustainable, and community-driven development.

Creatively Defined Educational Space

As a parent, I ponder the world my young children will inherit and what their outlook will be compared to mine. I think about how educators will shape and mentor their creative development. I think about the conditions that will support them throughout their educational journey to respond to everyday challenges and ones yet to emerge. As a designer, I think, too, that in solving problems, we are often prone to create others. As such, I recognize that we must elevate our expectations for more imaginative thinking and to demand more innovative design in response.

Many aspects of the educational spatial environment are fair game for a redesign conducive to creative development, and adding space for creative collaboration is key in that redesign. As Goldbard (2013) notes, we must recognize creativity as "a repository of wisdom, social imagination, empathy, beauty, and meaning . . . [that] provides the container, the matrix for all human knowledge" (p. 110). When creativity is paired with collaboration as a function of extraordinary listening, of cultivating presence and mindfulness, it enables connectivity to be invited into the design process. When multiple voices are engaged, design practice is rewarded with a multiplicity of dividends that bring robustness to ideas, resiliency to projects, and involved, community stewardship to place.

A Spatial Design Journey for Educators

This design journey proposed for educators is built around three design phases consisting of

- performance-based inquiry,
- spatial relationship fieldwork, and
- imagining of an innovative education place.

These phases combine to explore an embodied examination of spatial relationships and to initiate design thinking to transform underutilized educational spaces into more productive places for creative development.

PERFORMANCE-BASED INQUIRY: BECOMING PERSONALLY AWARE OF SPACE

It is important for learners to cultivate an awareness of themselves, their relationship to others, and their surrounding space. To establish this perspective, we employ a method used by stage performers that moves in a sequence from self-mindfulness (sensory and body awareness) out to ensemble engagement. With intent to cultivate an awareness of an embodied consciousness—a presence of being—and to employ extraordinary listening among participants, this process establishes interrelationship awareness to inform spatial design thinking.

The journey begins with the group taking a predetermined trip before arriving at the "classroom" for the day—an open space free from distraction. The group walks through the city streets and becomes immersed in identifying and understanding space from the scale of their own bodies. They note spatial conditions, such as the texture of facades, the cadence of doors on the street, the width of sidewalks, and the conditions of entryways. In this observation, they note the spatial qualities of the cityscape and the effect these have on lived experience.

By building an awareness of the different scales of urban architecture and the body in space, group members recognize how experience is shaped in relation to other things. For example, they realize how a knob within a door, a door within a room, a room within a building, and a building within a city are each contextually connected. In sensing the thresholds between the departure from one space and the arrival in another, group members develop a heightened understanding of interrelationships that is critical for spatial design.

The intent of this process is then continued in an open space free of distraction, such as a rehearsal space, where group members can be taken through exercises focused on meditation and body and sensory awareness. Going through these exercises helps group members connect with their immediate experience before building upon individual consciousness out to dynamic engagement with other participants. Taking inspiration from the "viewpoints" work of Bogart and Landau (2005), exercises aim to cultivate a

Figure CD5.1 Exercises focused on meditation and body and sensory awareness

sense of presence, where personal moment-to-moment interest and shared wakefulness of the collective is built, where extraordinary listening is experienced with the whole body. Activities described in Creating Development 2 (Building Trust and Accepting Ideas) can also be used to enhance interrelationship awareness.

Participants are encouraged to creatively capture these ideas in journals, to reflect, and to sketch throughout the exercises. This involves documenting the experiences from a personal point of view and articulating observations from varied perspectives that offer insight into spatial relationships from this performative approach.

SPATIAL RELATIONSHIPS FIELDWORK: BEING INSATIABLE DATA COLLECTORS

After a foundation of extraordinary listening and embodied presence is explored in the performative phase, the next objective is to focus on research and data collection. Any space has the potential to be transformed, and group members can focus on finding space within existing educational environments that may be transformed into places conducive to collaboration and creative development.

By exploring design in relation to objects, architecture, and the urban realm, group members begin to appreciate that educational spaces have implicit material qualities, adjacent spatial conditions, and broader connections, such as the communities they occupy, that inform our experience of them. Participants may be introduced to design techniques that translate physical objects and spaces into the language of plan and section, orthographic projection, and axonometric drawings to support their learning.

Figure CD5.2 Exploring design in relation to objects, architecture, and the urban realm

One method to heighten awareness and to collect data is to have group members use drawings to more actively capture site qualities. While photography should also be employed, it is important to recognize that the camera may limit participant's views; resonant connections to places are enhanced when they are captured in drawings created by hand. Group members may use other fieldwork collection methods including the following:

- Creating day-in-the-life scenarios of users of the space
- Walking and stopping to sketch atmospheric qualities
- Collecting site artifacts to convey the materiality of the space
- Initiating creative writing and drawing exercises to build alternative future and historical perspectives
- Developing surveys for detailed user data
- Using video drones to capture alternate views
- Developing circulation, sun path, and shading studies
- Observing and interviewing occupants
- Capturing soundscapes and sensory studies
- engaging in real-life spatial interventions

Throughout the fieldwork process, group members are encouraged to become insatiable collectors of data by employing unique subjective and objective investigations. A rich composite of field-study tactics and data will reflect how both sensory experience and quantitative data contribute to deepening our understanding of places and informing design intent.

INNOVATIVE PLACE IMAGINATION AND DESIGN: IMAGINING AND DESIGNING AN EDUCATIONAL PLACE FOR INNOVATION

In the next phase, group members create an ambitious design goal to transform an underutilized space into an environment conducive to creative development. The challenge is for participants to ambitiously imagine how a proposed design might lead to greater system change in keeping with emerging educational and world demands.

The group is encouraged to develop design questions around a structure of transforming X space to encourage Y innovative practice and set a precedent for greater Z change. The third variable is intended to drive participants to question "culture change" within a school environment and to imagine the ripple effect beyond classrooms into the community.

This exercise may require group members to extend beyond their comfort zone, yet through collaboration with peers, inspired design questions will emerge. For example, groups might ask how a library atrium could be transformed to create a sanctuary for deepening our awareness of sustainability and transform education globally or spark urban revitalization. This process challenges group members to think beyond immediate and ready-made solutions in order to imagine greater potential for these spaces.

The next step is to bring design ideas into form by creating a design artifact or model through a digital platform or scale model. Doorley & Witthoft's, (2012) book, *Make Space*, is an excellent resource on spatial design thinking that is conducive to collaborative, creative practice with a focus on the adaptable and flexible arrangements that make spaces more multifaceted and resilient in their uses. For example, their Z-Rack, a modified garment rack that becomes a writable surface as well as a space divider and a space creator, as well as their lightweight, portable foam cubes that can be configured for any imaginative interaction, both provide good inspiration for participants.

Encouraging the reimagination of education space and collaborative design thinking is an engaging process. One example comes to mind in which students explored how an underused corner of a learning commons could be reconceived to create an inclusive place for the exchange of ideas to promote a greater sense of community within the school. This project employed tactics to document the space and conducted exploration and assessment of the spatial attributes with stakeholders before developing design intent. To explore how to enhance the potential of the space, the space was reconceived to permit performative opportunities through multiple configurations and expanded use. Diverse explorations of the spatial qualities included a consideration of the placement of objects within the space and a response to lighting, signage, and textural qualities along with moveable elements. These explorations were used to create a design proposal in the form of scale models that creatively imagined more potential for this space.

Figure CD5.3 A design proposal in the form of scale models

In conditioning divergent ways to embody, evoke, enable, and expand spatial relationship thinking through this learning journey, we can also see potential for culturing places where education and creative collaboration go hand in hand with ingenuity and innovative response. As artist, urban planner, and placemaker Theaster Gates (2013) describes, this design journey similarly provokes "a sincere appeal to imagine ourselves, as having the capacity to not only transform the thing that sits in our hands, but actually to have real transformative power in the world" and suggests that each of us can become agents of change for the betterment of the world—with a little encouragement to imagine it.

REFERENCES
Goldbard, A. (2013). *The culture of possibility: Art, artists & the future*. Minneapolis: Waterlight Press.

Bogart, A., & Landau, T. (2005). *The viewpoints book: A practical guide to viewpoints and composition* (1st ed). New York : St. Paul: Theatre Communications Group.

Doorley, S., & Witthoft, S. (2012). *Make space: How to set the stage for creative collaboration*. Hoboken, N.J.: John Wiley & Sons.

Gates, T. (2013). *Visual arts lectures by the Banff Centre: Leading ideas speaker series: iTunes U*. Banff, AB: Banff Centre.

4

Learning Experience Design
for Creative Development

ROBERT KELLY

The Disposition of Design: Teacher as Designer

We have taken a journey through engaging in creative practice through design thinking and design doing, guided by a disposition of design that applies to educators and learners. Just as the disposition of design is empowering for learners, it is equally empowering for educators equipped with the belief, and corresponding methods and tools, that any problem can be resolved by the application of creative processes through design practice. This heightened creative capacity leads to unlimited possibilities for educational design, which in turn leads to an exciting and engaging learning environment.

Heightened creative capacity can be applied in two distinct contexts for educators. The first context is teaching and learning creatively. Here, educators engage in the creative exploration of discipline fields that are typically associated with curriculum areas through exciting, novel, adaptive learning experiences. This makes the exploration of discipline areas fun and engaging, as it moves research from a typically passive orientation to a very active and interactive orientation. This expression of creative capacity is not enough, however. It is more important that the heightened creative capacity of educators enables learners to learn to create, which leads to student-initiated innovation and invention through original research, production, and action. Growing the creative capacity of educators is discussed in chapter 6 (Creative Development in Teacher Education, in the Field, and Beyond).

Educator as designer, facilitator, collaborator, and mentor

If the overall goal is to enable the creative development of learners, the traditional role of the teacher must change. Educators need to take on several mutable roles to accommodate individual learners at varying levels of creative development. This implies that educators have to move from a teacher-centric, authoritative pedagogy to one where they are able to allow for greater student autonomy and ownership in learning (Kalantzis & Cope, 2010). When this shift occurs, educators become designers of learning environments for learners who engage in active research leading to experimentation, prototyping, invention, and action. This process begins with educators assuming the role of designer, but it does not stop there. Educators must assume shifting roles to adapt to the developmental needs of learners as they engage in the various stages of design thinking and design doing. This encompasses becoming a facilitator to enable learners to access active research possibilities and to serve as an authoritative source for knowledge resources. It embraces the role of collaborator as educators co-construct inquiry and pre-inventive structures with learners, all with the goal of having learners assume complete ownership of the creative initiative. As learners move into a space of learner-initiated and owned invention and innovation, educators take on the role of mentor. The educational environment for collaborative creativity ideally starts with an educator with a disposition of design who can progressively assume the roles of facilitator, collaborator, and mentor to accommodate learners at varying stages in the design process toward the creation of original work. These progressive roles, the stages of the design process, and the notion of increasing student ownership of creative practice inform the three-stage learning experience design progression for creative development:

Stage 1—Explore is a stage of experiential, active research and
  investigation.

Stage 2—Inquire and Experiment is the stage for formulating
  questions that lead to experimentation and early prototyping,
  shaping pre-inventive emerging frameworks for innovation and
  invention.

Stage 3—Innovate and Invent is the stage for sustained student-
  initiated, emerging, curriculum-connected or pure original
  research, production, and action where prototypes are refined in
  real-world contexts.

Learning Experience Design Progression for Creative Development

The learning experience design progression is structured to assist in scaffolding students from the experiential exploration of discipline content to engagement in original research, production, and action across the discipline spectrum. The notion of setting real-world problems for real-world audiences and engaging in original research and producing original work involves students being able to do the following: conceptualize ideas for explorations independently; apply diverse research and investigation strategies, and bring appropriate stimuli to the evolution of these ideas; experiment through prototyping with a variety of outcomes; and assess alternatives and converge on a set of ideas after considerable experimentation.

This leads to the development of inventive momentum that can be carried through to further creative explorations in which resolutions to problems are driven and sustained through several iterations of idea generation and prototyping. This momentum is established in a collaborative environment and encompasses the eight interconnected creative development strands:

1. Collaborative development
2. Self-instigative development (intrinsic motivation)
3. Research/investigative development
4. Generative development (idea generation)
5. Experimentational development (prototyping)
6. Critical/analytical thinking development
7. Discipline complexity development
8. Creative sustain development

Learning experience design progression for creative development is built around three general learning experience stages: Stage 1—Explore; Stage 2—Inquire and Experiment; and Stage 3—Innovate and Invent. These stages are collectively designed to enable learners to progressively grow creative capacity with increasingly more complex engagement in creative explorations that move from being educator initiated through co-construction to learner instigated. It is important to keep in mind that the goal of this progression is to scaffold students into initiating original research leading to original production and action. This format provides a general progression for learning experience design. The progression enables educators to specifically tailor educational design to the developmental needs of learners through differentiation of learning experiences.

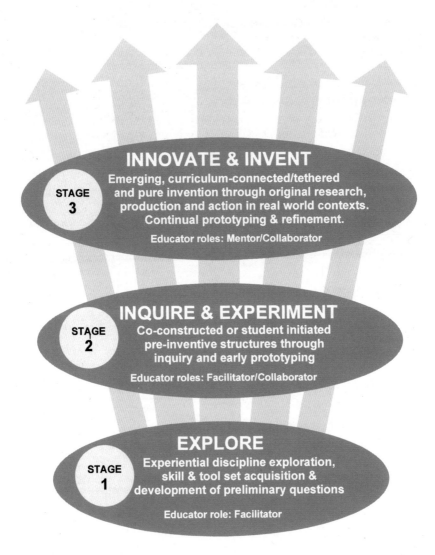

Figure 4.1 Learning experience design progression for creative development

Pre-inventive structures

A typical starting point for exploration that ultimately leads to innovation and invention is the development of a pre-inventive structure. The pre-inventive structure describes the challenge of the creative exploration that leads to design challenges and the field(s) where they are generally located at a developmentally appropriate level for each student.

The pre-inventive structure is designed to allow for enough room for experimentation and discovery without being so prescriptive as to choke off inventive possibilities and not being so open as to cause floundering from the paradox of choice. The pre-inventive structure can be articulated from the onset of the whole exploration, or it can be managed to emerge as the exploration evolves. If designed by the educator, the skill is in designing the pre-inventive structure for inherent transfer of ownership to the student. As such, the design challenge from the educator perspective is to create a pre-inventive structure that leads to learner-designed and owned pre-inventive structures. Educators can provide the initial description of the pre-inventive structure, or learners can develop the pre-inventive structure as they evolve through the three stages toward innovation or inventive problem resolution.

Stage 1—Explore: Active research and investigation

Principal Developmental Strands: Discipline complexity understanding co-development, research/investigative development, collaborative development, early generative development.

Primary Educator Role(s): Facilitator of the experiential exploration of the discipline or field of intended creative exploration and resultant design challenge. Co-constructor of emerging design questions.

At this stage, educational design works to support the collaborative and creative potential of active research and investigation. In IDEO's (2016) preliminary discovery and interpretive stages of the design process, research is a very active, experiential practice that sets the table for invention and innovation. Passive, literature-based research can certainly supplement the exploration, but given the infinite number of avenues available in an interactive, networked, digital world, information acquisition can be accessed through interactive dialogic means quite readily. Experiential research and investigation falls into the realm of highly contextual applied and action research (Parsons et al., 2013).

Engaging an area of interest through experiential learning gives the research greater personal relevance and the learner greater reason to explore. Active, experiential research for real-world problems and real-world audiences gives learners' activities an even greater personal relevance as their work is integrated into the broader world around them and not limited to an insular educational environment. This first-hand research gives their work deeper meaning while validating their capacity for a larger, positive role in the world. Also, just as collaboration is a natural human activity, so is communication. Learners can draw on this form of research by using interviews and conversations, which are readily accessible, especially in the world of social networking.

A REAL-WORLD PROBLEM FOR A REAL-WORLD AUDIENCE.

Early in my teaching career, a grade seven student approached me with an interesting project proposal. She was concerned with the behaviour of the two adult polar bears at our local zoo. They were housed in a substantial facility that included a concrete area painted to look like ice and snow, and a water component where the bears could swim and be viewed by spectators. Every time my student visited the zoo, she observed the two bears manically pacing back and forth within their enclosure on the same well-worn path. She concluded that these polar bears had developed this behavioural pattern because they were limited by the design of their enclosure. She saw the animals as unhappy. Her project proposal was to create an enclosure design that she felt was more compatible with their natural habits and habitat to address this perceived unhappiness. I was excited to see her wanting to engage in design and innovation in a context that was personally meaningful to her. I was not as excited by how she wanted to research and develop her project. As expected, she wanted to go to the library and do typical book research, and then make a diorama to present to the class for me to grade.

Instead of following this familiar path, I instructed her to contact the zoo and make an appointment with the polar bear keeper as a research visit and told her that I would accompany her. I also instructed her that her redesign of the polar bear enclosure would not be given to me to grade, but would rather be presented back to the zoo for their feedback. It was now a real-world problem for a real-world audience.

Our zoo visit revealed discovery in a very different way from passive research. Filtration plants, diet and food preparation considerations, veterinarian support, and polar bear behaviour and management were revealed and explored in ways that would not have been possible without this experiential approach to first-hand research. This acutely came to the fore as we walked though a hallway along the back of a caged area where the bears were fed. This hallway featured concrete on one side and cage walls on the other. Inside the locked gates of these cages, we could see the beautiful white bears resting peacefully. There was a small gap between the bottom of the gates and the floor, and we were warned to walk with our backs against the concrete wall as we went through the corridor. When I asked why, the polar bear keeper's answer was quite succinct: "If we are too close to the bottom of the gate, they could attempt to swipe at us. They are carnivores!"

Stage 2—Inquire and Experiment: Emerging frameworks for innovation and invention

Principal Developmental Strands: Collaborative development, research/investigative development, self-instigative development, generative development, experimentational development, discipline complexity, critical/analytical thinking development.

Primary Educator Roles: Collaborator in co-construction of design challenges where needed. Facilitator and collaborator in moving learning engagement from extrinsic to intrinsic motivation, and moving the design process from thought to form through idea generation and early prototyping.

This stage of learning experience design is one of inquiry and experimentation. As such, it is a transitional stage in many ways. In this stage, ideas are focused into creative, actionable opportunities to engage in the design process. As well, ownership of the design challenge is transferred to the learner as much as possible, if it has not happened already. It is the stage where the creative process goes from thought to form. It is a stage of both divergence and convergence.

The experiential exploration of Stage 1 leads to preliminary questions and curiosities that will inform the driving questions and goals of the evolving research and design challenges. IDEO (2016) describes the difficulty in shaping preliminary questions into concrete design challenges and notes that "finding meaning . . . and turning it into actionable opportunities for design is not an easy task" (p. 46). They go on to describe how important it is for learners in truly interactive environments to work to find emerging themes, make sense of their active research, and develop new insights and questions that will frame a potential design challenge. Mind mapping (Buzan, 2012) and idea charting can be useful tools to uncover concentrated areas of interest and inquiry out of a sea of potential idea candidates. This leads to discovering design challenges that are potentially actionable and personally relevant to learners.

At this point in the learning design process, clearer pre-inventive structures begin to form and intrinsic motivation becomes the inventive driver. The emerging pre-inventive structures will provide the basis for early prototyping, where the process moves from thought to form.

All stages of the design process require fuel in the form of new ideas and new information. Maintaining a continual flow of stimuli into shaping pre-inventive structures and corresponding early prototyping is essential to maintain inventive momentum. This involves engaging in recurrent iterations of divergence and convergence as the design process evolves. John Sweeney's (2004) Brave New Workshop theatre group applies a practice for developing new productions of generating a minimum of 600 ideas to fuel the process at the onset as the pre-inventive structure is shaped. The active idea exchange described in Creating Development 3 (Introducing Design Practice) is a great strategy for interactive cross-fuelling that leads to refinement of the shaping of pre-inventive structures and refinement of early prototypes that lead to Stage 3 (Innovate and Invent).

The thought-to-form transition in Stage 2 is a critical transition. Learners can only stay in a state of pure ideation for a certain length of time before diminishing returns slow inventive momentum. Eventually learners have to converge on potentially actionable design challenges that undergo preliminary testing through early prototyping to test out ideas. There are several ways that early prototyping can manifest itself, as described in chapter 3 (Engaging in Creative Practice). This enables the continuation of traction in the design process while maintaining inventive momentum. What emerges from Stage 2 (Inquire and Experiment) are more clearly defined design challenges that are ready for Stage 3 (Innovate and Invent) in the actual context for which they were planned.

Stage 3—Innovate and Invent: Original research, production, and action in real-world contexts

Principal Developmental Strands: Collaborative development, research/investigative development, self-instigative development, generative development, experimentational development, discipline complexity development, critical/analytical development, creative sustain development.
Primary Educator Roles: Mentor to intrinsically motivated learners involved in tethered or pure invention. Co-collaborator and mentor to learners involved in co-constructed emerging invention.

As learners transition from Stage 2 to Stage 3, prototyping moves from soft convergence, where a small set of prototyping candidates are in play, to hard convergence that often results in a single prototype that will potentially be brought into real-world application. A prototype by nature does not have to be perfect from the outset. It is a convergence point where various ideas are merged and brought into a form in the currency of the discipline in which the design challenge is taking place. It is only when ideas are brought into form that learners can verify if the proposed design solution will work. Stage 3 is the stage of final prototyping in the context of the actual problem where the prototype is subjected to constant feedback and refinement. This speaks to the developmental strand of creative sustain: the capacity to maintain creative sustain through innumerable refinements of prototype resolutions is one of the benchmark indicators of creative maturity.

Establishing sources for quality feedback is essential at this stage to move the design process forward. This is an excellent opportunity to move outside traditional educational spaces to seek feedback from broader expert communities. Learners can recruit local, regional, and global experts for this purpose. They can form intended audiences for the design resolution into focus groups for feedback to inform their continual design refinement. At this stage, divergent thinking is largely in the form of bracketing, with learners focused on refining, designing, and testing prototype components toward problem resolution. The demand for continual refinement and prototype modification requires creative sustain development to maintain inventive momentum throughout this process.

As learners move into Stage 3, there can be varying degrees of ownership and instigative context depending on their developmental level and the impetus for innovating and inventing. Co-construction of innovation and invention between educators and learners can go into Stage 3 if co-constructive support is needed by the learner to engage in innovation and invention. The developmental goal and educational dynamic here would always be toward moving learners to complete self-instigative intrinsic motivation, though. In the co-constructed configuration, the learner would be seen to be in the phase of *emerging invention*. If the impetus for the design challenge is rooted in mandated curricular fields, it is certainly possible for learners to construct their own design challenges and take complete ownership for them. In this context, Stage 3 design challenges would be described as *curriculum-connected* or *tethered innovation* and *invention*. If the learner is intrinsically motivated to instigate the design challenge over and above mandated curricular contexts, or independent of them, this would be described as *pure invention* or *innovation*. Emerging, curriculum-connected or tethered and pure innovation and invention can all exist in Stage 3. The ideal educational and developmental dynamic is to enable all learners to initiate and undertake pure innovation and invention.

Students Enter Progression at Their Developmental Level

It is important to note when applying the learning experience progression for creative development that a student can enter the progression at the level of their creative capacity. If they are already functioning at a Stage 3 level of creativity capacity, then it is perfectly okay for them to start in Stage 3, as they have already internalized the mature practices to get them to innovate and invent. Early in my career while teaching grade twelve art and design, three students approached me at the very beginning of a semester with an interesting proposition. They asked if they had to attend my art class because they wanted to do something different as an equivalent. They wanted to make a twenty-minute movie that would be original from start to finish. My initial response was to ask why they would not want to take my class after being my students in grades ten and eleven. These three students had already exhibited that they were capable of complex original work and they were clearly functioning in Stage 3. I quickly reeled in any thoughts of holding these students back and agreed to allow their proposition—dependent on their presentation of a thorough, detailed plan. When their plan was completed and accepted, we found a room in the school where they could work for the semester. We met every week and they successfully created a great movie. Imagine what would have happened had I held them back to comply with the typical educational script. One of these students went on to make movies for the Bravo network, another went on to win a Grammy Award as a music producer and sound engineer, and the third member of this group I lost track of. They are still in Stage 3.

Problematic Educational Archetypes for Creative Development

There are several educational archetypes that preclude maximum creative development potentials. On the surface, they appear to enable innovation and invention, but their fundamental structure is inherently flawed to enable a systematic developmental approach to growing the creative capacity of learners. These educational archetypes generally fall into these patterns:

a. **Skill and discipline content acquisition (Stage 1) activities are the exclusive focus.**
   This instructional disposition assumes that discipline competency equates to increased creative capacity. This is not the case. However, discipline competency, as part of the ecology of comprehensive creative development, is one of many developmental strands that will enable growth in creative capacity. The focus in this archetype is exclusively on acquisition of discipline competency.

b. **Inquiry and experimentation (Stage 2) experiences are omitted.**
   This essential transitional stage is left out, leaving learners to

go from Stage 1 (Explore) all the way to Stage 3 (Innovate and Invent). This archetype assumes that all learners have a relatively high creative capacity and that students have acquired the self-discipline and design process patterns of mature creative producers. This archetype assumes development instead of enabling development.

c. **Innovation and invention (Stage 3) activities are completely omitted.**
In this archetype, Stage 2 (Inquire and Experiment) is considered to be the creative peak of the program. This archetype falls prey to the reluctant release of creative ownership and design instigation to the learner, which would enable them to grow into self-instigated creative space. Co-construction is the limit of design practice. This issue is discussed in Creating Development 6 (Learning to Let Go).

d. **Innovate and Invent (Stage 3) is the only stage explored.**
This is the laissez-faire approach to invention. There is some value here in enabling play and experimentation for discovery and possibly invention. This approach is subject to the same limitations as Archetype b (above), where there is little or no developmental scaffolding in place to optimize growth in creative capacity and also to address the developmental needs of the learner.

The learning experience design progression for creative development, when applied in a flexible manner, precludes the failures of these archetypal program patterns.

The learning experience design progression for creative development can be scaled to apply within a designated unit of study, a semester, a school year, or the complete educational journey of a learner. The direction dynamic of this developmental progression is always toward the intrinsically motivated third stage of innovation and invention. When this progression is applied in an educational environment, the option always exists to deploy learning and design experiences from the three stages as dictated by individual student developmental needs. Keep in mind that these stages are not designed to be hard and fast, but rather to inform the fluid learning experience dynamic of enabling learners to evolve into an innovative and inventive educational space.

Examples from the Field

The following are vignettes from the field to illustrate how learners can be enabled to engage in innovative and inventive practice. These snapshots of practice span the range of co-constructed emerging invention, curricular connected or tethered invention, and pure, student-instigated innovation and invention.

These vignettes were provided by the Étude Group of Schools in Sheboygan, Wisconsin, which places a high value on design, creativity, innovation, and invention in authentic disciplinary contexts. They are a set of three, tuition-free, public charter schools within the Sheboygan Area School District: the Elementary School for the Arts and Academics (ESAA); the Mosaic School, a middle school; and the IDEAS Academy (Innovation through Design, Engineering, Arts, and Sciences), a secondary school. Étude director, Ted Hamm, and members of the faculty from the three schools compiled these vignettes.

There are many examples of innovative and inventive educational practice in North America and beyond as discussed in *Education for Creativity: A Global Conversation* (Kelly, 2012). They range from the previously mentioned boats designed by six- and seven-year-old students at Brightworks School in San Francisco to an album of original music written and performed by a grade twelve student at Puget Sound Community School in Seattle. These examples are from private institutions that operate largely outside state, provincial, or nationally mandated curricula. Regardless, systematic creative development must be intentionally enabled in any educational setting with the goal to transform educational practice and the concept of schooling whether within an established system or through the invention of something new. The vignettes that follow are here to provide a variety of examples across traditional grade levels and discipline areas of how learning experience design could possibly be structured in a variety of contexts to enable innovation and invention through original research, production, and action in co-constructed, tethered, and pure invention contexts.

Example 1. The chicken coop—Kindergarten

TED HAMM—BASED ON AN INTERVIEW WITH RACHEL PEKAREK AND SUSAN GRIFFITHS, TEACHERS, ELEMENTARY SCHOOL FOR THE ARTS AND ACADEMICS

Young children are natural designers. They are inherently inquisitive about how the world works and imaginative with solutions to problems. Through a process of observation that leads to questioning, and questioning which leads to discovery, young children are able to solve design problems in a sophisticated manner. Through this course of study, students collaborated with a farmer, knowing that they wanted students to have the experience of raising hatching eggs. The purpose of the unit

Figure 4.2 The first phase of the Chicken Coop project is for students to make an initial visit to a farm to better understand how chickens live on the farm. Teachers use routines such as What Do I See, What Do I Think, and What Do I Wonder to guide student observation.

was to study life cycles, which was to be done through observation and care for chicken eggs but design emerged as an opportunity around the essential question, "How do we make life better for the next generation of chickens?"

STAGE 1—EXPLORE.

How do we make life better for the next generation of chickens?

Using butterflies as the initial entry into understanding the life cycle, students observed the life cycle of a butterfly from the egg stage to the caterpillar and chrysalis stage to the butterfly stage. Throughout this study students used a "See, Think, Wonder" approach to record and guide their observations through each phase of the life cycle. Students measured how the butterflies grew and how the eating habits of the butterflies impacted their growth. This same process was followed for the study of plants.

The butterflies opened up the opportunity to explore the life cycle of chickens and apply students' knowledge through design. The introduction to this phase of the project started with the farmer bringing chicken eggs to school for the students to hatch and raise chicks. The students followed that up with a visit to the farm, where the farmer introduced the design challenge of making a better chicken coop for the generation of chickens the students were hatching. To guide the process of observation at the farm, students went back to "See, Think, Wonder." This process allowed students to ask informed questions of the farmer (e.g., How do birds clean themselves? Where do the birds go to roost?). Through this process, students uncovered many issues, including that chickens clean themselves using dirt to keep off mites. Throughout this study, students used read-alouds and individual research to better understand chickens and their life cycle.

STAGE 2—INQUIRE AND EXPERIMENT.

How do birds clean themselves? Where do birds go to roost?

Following the visit to the farm, the students began work on creating a better chicken coop for their chickens. Students chose what they wanted to design (e.g., chicken bath, water drinking system, roost). They were taken through a process of creating mind maps and word webs to generate ideas. During this phase of the process, the teachers resisted constraints and emphasized with the students that nothing was too big. As designs were created, they were drawn out and presented to the farmer for feedback. One issue the farmer raised was the need for the chickens to eat a more natural diet that required chickens to be out in the field. The students drew up plans for a portable chicken coop. The plans were reviewed by the farmer and teachers, and it was determined that a portable chicken coop could not be built in the classroom. This resulted in the student design team switching to building a scaled-down version of the portable chicken coop.

Following this work, a few design constraints were introduced. Students needed to start to factor in the cost, materials, and functionality of their designs. Costs were explored in a field trip to the local hardware store where students also factored in the type of materials they felt would best fit the process. Once these design constraints were factored in, students had to decide on a single design, or a combination of designs, to follow through on as a class.

STAGE 3—INNOVATE AND INVENT.

To facilitate the building process, adults were brought in to take direction from the students and to offer strategies for bringing the designs to fruition. Through this process students built dust baths, a watering system, raised roosts that were designed to keep the eggs from rolling out, and a scaled-down portable chicken coop. The actual pieces were then presented to a group of experts consisting of the farmer, a veterinarian, a handyman, and a high school life sciences teacher. Students presented what they had learned and observed about the chickens in their various stages of life and how their designs addressed the issues of hygiene, natural nutrition, watering, and habitat. Ultimately, the farmer took all of the designs and still uses them at her farm.

Example 2. Mathematics—Triangles, Home Alone, and probabilities

PETER WOODS—MATHEMATICS EDUCATOR, IDEAS ACADEMY

This may seem like an obvious statement, but students often have trouble innovating in the math classroom because they do not know what that phrase actually means. This lack of understanding stems from the fact that most math classes never actually show students how mathematicians or other professionals working with math create something new from the skills and tools they developed as students, despite the fact that new innovations developed through research and production arrive from mathematical thought processes all the time. More often than not, students only ever see their teachers walk through algorithms without explanation of how those pioneering thinkers developed their ideas (they may see a few proofs, but how those thinkers arrived at a proof is a different story). Hopefully, these examples illuminate how teachers can help students uncover the processes of experiential exploration, inquiry and experimentation, and innovation and invention through mathematical thinking.

STAGE 1—EXPLORE: "INVENTING AREA FORMULAS."
The following lesson took place over one day in a geometry class. The objective for the day was to understand the formulas for calculating the area of various quadrilaterals. Students had previously worked with the areas of triangles, squares, and circles.

The workshop started with a general review, making sure students remembered how to find the area of a rectangle and a triangle. We also worked through a couple of examples as a class. After that, I asked the class where the formula for a triangle comes from. They were stumped, so I drew a rectangle on the board, and then drew a line from one corner to the other, showing them that the area of a right triangle is very literally one-half the area of a rectangle. I then erased the diagonal line, drew a non-right triangle inside the rectangle and asked students if the same logic applied. After thinking about it for a second, a student raised her hand and said, "Yes, because you can put the smaller triangles together to make a bigger one that is the same as the triangle you just drew." I told the student she was correct and commended her on her logic. This simple response shows the beginnings of her innovative thought processes in this medium, as the student's solution came from her own mathematical thinking as opposed to applying someone else's logic to a new set of numbers.

After this, I gave the students a bunch of paper quadrilaterals, a ruler, and scissors, then told them to do the following:

1. Find the area of each shape, and
2. Create an area formula for each shape.

After a lot of brainstorming and discussing in groups, students got to work chopping up the quadrilaterals into rectangles and triangles, finding the area of these smaller shapes, adding them all up, and then generalizing their findings by replacing the lengths of each side with variables. Along the way, I answered questions and reoriented their thinking when they became completely stuck (but always as a last resort). Once students had found the various formulas, they presented their findings to the class. When a student presented an overly complicated formula, the class collaborated on simplifying their findings and then compared their work to ensure accuracy.

STAGE 2—INQUIRE AND EXPERIMENT: "THE MATH FROM *HOME ALONE*."

As part of the mini-project week at IDEAS Academy (a week-long crash course that models the phases of our school's semester-long projects), students gathered in various academic and creative disciplines to create something new involving the theme "home." Five students were brave enough to try out math as their discipline of choice.

First, students developed a list of concepts that mathematicians found important, then moved onto all of the ideas they associated with home. After these thoughts were collected, the group organized their ideas into subcategories and started making connections between the two larger groups. One of the students brought up the concept of safety and another built off this, mentioning the booby traps in the film *Home Alone*. The conversation suddenly jumped to whether these traps would work, if they would be too dangerous, and how they could prove their theories without injuring anyone in the school. They decided to make these their guiding questions for the week.

After developing this plan, the students dove into research, picking one of the traps from the movie to focus on (we went with the swinging paint cans) and determining the amount of force needed to be effective but not deadly. They decided to go with the minimum amount of force needed to break a bone, which students found by averaging the values pulled from a collection of scientific articles. The group then started working on individual aspects of the problem. Some students went to the stairwell in the school to get measurements, others took these measurements and used trigonometry and the properties of circles to flesh out the design of the booby trap, and a final group found the physics teacher and asked him which formulas were needed to calculate the force of the paint can. Since all of these students came from different math classes, this process worked exceptionally well due to the differentiation that occurred.

Finally, after all the calculations were completed, students wrote up a mathematical paper, complete with abstract, literature review, and figures. Students presented this work to the school during the mini-project presentations. A few of the members on the project team extended the work, redesigning several traps to become mathematically more effective. They increased the probability of the Wet Bandits engaging some traps as well as adjusting the levels of force, heat, and electricity associated with others.

STAGE 3—INNOVATE AND INVENT: THE CASINO AND "HOW MANY SONGS ARE THERE?"

In this example, an Algebra II class was learning about combinations, permutations, and the fundamental counting principle. Students started by engaging with these concepts collaboratively, answering questions that slowly built into the three topics mentioned. Almost every math class that teaches probability incorporates these exact questions or other questions like them (e.g., How many different hands can a player get in five-card stud? If I roll six dice, how many different ways can I get a total of twenty-one?), but students found answers to these problems without the usual formulas. Only after the class had solved several similar problems and compared their solutions would we discuss what a formula for these problems might look like.

We decided, as a class, to host a casino night for the rest of the school. To accomplish this task, students created their own casino games that ranged from simple variations of blackjack and poker to hybrids of roulette and bingo involving air cannons that shot rubber balls around the inside of an empty aquarium. For each game, students used permutations and combinations to calculate the probability of winning, and then used these values to determine the payout of each game (just as game designers do). Students then created playable models of each game (if the game involved more than a deck of cards or some dice) and invited the school community to place their bets.

An example of student-initiated pure research finally arrived about a year after this class took place. One of the students from this class approached me after school with an idea: if there were a limited number of notes, would there not be a limited number of songs? I asked the student how they would solve this problem, and they said that they could use concepts like the fundamental counting principle and permutations to figure it out.

The student-initiated question led us to consider a few more basic questions to help frame their thinking. For example, "Could a song be infinitely long?" "Even though notes repeat, can they go infinitely high or low?" and "How can you restrict these things?" At this stage, I became a mentor and did not give the student a solution to this brand-new problem. Instead, the student went through the exploration, inquiry, and experimentation stages to build toward student-initiated research. As this example shows, educators must be prepared to allow for greater student autonomy as learners take ownership of innovation and invention while changing roles to support student research.

Example 3. Humanities and movement—Grade seven

TED HAMM—BASED ON AN INTERVIEW WITH MOLLY KING, MOVEMENT TEACHER, THE MOSAIC SCHOOL

Students at The Mosaic School are simultaneously enrolled in disciplinary classes in the academics, like social science, and creative seminars of their choice: animation, engineering, theatre, modern dance, or ensemble. The school is designed in a way that provides students with scaffolded opportunities to interpret ideas through different art forms. They explore interpretation of disciplinary ideas through projects in the classroom, exploration of art forms for interpretation in seminars, and in a unique class called Project Seminar, where they have the opportunity to select a discipline of their choice and an art form of their choice to study in depth through the creative process. In the example that follows, a seventh grade student chose to use modern dance to interpret a concept in social studies.

STAGE 1—EXPLORE.

What does it mean to be a social scientist or a choreographer?

All students at The Mosaic School are enrolled in social studies, wherein students explore the different lenses of social science. In this example, the focus of the year was cultural anthropology and students were exploring the course question "How do ideas affect and reflect our identity?" They explored this question through the guided study of different cultural periods, such as the Renaissance, and developed their rhetorical skills for creating claims and supporting them with evidence. In one instance, students created claims about how ideals of beauty spread across the world and influence consumers and plastic surgery.

Concurrently, students who selected the modern dance seminar engaged in eight weeks of skill development in that art form. During that time, the movement teacher taught students choreography that she created to introduce the elements of modern dance and share her creative process as a choreographer. In exploration, students also responded to the work of professional choreographers by observing their work and mimicking movements in the discipline, such as fall and recovery, swing and release. They also analyzed the creative process of professionals using "Think, Puzzle, Explore" thinking routines. This process situated students in the role of choreographer, where they had to identify the creator's intent, the questions they had to ask themselves to fulfill intent through movements, and the opportunities they had to explore in their own creations.

STAGE 2—INQUIRE AND EXPERIMENT.

How does the spread of ideas affect cultural identity?

When students were familiar with the vocabulary and constraints of cultural anthropology, they were challenged to develop original questions derived from the class question "How does the spread of ideas affect cultural identity?" Through a process of generating, sorting, and categorizing possibilities, students generated more specific questions, such as "How does the spread of ideas affect traditions and beliefs as part of cultural identity?" They were then guided through research in which they focused on defining key terms within their questions and evaluated sources to develop even more specific questions. As a result of this process, one student arrived at the question "How is religion altered or stripped away because of war and politics?"

In modern dance class, students began creating original choreography while still responding to professional models. In a series of low-pressure movement experiences, students were asked to translate keywords or themes into movements. For example, they watched a professional model and analyzed the significance of the piece as a class, and then each student summarized the theme of the model through feeling, shape, and movement. Then the teacher facilitated collaboration between students to place these movement summaries into a sequence or original movement, with each person contributing a small part of the choreography.

STAGE 3—INNOVATE AND INVENT.

How can I use dance to show the relationship between war and religion?

Invention in Mosaic's modern dance project seminar stemmed from a survey of all disciplines. As a class, students generated multiple possibilities and collaboratively created a menu of project ideas that lead to the interpretation of the discipline through the art form. In this example, students were responsible for bringing their cultural anthropology lens to modern dance choreography.

One student choreographed a modern dance that interpreted the relationship between war and religion. She intentionally chose the modern dance elements of contract and release to represent the contrasts between war and religion in her dance. She employed an ensemble of dancers to represent war and choreographed rigid, repetitive movements to capture the structure of the military. In her project proposal, which follows, she also discusses how she will seek feedback from peers.

STUDENT PROJECT PROPOSAL.

Right now I'm in the modern dance project seminar and I want to express what I'm learning in social studies. My driving question will be "How can I use dance to show the relationship between war and religion?" I will focus heavily on the modern concepts of contract and release and experiment with the contrast in war and religion through dance.

In social studies we developed our driving questions based off of sub-questions. I already had an interest in the religions of different cultures so I choose the sub-question that is "How does the spread of ideas affect traditions and beliefs as part of cultural identity?" Knowing already I wanted to do religion I had to think about ways that ideas about religion are spread. This made me think about all the wars that either start with religion, not start with religion but turn into a war about religion or the war ends up affecting a religion. I then formed my own driving question for social studies, "How is religion altered or stripped away because of war and politics?" I then slightly altered it to fit modern dance, "How can I use dance to show the relation between war and religion?" I really like doing this because even though I'm not a religious person myself but I think religion is really interesting and for some people it's a huge part of them. I think that religions in other countries are especially interesting.

To create a modern dance around this topic, I'm going to need a song that portrays the emotion, which requires me to first find out what emotions I want to show through the dance. I will need a couple of dancers depending on my choreography. I want to use an ensemble of dancers to represent war. I want to capture the structure of the army through rigid repetitive moves that are in sync. I will show religion through solitary movements that will contrast to the more small movements of the army and use bigger movements that are less repetitive and move around the space more. I still have to do some more research before I can exactly figure out how I want the movements to look.

I will ask people in my class for feedback throughout my process to make sure I don't forget about the modern concepts and I don't lose my meaning. I will also try to get feedback from people who aren't in my class to see if non-dancers can tell what my intention is. I'm also considering showing it to Mrs. Machut to make sure she thinks I'm doing a good job of portraying my topic.

I want to show my dance first in my presentation even though this could confuse the audience; I want to see the meaning they take out of it. I have done this in other projects before and it actually worked out fairly well. After I show the dance I will explain the concept and more of my research. I will also explain part of my research and then connect it back to the dance by doing a move again after saying part of my research. I want people to see different sides of war because a lot of times when we think of consequences of war we think of the lives lost, the money spent, families being torn apart, which are all very important things but I want to show how war can destroy other parts of people.

This is going to be a challenge to me because I haven't done a dance that relates to an academic area before so I will need the help to make sure I'm getting my intention across. I'm also going to be looking at using more quick, rigid, big movements that are more out of my comfort zone in my choreography and dance abilities so to create choreography like that I will need to use the professional models we look at on Mondays and source other videos to look at for ideas. Even though these are all things that are challenges to me they are at the same time excitements because I am excited to work outside of my comfort zone and do something different.

Example 4. Community health—Secondary school

TED HAMM—BASED ON AN INTERVIEW WITH KAREN ROBISON, LIFE SCIENCES TEACHER, IDEAS ACADEMY

High school students at IDEAS Academy have the option of taking a Human Anatomy and Physiology class. Prior to taking this class, most students have foundational experiences in biology and chemistry. The experiences that are most conducive to student creative development in the example below include experiences in scientific exploration that lead to an analysis of trends, rather than predetermined lab outcomes or those that lead to yes or no conclusions. In this service learning example, student engagement and invention go hand in hand.

STAGE 1—EXPLORE.

What does it mean to be healthy?

Exploration in science requires an understanding of how things work. In a Human Anatomy and Physiology class, students prepare to explore by sorting body systems from most to least familiar. This sets up the foundational knowledge needed at the outset of the class. Students in a particular class identified the endocrine and immune systems as areas where they needed better understanding. The teacher then set up a series of opportunities, ranging from digital flash cards to current event discussions, for students to play with and come to know these systems. When students were more familiar with the academic foundations, they re-sorted the list of body systems according to which ones they felt were most important for human health.

An additional exploration in this class included an introduction to how professionals interested in public and community health go about their work. For example, students looked to the Centers for Disease Control's examples of how professionals in the field approach community health challenges. They also examined community health challenges in their own community by looking at teacher-analyzed data from a Sheboygan County Health and Human Services report called "Sheboygan 2020." Students used this data and analysis to identify areas of interest for their own IDEAS Health Fair projects. Within these projects, students would need to design and conduct a scientific experiment that would impact the health of teens in their own community.

STAGE 2—INQUIRE AND EXPERIMENT.

What do we need to know about our genetic heritage, environment, and culture to live a healthy life?

To identify authentic community needs for their Health Fair projects, students used scientific structures to explore community-based understandings. For example, students were responsible for collecting data on their community's perception of healthy living using a collaboratively designed survey. They also consulted an Aurora Health Care Community Outreach representative, who provided resources specific to teen health. Another form of student-centred research included collecting and documenting their own family histories and looking in-depth at their own genetic heritage.

Throughout this project, the class regularly examined current events, current research, and technical articles regarding health. The discourse around these readings reinforced foundational understandings of human body systems, offered professional models of scientific application, and sparked potential project ideas. One article took up the health implications of urine colour. The resultant discussion and research became the source for the teacher's model project, which was an effort to increase the amount of water consumed by the school community. The teacher modelled each phase of the creative process, engaging students for feedback throughout the design and completion of her experiment for the Health Fair.

With data from their community and problem-solution models, students began generating questions about the needs of their community. Knowing they would have the venue of a Health Fair to engage their peers, students began their own research.

STAGE 3—INNOVATE AND INVENT.

How can we, Human Anatomy and Physiology students, improve student health at IDEAS?

To pursue their own experiments for the Health Fair model, students had to respond to the question "What does it mean to be healthy?" and design a course of research that would be scientifically and locally relevant. Some students chose to visit local health care facilities and interview employees. One student visited local resources for teen pregnancy to make recommendations for where to find the best care and largest range of resources. All students continued reading current research to support their projects.

Inventive and innovative work in this project came through the solutions students offered and how they engaged their peers at the Health Fair to activate those solutions. One group took up the issue of healthy snacks and redesigned recipes to make them healthier, then had students sample them at the fair. Another group provided a menu of strategies for peers to use to manage their anxiety in class without having to miss experiences or instruction to cope outside class. With authentic work in public health, students carefully designed their interactions with their peers as clients or audience members. One student made origami frogs and cones to simulate the spread of communicable diseases through a population. Another student developed a crowd-sourced map to depict popular places in the community where people would like to ride their bicycles if there were safer lanes.

As students reflected on the long-term impact of their process, they acknowledged how difficult it is to change unhealthy habits and patterns.

Example 5. The SeaPerch project

*TED HAMM—BASED ON AN INTERVIEW WITH TIM PASCHE, ENGINEERING
TEACHER, THE MOSAIC SCHOOL*

At The Mosaic School, students select seminars based on their interests and the habits that they are developing. One seminar offered is an engineering course called Discovering with STEM, which focuses on design and modelling. In the class, students learn the engineering and design process, sketching, technical drawing, 3D modelling, and how to develop new ideas based on professional models. This class also covers the disciplinary content standards relating to measurement, density, buoyancy, and scale drawing.

Figure 4.3 A Mosaic School student in the rebuilding phase of the SeaPerch project, in which students redesign the remotely operated vehicles (ROVs) after the initial build and testing process.

STAGE 1—EXPLORE.

How does air density affect movement and resistance?

In the Discovering with STEM class, one of the first experiences students had was the observation of two containers with clear liquid and a candle in them. In one container, the candle was on the top of the liquid, and in the other, the candle was at the bottom. Students used a "See, Think, Wonder" thinking routine to begin reasoning as engineers. Engineering classes emphasize many skills, including on observation and reasoning. The observations, conclusions, and questions from this experience were used as a baseline for developing understanding of density through the first STEM project in the class.

As an initial project in this course, students were challenged to make a hot air balloon. They copied an existing design for a hot air balloon and made minor adjustments to the design. In this way, they were introduced to the engineering and design process experientially, while applying their understanding of density.

STAGE 2—INQUIRE AND EXPERIMENT.

How does water density affect movement, resistance, and buoyancy?

In another project, students in the Discovery with STEM class were provided with pieces of pvc pipe, tools, and directions for assembling the SeaPerch, a remotely operated vehicle (ROV), based on a kit from the Office of Naval Research. Students assembled like copies of the SeaPerch and tested it using an underwater obstacle course. To navigate the course efficiently, students found they had to make adjustments to the design's buoyancy. Using the engineering and design process, students engaged in observation, feedback, redesign, and rebuilding to meet their group's navigation goals. While doing this, they also honed their skills in sketching, measurement, and calculating density and buoyancy.

STAGE 3—INNOVATE AND INVENT.

So what? How can we redesign an unmanned underwater vehicle to include more functionality?

Following the SeaPerch build, students used a "See, Think, Wonder" thinking routine to slow down their thinking and generate possibilities. Their observations were broken down in the "See" portion of the routine, segmenting different parts, behaviours, and steps. In the "Think" part of the routine, students began imagining how the design and purpose of each piece might change. Resisting closure, students generated many "Wonders" about how the principles of an ROV might be used more effectively. As a class, they identified that it would be most useful to create a version of the SeaPerch that could easily navigate underwater and have the capacity to pick up items. Students posited that this functionality might be used to collect scientific samples for further study in a lab, for example.

For these designs, students were put into multi-age teams. Each team had to design, sketch, calculate buoyancy, create 3D models using CAD software, and assemble and test their designs. The outcomes of navigation and picking up objects underwater were shared; however, groups had complete latitude on their designs. In the testing process, students had to determine whether their calculations matched their observations of the vehicle in the water. They also had to assess how efficient their design was and went through several rounds of testing and tweaking of designs.

One of the more divergent designs transformed the cube frame of the SeaPerch into a more two-dimensional plane, giving it maximum manoeuvrability and precision. It also made driving more complex and required further development.

Example 6. IDEAS Academy block project— Psychology's influence on culture

TED HAMM—BASED ON AN INTERVIEW WITH HANNAH STAATS, GRADE TEN STUDENT, IDEAS ACADEMY

IDEAS Block is a core part of the educational program at IDEAS Academy, providing a place where students explore and research their own interests and concerns and ultimately create original works of art, engineering products, policy papers, or experiments. Students move through a process of ideation, research, creation, exhibition, and reflection for a project in each semester over their four years in grades nine through twelve. Through this process, students learn to generate ideas based on observation and experience, research those ideas, and create original works that clarify, interrogate, extend, or challenge them. These classes can grow from academic coursework and arts or engineering seminar courses that provide students with the skills and knowledge in each discipline. The IDEAS Block provides students the opportunity to take the skills and explore topics of interest through the creative process.

The example that follows is an independent IDEAS Block project wherein a student began with an art form, drama, and broad academic foci, psychology, and culture already in mind. She then used the phases of the design process to continually narrow her inquiry, constraints, and creative intentions. After initial research, she arrived at the question "How does the way we perceive our own psychological mindsets further biological and cultural evolution?" The student had background in theatre from school seminars and from drama in the community. She also relied on her practices as a creative writer and involvement in forensics.

STAGE 1—EXPLORE.

How have people's perceptions of their own psychology changed over time?

Exploration in IDEAS Block projects takes place on several levels throughout the school; however, an intentional exploration of the creative process that is shared community-wide takes place at the beginning of the school year. Students first practise drawing project ideas from their own observations and developing a project in advisory groups of fifteen to twenty students. (Students work in advisory groups primarily to build community and a safe environment for expressing and experimenting, and to ensure diverse backgrounds.)

In this example, advisory groups focused on the theme of home in the first week of school. With this focus, students went through facilitated observations of their community, an exhibit at a local arts centre with the same theme, and reflections on their own experiences. Students then went through all of the phases of the creative process in one day: ideation toward a specific guiding question, research, creation, exhibition, and reflection. These projects were based on student ideas, while the teacher facilitated collaborative decision making. Through the school-wide exhibition, students could see how one theme could diverge into a range of questions, courses of research, and interpretations. Groups interpreted their ideas through building designs, proposals for community programs, visual art, movement, and spoken word poetry. Part of this experience involved students understanding how the ideas they wanted to communicate influenced their choice in discipline medium. These explorations are about process for most students, especially those returning to the school. Those new to the school have the additional explorations of learning about how the community collaborates, shares ideas, provides feedback, and participates.

In the next phase of exploration, students were arranged in affinity groups by discipline. Students chose to work with a teacher in theatre, movement, engineering, visual art, creative writing, science, social science, or math. They then built on the community brainstorm on the theme of home and went through the same phases with less teacher direction but with more constraints on their discipline. Knowing that they had to create a film, for example, affected the academic research and what they were looking for in terms of understandings to communicate.

Since psychology is not a discipline offered in the school, the student relied on her disciplinary learning experiences in the classes that are offered to chart a course of study for herself in IDEAS Block. She understood that the field of psychology, like other disciplines she was more familiar with, involved certain common principles, many sub-disciplines, and a range of careers and institutions applying the principles to various degrees. With that understanding and focus, the student set out to map the discipline of psychology with a specific focus on evolutionary psychology. She sought first the history of the study of psychology to understand how people's perceptions of their own psychology have evolved.

She then identified specific theories that spoke to her driving question "How does the way we perceive our own psychological mindsets further biological and cultural evolution?" One theory that she pursued was the self-enhancement bias, where people inherently perceive themselves as more attractive and more successful than other people around them. She connected this theory to her question by claiming that this bias would be an advantage in evolution.

We think this could be categorized as exploration in creative development, though it is also innovation, because the student was able to essentially design a course of study around her understanding of disciplinary learning. This is the same thing that a teacher would do. She created essential questions, specific disciplinary questions, and ways to make academic research accessible to herself while also imagining how she would interpret these things through a dramatic piece for an audience of her peers. One way she did this was by outlining her reading in traditional academic notes as well as in visual sketches; this may have come from prior experiences in learning a second language. She also asked her peers questions that would expose self-enhancement bias to them while also clarifying it for herself; this may have come from prior experiences in learning dramatic improvisation. In addition, the student envisioned the character arc for her dramatic piece during, instead of after, her research process; personifying psychological theories made the abstractions tangible for understanding, but also malleable for innovation and invention. It is important to note that she made these choices independently.

STAGE 2—INQUIRE AND EXPERIMENT.

How does the way we perceive our own psychological mindsets further biological and cultural evolution?

IDEAS Block provides students a semester to pursue a project of their choice, using the phases of the creative process to create original work. With students at so many levels of project experience and self-direction, each phase has a set of supporting structures and rituals. Students also receive project-specific feedback and support from an advisor in their discipline and peers working in their discipline.

In this example, the student creating this dramatic art project participated in ideation, research, and creation phases alongside a peer group of creative writers. She selected this environment as a way of observing patterns in character development through professional models and her peers' work. From the beginning, she also made the choice to diverge from the sequence of the IDEAS Block class and create her dramatic work during her research phase. This innovation in the process allowed for extensive revision, or prototyping, opportunities and ensured that all of her creative choices would be reinforced by research and support her specific intentions. In this way, her writing was not just a way to understand and interpret her research, but became somewhat of a psychological experiment, playing with a character's degrees of awareness (conscious and subconscious) to achieve different narrative outcomes.

Like other disciplinary groups, the creative writing group looked at professional models on a weekly basis. Because of the range of project topics and forms of creative writing, students worked with their advisor to develop individual catalogues of professional models specific to their own work. So, for example, they collected poems, monologues, or other forms. They used the protocols of "Connect, Extend, Challenge" and "See, Think, Steal/Write Beside" to understand the parts and purposes of the forms they were creating. With the "See, Think, Steal/Write Beside" routine, students identified choices that writers make, analyzed what effects they think the choices have or are intended to have, and then practised writing in the same form using the author's language and/or structure as a template. This writing was experiential, giving new writers the feel for a certain pattern or rhetorical element that cannot be used after only reading it.

The individualized ways that students interacted with professional models was similar to how students were supported in their research process. For the project in this example, the advisor served as somewhat of a mentor. When the student had a piece of difficult research to interpret, she would break it down with the advisor and they would look for examples of psychological theories through current events. In this individualized process, the student even scheduled the conferences with the advisor and identified intended outcomes.

STAGE 3—INNOVATE AND INVENT.

How can we redesign institutions based on understandings of our conscious and unconscious to nurture and not constrain our biological and cultural evolution?

In this example, the student's project was pure invention from the development of a research question and sub-questions, to the modification of the order of the phases in IDEAS Block, to the creation of an original academic argument (in academic writing and an original dramatic narrative and performance) for which she determined her own constraints.

When students are engaged in truly self-directed processes as part of a class, it is sometimes difficult to understand exactly how creative development is realized. We ask students to share their process in a few ways: an artist statement (included below), a public exhibition of learning, and a reflective conference with an advisor. Conferences are focused around habits of mind: observing, wondering, connecting, interpreting, reasoning, and innovating. We have found that by breaking down these habits with students after a creative process, it exposes their development toward inventiveness.

In this project example, the conference revealed some of the following about the student's self-imposed constraints and depth of understanding about the art form. For example, the student realized that her research on the conscious and unconscious use of the self-enhancement bias was really, also, a study of subtext. She said, "It is natural to have multiple layers of thought at one time, some of which we are conscious of and others we are not. The ones we are not aware of are still present. This lends itself to theatre in the ways that the character is not always aware of all the information that the audience has access to." With this observation, the student realized that exposing what a character is unconscious of is an intriguing way to develop a narrative. Throughout her script, the student applied the self-enhancement bias by playing with real time and reflective monologues to put the character in crisis. The audience saw the character of Olivia acting out the self-enhancement bias and heard the character retelling the act as a way of bringing the faults to the surface and into consciousness. The success of this in her project, according to her, was related to her choice to have a single, female actress in the play. (She made this choice based on her study of professional models and her performance of other writers' works in forensics.) The lack of dialogue allowed for a kind of depth and flexibility needed to make transitions from real time to monologues.

ARTIST STATEMENT.

Olivia struggles with understanding the irrational behaviour of the people around her, but cannot perceive her own behaviour as anything but logical. As an individual, this is something she simply cannot do, something that none of us as human beings can do, because the cause of these behaviours that break the mould of what is predictable and rational is the part of our minds that operates unconsciously. We are in the dark when it comes to this part of our brains, and even an infinite amount of study cannot turn on the light and bridge the gap between understanding and awareness. This is one challenge we cannot overcome because it sets a fundamental basis for our evolution and is an essential portion of the definition of humanity. And as the human parts and pieces of our entire species and our culture, we construct around ourselves institutions, media, studies, and art that reflect a flawed understanding of ourselves. However, while incomplete awareness is inevitable, incomplete understanding is not: we can understand our minds even if we cannot know what is happening in them as it happens. It is possible to design ourselves a world that works if we arm ourselves with knowledge of ourselves, complete with conscious and unconscious. Just as Olivia is frustrated by the lack of intention she sees in the world, we will be fighting with the workings of the culture we've created until we design it intentionally and based in understanding.

REFERENCES

Buzan, T. (2012). *Modern mind mapping*. Cardiff: Proactive Press.

IDEO. *Design thinking for educators toolkit*. Retrieved January 19th, 2016, from designthinkingforeducators.com.

Kalantzis, M., & Cope, B. (2010). The teacher as designer: Pedagogy in the New Media age. *E-Learning and Digital Media*, *7*(3), 200–222. http://dx.doi.org/10.2304/elea.2010.7.3.200

Kelly, R. (2012). *Educating for creativity: A global conversation*. Edmonton: Brush Education.

Parsons, J., Hewson, K., Adrain, L., & Day, N. (2013). *Engaging in action research*. Edmonton: Brush Education.

Sweeney, J. (2004). *Innovation at the speed of laughter*. Minneapolis: Aerialist Press.

Learning to Let Go: Transferring Creative Ownership to Students

CARLA-JAYNE SAMUELSON

Carla-Jayne Samuelson is an educator specializing in English and Drama with an extensive background in theatre, singing, and songwriting. She is also a Learning Leader with a focus on creative development through the arts.

Perhaps one of the most difficult things for many educators to do is to transfer creative ownership to young learners. After all, educators are usually the class experts and there is a great deal of pressure for them to put their best foot forward when presenting student work for parents and school administration. However, educators must learn to shift roles as learners move through teacher-initiated to co-owned to student-owned creative development. Throughout this progression, educators' roles shift from teacher to facilitator to mentor/collaborator as students are scaffolded through the three developmental stages on their way to creating original work. And, of course, resisting the urge to intervene in final student productions, whether one likes the end product or not, is always difficult.

The following narrative takes us on a journey through the Theatre School Project of a grade six public school team that collaborated to enable the creative development of all students while learning to let go at the same time. –Robert Kelly

The Theatre School Project

I started my first year of teaching at a school that had a long history of a yearly spring musical that included the entire grade four to six populations. Each grade six class was responsible for writing a short play, thirty minutes' maximum, based on a common piece of literature that was read by all the grades involved. With the support of the music teacher and an artist in residence, grade four and five students had a hand in writing lyrics and creating the music to go along with each of the plays.

For both students and parents, anticipation of the new production began building at the start of each school year. Grade four students knew their introductory roles as choral support, grade five students knew they were a step up as musicians, and grade six students enjoyed the most coveted role at the level of writers and actors. Grade six students had the opportunity to audition for parts and solos in the plays their classes had created over the previous eight months.

Even now as I write this process it seems so simple and well defined—a good idea even—but those of you that have ever tried to put on a performance that included three grade levels while trying to teach your own class-mandated curriculum, know how taxing something of this magnitude can be. My background was in theatre and my principal was excited to have me on staff and thought, along with my full classroom teaching load, I would be a perfect fit to help staff with the yearly production. I agreed and was excited to be a part of such a huge collaboration of creative practice. What I began to see, however, were time constraints in the classrooms, partly due to the enormity of the project, leading to vertical comparisons between teachers of their classes' work on the productions, and inevitably social isolation of the teaching staff. The trust and culture of collaboration that should have been developing within the staff greatly diminished because no one had time to work together, so instead, teachers retreated to their classrooms to struggle alone. There were rumours of parents and students each year requesting to be in certain teachers' classrooms simply because they had better end products for the spring performance. Students were extrinsically motivated to land lead roles and solos, which in turn led to competition among them and extreme anxiety for everyone involved. The spring musical had become well defined over the years as an end-performance extravaganza but the process of getting to that end was lost.

Seeing this problem and wanting change raised several questions to our staff:

- How do we transform this competitive school culture and end product addiction?
- How do we as teachers let go of our own hubris and let the students' work stand on its own?
- Where do we find the courage to let the students' work be the students' work without us tweaking it so that we inevitably look better?
- How do we engage students in the process to be co-creators?
- How do we help students and parents let go of the end spectacle?

The biggest challenge lay with the grade six classes. These five classes provided the writers, actors, and soloists for anything new we could plan, and so this was where we began our plan. We returned to our mandate as teachers by rooting our rationale for change in the competencies of twenty-first-century learning. Our grade six team looked to creativity and innovation, communication, collaboration, and leadership as our focus to help us let go. Enter stage right—G6TS (Grade 6 Theatre School) was born.

Levelling the Playing Field

The first thing we needed to do as a team was to level the playing field. Instead of each teacher (and their class) being responsible for writing a script; making the set, props and costumes; doing makeup; teaching and learning acting techniques; directing and blocking; creating and running lighting; and managing sound and backstage for each of their classes, we embraced the concept of a theatre company. We let go of the notion of six autonomous groups and began to share the load within our own areas of expertise and passion. Instead of hiring one artist in residence for the better part of the year for music alone, we instead hired three artists for shorter stints to assist teachers in script writing, set design, and music. Instead of each class recruiting and organizing countless parent volunteers to design sets and props and make costumes (sometimes in the back of the classroom with numerous machines droning away during math class), students took on the responsibility of the artistic design of the entire show themselves.

We broke down each area of the process into five design studios called *Creative Development Workshops*.

- **Design one** was responsible for designing sets, props, and lighting. They were also responsible for training the technical crew and managing the backstage area for the entire show.
- **Design two** was responsible for creating makeup and costume designs for every character.
- **Design three** was responsible for producing the show: website, advertising, documentation throughout year, bio boards, programs, tickets, and posters.
- **Design four** was responsible for musical vocal training, which was accomplished during students' regularly scheduled music times.
- **Design five** was responsible for teaching acting techniques in drama studio classes.

Students had team leader roles in each of the workshops and were partnered with teachers as co-creators. All one hundred grade six students were divided into the studio times according to their own interest areas.

Letting Go of Vertical Comparisons and Star Roles

To reduce vertical comparisons, we eliminated the need for auditions and star roles. We did this by asking students to identify who wanted major or minor roles. We did this before the script-writing process began, and thus students were able to write scripts that accommodated student requests.

There was only one class in which every student wanted a major role, and therefore students had to work within those constraints to write a script that gave twenty-five students an equal number of lines. Surprisingly, there were many students within each of the classes that did not want to act at all, but were very excited at the prospect of learning how to be designers and technicians.

Writing and Refining the Script

Our theatre company was now creating an entire play from the genre of fairy tales with the overall theme of "We're Not Out of the Woods Yet." Students generated the idea of a common set that featured a forest with a large oak tree in the centre. Each grade six class was responsible for writing a scene, no more than twenty minutes long (including music), based on the conventions of fairy tales, the chosen theme, and the selected setting. Each class workshopped their scripts through the writing process four times with all the other classes for feedback. Students were instructed to ask specific questions that would help to move the work forward, such as "Does the skit make sense?" If not, "Where was it confusing?" In this process, students encouraged one another through plussing and using "yes and" responses to all feedback. In addition, when students received feedback on their work, they were instructed to not defend their ideas or become precious about their work, but rather to receive comments, ask clarifying questions, and use or bank the ideas.

The Residual Effect of This Process

The residual effect of this process shift on both staff and students was invaluable. Students took ownership of the entire G6TS company and were proud of the end product, as we all were, but through the process, they also built leadership and collaboration skills, which would not have been possible in the previous model. Students were designing and problem solving an entire production. In that process, each student had their own portfolio, which grew over the year, and was full of sketches and notes for costumes, designs, and makeup; or checklists of productions items; or notes from artists depending on what design team they were involved with. Students had the time to generate ideas, test them out, and add to those ideas or scrap them and start again. It was so inspiring to see the costume designers draping material over an actor and asking if they felt they could move in the piece or if a certain design would help them feel their character more. Set designers had actors come into the workshop to try set pieces, and actors asked if certain pieces could be made stronger to support their weight. One class needed a growing beanstalk, and the set design team went through many prototypes experimenting with pulley systems to make it work just right.

Figure CD6.1 Sketchbook costume design from Design Studio 2

Figure CD6.2 Prototyping a makeup design in Design Studio 2

Through this process, staff became better communicators with one another as we learned how to work with, trust, and depend on each other. We became more open to sharing and listening to one another and generating idea after idea. As a group, we learned to let go of our own ideas and allowed students to explore and try new things. We learned to trust their voices. One of the many examples of this occurred when staff was reviewing submissions for the production's poster. Although there were many great submissions, students voted for the one that we as a staff would never have picked. We were tempted to override the students' choice and slip in what we would have wanted, but in the end, we stayed true to our goal of letting go and handing ownership over to the students.

> Once upon a time . . . a group of students embarked on a journey to create a theatre production from the ground up. The group of travelling artists became known around the land as G6TS (Grade 6 Theatre School). There were twists and turns along the path as they developed their creativity. In the deep, dark woods, each character became a specialist in the areas of makeup, costumes, set design, production, lights, and sound. They encountered experts in the field of theatre who helped them in their journey. We welcome you to feel the magic of . . . Happily Never After!

Lingering with Words: Developing Creative Writing and Living Creatively

CARL LEGGO

Carl Leggo is a poet and professor in the Department of Language and Literacy Education at the University of British Columbia. Each day he seeks to know the heart of living poetically.

> *To create an educational environment conducive to the creative development of the writing of learners, it is essential that both educators and learners know themselves as creative writers. This piece is directed at both educators and learners and encourages them to engage in the writing process to foster the growth and development of creativity. Educators engaging in the writing process are engaging in action research, and that is perhaps the surest path to understanding and enabling the creative writing of learners. —Robert Kelly*

Know Yourself as a Creative Writer

As a professor of language and literacy education, I encourage educators and learners in elementary and secondary classrooms, in undergraduate and graduate programs, and in a network of community life writing groups, to pay attention to language by lingering with words. Above all, I invite writers, whether English is a first language or an additional language, to know themselves as creative writers who can live creatively.

As a poet, I seek to see the world with a poet's senses, heart, and imagination. As a beginning professor in the early 1990s, I was asked by a senior colleague, "What courses do you teach?" I responded with a wry smile, "Whatever I teach, I always teach creative writing." The colleague indicated she was neither amused nor enthused by my answer, and later reported to other colleagues that I taught "nothing" but creative writing. Almost twenty-five years later, I cheerfully acknowledge that, indeed, all I teach is creative writing. I am a poet who seeks to live poetically. And I always want others to explore the possibilities of living creatively, too.

In all the courses I teach, whether focused on writing, narrative inquiry, or creative expression, I invite learners to know themselves as creative writers. I explain how school did not serve me well and share the story of one respected teacher who told me, "You'll never be a writer!" Sadly, I believed her. I have lived much of my life as a wounded writer. As a writer and educator, I am committed to nurturing writers and writing. I ask students to listen to their hearts, to the rhythm of their hearts, to the metrical measure called the iamb (unstressed syllable/stressed syllable), the first poetic rhythm we know in our bodies. I offer words of hope that when we listen to our own hearts, we begin to know the lively creativity that dwells in all of us. I then share a few anecdotes about how I finally heard my own heart's rhythms when I began writing creatively in a journal. I was in my twenties, and life seemed like it was falling apart. I wrote in a journal to organize the chaos of experiences and emotions I lived daily. As I wrote, I heard a vibrant voice of hopeful wisdom, and I realized that I was a writer and that writing could heal and teach me how to live in the world with more joy.

After introductions at the beginning of a course and sharing hope that we will all journey together in writing, I ask students to leave! Actually, I invite them to leave the room and "wander for wonder." I ask them to take their journals and smartphone cameras, and walk outdoors and attend sensually to the abundant world all around them. I also ask them to return after a half-hour with an observation, a sentence, an image, or a metaphor—a hint of wonder gathered in their wandering. When they return, we share the gifts of wonder we received in our wandering.

Next, we explore the reasons for writing. We typically identify four or five main reasons, including self-expression, exploration, communication, entertainment, and utility. We quickly acknowledge that we are all writers, story makers, and poets. We are born into language and we revel in language. As a grandfather to four granddaughters, I have enjoyed the privilege in recent years of observing the insatiable desire of young children for creative adventures. In my writing classes, I remind writers that their creativity might seem dormant, but it is really just waiting to be called and nurtured.

The Process of Writing

Students are then introduced to free writing, an approach to writing as a process that has been invaluable in own my writing. A prompt is offered, and an invitation is given to write for a specific amount of time, perhaps five or ten minutes. In free writing, students are asked to keep their pens and fingers moving. They don't have to be concerned about punctuation and grammar. They don't have to be concerned about making sense or nonsense. Their goal is to keep on writing! Free writing is a way of thinking on paper, a way of letting words surprise the writer. What often happens in free writing is that the conscious mind loses some of its control, and suddenly memories that have been long forgotten call out, and connections between events that have been little understood emerge, and emotions that are often suppressed laugh and cry out. Above all, free writing is a way of tapping into the energy of words and word making. Free writing reminds the writer that writing is both conscious and unconscious. There is a sturdy sense of design in laying down words on the page. Like a bricklayer, a writer is following rules of syntax and semantics and grammar to connect words, one by one, in a pattern or arrangement that communicates an idea or emotion or story or argument. But writing is also full of mystery. I recommend to students that they avoid seeking mastery in writing to be open to mystery.

As a writer in school I almost always felt inadequate, not quite sure where to put commas, concerned that I didn't have anything worth saying, fearful that I was not as humorous or witty or bold or eloquent as my classmates, convinced that I was inferior because I wrote slowly, ashamed that my drafts were messy and chaotic and confusing, a litter of letters sprawling over scraps of paper. I was sure everybody else wrote as if transcribing dictation from speakers inside their heads. Now I revel in the process of writing. I don't know what I want to write until I can read what I have written. Therefore, I like to fill blank pages with writing to discover meaning, to discover what I want to say.

The writing process model emphasizes writing as a process, not writing as a product. The chaotic nature of the writing process is acknowledged. Writers don't begin with a clear understanding of what they will write. Instead, they discover meaning during the process of writing. The writing process model stresses the significance of writing as a meaning-making venture. Writers don't begin with a mentally constructed text that needs to be transcribed. Writers engage in an ongoing dialogue with their written words. Out of that dialogue meaning is produced and constructed and revealed.

Generally the writing process comprises five main stages: pre-writing, drafting, revising, editing, and publishing. But the process needs to be understood in more complex ways. Therefore, I suggest that the writing process include the following forces or dynamics: writing, reading, collecting, selecting, connecting, talking, thinking (convergently and divergently), doubting, guessing, reducing, paraphrasing, ordering, seeking, hypothesizing, wondering, deducing, inducing, constructing, deconstructing, reconstructing, reflecting, listening, viewing, representing, drawing (in, out, through), conjecturing, questioning, (day)dreaming, rehearsing, exploring, clarifying, revising, reviewing, drafting. The process is not linear, at least not for most writers; it is more like a spiral or a maze. The path is not always predictable.

I begin most of my poems and stories with a remembered image or word, which in turn generates a free-writing exercise. I like to get a block of words on the white page. I then have something concrete to react to, to question, to expand and compress, to revise and revisit. After free writing and composing a block of words, I suggest that writers next attend to sculpting. I invite them to linger with their words to highlight any thoughts or memories or stories that they would now like to focus on. This sculpting stage often involves chipping and chopping away at the block of words to reveal the poem or story or essay that is calling out for attention. I don't want writers to think that they are entirely in control of the process. I want them to be open to surprise. I want them to engage with their words full of possibility. My main goal is to promote child-like wonder in the midst of adult-like wisdom.

As prompts for free writing, I often invite students to write about their names, or about experiences with bread, or about memories of cars or shoes, or about childhood stories of backyards. I want students to realize how many stories they have already lived and are living. I suggest that we are awash in stories, the stories of memories, present moments, dreams, and hopes. I make the simple point that many of us don't recognize the power of our stories and how we live storied lives. When I speak about story, I also speak about discourse. While story is "what happened," discourse is "how we tell the story." I emphasize discourse because many of us don't know how to write our stories, how to compose our stories creatively. Stories can be composed in countless ways, including photography, art, music, fiction, dance, and movement. We need to attend to the possibilities of discourse.

The Elements of Narrative

As we focus on writing stories, I invite students to brainstorm all the elements of narrative. I recommend using the heuristic of an abecedarian to name at least one element for each letter of the alphabet. Some of the elements of narrative writing include action, allusions, antagonist, anticlimax, atmosphere, biography, change, character, cliffhangers, climax, closure, communication, conciseness, conflict, constraint, continuity, denouement, details, dialogue, drama, emotion, ending, events, exposition, falling action, flashbacks, flow, foreshadowing, generation, history, imagery, intrigue, irony, jouissance, knowledge, laughter, life writing, metaphor, mood, motif, narrator, opening, pace, parody, plot, point of view, precision, problem, protagonist, question, resolution, rhythm, rising action, satire, secrets, selection, setting, silence, structure, style, suspense, symbols, tension, theme, transitions, utterance, voice, X-rated, yarn, and zoom.

I especially focus on the element of voice. I encourage students to know their voices in their writing. So much of school experience is focused on homogenizing voices. Everybody is expected to learn to write a kind of school writing that avoids the passive voice, the pronoun *I*, as well as emotions, and opinions. I invite students to revel in the multiplicity of voices, to experiment playfully with voices, to explore the effects of different voices, and to write in voices filled with desire.

To explore some of these ideas, we then write about memories. I invite students to complete the sentence stem, "I remember . . ." with sensual memories of elementary school. I ask them to write at least five sentences for each of the memories of sight, hearing, touch, taste, and smell. Then, in small groups of four or five students, we braid our memories together and consider how to perform the group *métissage*. I encourage students to consider how they will use their voices, how they will position themselves in the space of the classroom, and how they will collaborate to evoke the complex experience of elementary school.

The Poem

We then move on to poetry as another kind of discourse. I often cite Jane Hirshfield (1997), who claims that the "central energies through which poetry moves forward into the world it creates" are "the concentrations of music, rhetoric, image, emotion, story, and voice" (p. 7). Hirshfield reminds us that poetry is made (from the Greek *poiein*, to make). While I enthusiastically open complex possibilities for imagining poetry, I also explain that a poem can be understood with two simple and playful terms. Borrowing from Northrop Frye, I claim that a poem is babble and doodle (Leggo, 1997). I have been making this claim for a long time, and I continue to be intrigued by how poetry is both comprehensively complex and remarkably simple. Everything in a poem that appeals to the ears, the sense of hearing, is babble, including rhythm, rhyme, alliteration, consonance, and onomatopoeia. Everything in a poem that appeals to the eyes, the sense of seeing, is doodle, including figurative language, imagery, similes, metaphors, layout on the page, shape, and stanzaic structure. I invite students to attend to a poem as a construction of elements or signifiers that appeal to the ears and eyes.

I invite students to ask again and again "What is a poem?" Then, we often consider four kinds of poems that expand our understanding of poetic possibilities. As we attend to the capaciousness of poetry, we consider found or erasure poetry. I bring in newspapers and magazines and invite students to find poems by taking away many, even most, of the words in articles or editorials. By erasing words, students create poems that represent their responsive engagement with the original texts. I suggest to students that poems are everywhere, just waiting to be found. As we continue to ask "What is a poem?" we also consider the *visualizt*, or concrete, poem, where the shape or design of the poem on the page illustrates the subject of the poem. A concrete or *visualizt* poem emphasizes the doodle of poetry and often militates against an oral reading. Next, we explore sound poems, which emphasize the babble of poetry and invite oral performances. I love playing with the sounds of words. Finally, I am especially fond of the prose poem. We often recognize a poem by its visual representation on the page. A poem often looks like a poem, especially because of the line breaks. Unlike prose, a poetic line doesn't usually extend from left margin to right margin. The prose poem shakes up even this basic understanding of what a poem typically looks like.

A Journey That Doesn't End

We continue in these ways to investigate the possibilities of descriptive writing and expository writing, including argumentation and persuasion. In all the activities and dynamics of the writing course, the focus is always on creativity and imaginative thinking. We focus on creative ways of re-imagining possibilities for using language to understand our living experiences and communicate our understanding to ourselves and others. In the course, we write and we share our writing. We spend time together in the joy of lingering with words and living creatively. The following poem of mine represents the journey of the course as a journey that doesn't end.

ALPHABET
the alphabet we learned
to write in school was spartan
pressed between parallel lines
eschewing swirls curls whirls
but we need to ask always, all
ways, with tireless wonder
what lies beyond the alphabet?
for the alphabet, the creation
in letters, is a letter
inviting the imagination
beyond the alphabet in lines
that do not begin, do not end

REFERENCES
Hirshfield, J. (1997). *Nine gates: Entering the mind of poetry.* New York: Harper Perennial.
Leggo, C. (1997). *Teaching to wonder: Responding to poetry in the secondary classroom.* Vancouver: Pacific Educational Press.

Creative Development in Mathematics Education

A CONVERSATION WITH CONRAD WOLFRAM, EDITED BY ROBERT KELLY

Conrad Wolfram, CEO and cofounder of Wolfram Research Europe in the United Kingdom, has been a prominent proponent of Computer-Based Math—a reform of mathematics education to make greater use of information technology. He is the founder of www.computerbasedmath.org, which is designed to align global mathematics education with its real-world application.

A lot of what we really do in life is to try to define and answer problems in ways that make sense. That requires creativity; just defining problems requires creativity because there are so many routes and tools to know, visualize, and figure out what to abstract to, to get the kind of answers we want. Traditionally, the required real-world tools that actually did require extensive machinery and physical spaces were not available in typical educational settings. That's not true any more. The required tools are actually for the first time largely available in schools. There is little excuse for not having the real context for problem creation and problem solving in contemporary mathematics education. The fundamental problem with today's education is that the outside real-world subject has just fundamentally been turned on its head by mechanization in the last fifty years without a corresponding shift in education. An analogy often used with reference to current educational practice perceives a do-it-yourself kit where you're not allowed to use a tool until you've learned how to make it. You can't use a hammer until you have learned how to make a hammer. You can't use a screwdriver until you've learned how to make a screwdriver, etcetera. The result is that learners don't have a very large tool set. Then the problem becomes that they cannot do anything very creative with the tool set because there is not a lot they can do with just a hammer. What we are saying is give people the whole tool set right at the beginning.

Starting with the Problem

Current mathematics education follows a specific process: educators start lessons with the abstract and teach learners to use the abstraction to do the calculation, and then they go through all that process in great detail, and if they are very, very lucky, learners are able to practically apply the abstraction to solve a problem they might care about. What we should do is exactly the opposite. The role of abstraction in math is that it is a fantastic tool for solving problems. The reason we abstract in math or code is so that we can put many apparently disparate situations into a similar situation for which we know how to calculate a solution. Today, coding is central to practical abstraction. The point is that when you abstract, you have to abstract to a set of tools, language, and notation to be able to work out the calculations. In the modern world, we should teach students to abstract to code, rather than traditional mathematical notation, for two key reasons:

- Computers ultimately do the calculating.
- Traditional mathematical notation lacks many constructs for describing algorithms.

Traditional mathematical notation is a sort of narrow coding language that does not allow the use of many of the algorithm tools you can use in a modern coding language. This is a crucial way to look at the importance of coding (which governments usually miss). Coding is central to math education because, in a sense, it is a way to write mathematical abstraction.

However we write down the abstraction, it is critically misguided to start with it, yet that is what is happening in math education. We start with the abstraction, totally dissociated from everything else, and then we grind students through how to do all this procedural stuff by more-or-less rote learning instructions. Most learners do not care, nor do they learn to engage with math, with this approach. If learners are very lucky, they may learn to associate the abstraction with something that seems to be practical, though probably is not. In this common scenario, learners are only allowed hand techniques, but the real practical things need mechanized calculating for the math to work in practice. Word problems are a great example of this failed contextualization of math education. These problems are supposed to put math in context but are actually impractical and not something where math seems to be much help. This backward use of abstraction is essentially killing math education and is totally killing any potential creativity. We should be starting with the problem, taking the problem and learning how to abstract the problem, including much harder problems than we do right now. We explain this in a four-stage problem-solving sequence: define, translate, compute, and interpret (computerbasedmath.org, 2016).

1. Define Questions
   Think through the scope and details of the problem; define manageable questions to tackle.

2. Translate to Math
   Prepare the questions as math models ready for computing the answer. Select from standard techniques or formulate algorithms.

3. Compute Answers
   Transform the math models into math answers with the power of computers or by hand calculating. Identify and resolve operational issues during the computation.

4. Interpret
   Did the math answers solve the original problem? Fix mistakes or refine by taking another turn around the Solution Helix.

There are several benefits to thinking this way. First, it is what happens in real life. That's what we're educationally preparing people for. Second, learners who find it hardest to see abstraction in its own right, often at the outset, get switched off immediately if you start with abstraction. By contrast, if we follow this four-stage sequence, we can pick problems a given learner might find interesting, and then that learner can see how abstraction really benefits solving the problem. Most real-life problems are a lot messier than you can do by hand calculation. So then you get into this loop where learners are not dealing with real problems, so then they don't understand why they are using math when they don't see the context. This results in dissociation where students become disconnected from what they are learning. Without the computer, you lose the context. Basically, very little math can be done without a computer and the real stuff in the real world, and so people just disconnect unless they happen to be from the beginning very interested in the abstraction. Abstraction is a useful tool for solving problems, not a mechanism of putting students off trying.

A Wider Toolset for Problem Seeking, Problem Setting, and Problem Solving

One issue we have confronted is that in building Computer-Based Math education, we could not find an effective list of outcomes to reflect mainstream math education, so we built a model comprised of ten dimensions. We call it a ten-dimensional outcomes tree. We are using this to answer the question "If it is a given that most learners are engaged in mathematics education for at least ten years of their life, what is it that you're hoping the outcomes are going to be from that education?" Aspirations of critical thinking, or really detailed content (e.g., students must be able to place ticks on bar charts accurately) does not seem likely to advance math education. To get math to where we want it to go, we (Computer-Based-Math.org, 2016) created this draft of our ten-dimensional outcomes tree:

1. **CT** Confidence to Tackle New Problems

   CTA Applying existing tools in new contexts

   CTK Knowing how to teach yourself new tools

   - Reading documentation
   - Self-testing understanding
   - Critiquing attempted use

   CTI Interpreting others' work

   - Working out what a formula means or what a program does

2. **AM** Abstracting to Mathematics Concepts

   AM1 Filtering the relevant information from available information

   AM2 Identifying missing information to be found or calculated

   AM3 Identifying relevant mathematical concepts

   AM4 Using diagrams to structure knowledge

   AM5 Identifying applicable tools of math

   AM6 Composing input for the chosen tool from the information

3. **PM** Planning and Managing Computations

   PMB Breaking a large problem into steps

   PM4 Learning how to manage the application of the four-step Computer-Based Math process

   PMP Programming

   PMR Identifying and resolving operational problems (e.g., will take computer too long to calculate, answer is wrong, etc.)

4. **IN** Interpreting

   IN1 Reading common representations (e.g., visualizations, notations, values)

   IN2 Relating values to the original problem

   IN3 Relating features (e.g., max, min, slope, etc.) in output to real-world meaning

   IN4 Relating questions about the original problem to features to seek in the result

   IN5 Identifying interesting features in a result

   IN6 Inferring about a wider level

5. **CV** Critiquing and Verifying

   CV1 Understanding assumptions

   CV2 Understanding limits of tools and concepts

   CV3 Listing possible sources of error from computation failures or limitations

   CV4 Listing possible sources of error from concepts' limitations

   CV5 Testing whether errors are present

   CV6 Quantifying reliability or scale of errors

6. **GM** Generalizing a Model/Theory/Approach

   GM1 Using a concept or tool in a new context (e.g., use significance in both a scientific experiment and in fraud detection)

   GM2 Being able to explore the effects of assumptions on a concept (e.g., adding drag to a projectile motion problem)

   GM3 Being able to draw wider conclusions about the behaviours of a type of problem (e.g., confidence intervals usually contract as more data are used)

   GM4 Making associations between different concepts

   GM5 Implementing a generalized model as a robust program

7. **CC** Communicating and Collaborating

   CCV Distilling ideas through visualization

   CCD Distilling ideas through description

   CCP Verbally presenting ideas

   CCR Making a detailed complete report

   CCG Working in a group

   CCA Making a case (debating)

   CCQ Questioning/interrogation

8. **CM** Conceptual Understanding for Each Mathematical Concept

   CM1 Being able to describe the concept

   CM2 Recognizing whether the concept applies

   CM3 Knowing which tools are relevant to this concept

   CM4 Interpreting the measures and computational results (of tools) in terms of the concept ("Step 4")

   CM5 Understanding the relative merits of different tools for use in the concept (intuition about the tools)

9. **TM** Tools of Math for Each Mathematical Tool

TM1 Being able to interpret documentation for a tool

TM2 Being aware of the existence and relevance of related tools

TM3 Having experience interpreting the tool's output

TM4 Having intuition about its behaviour (strengths, weaknesses, competitive advantage)

TM5 Having experience in application of the tool

10. **IF** Instinctive Feel for Math

IFE Having the ability to estimate

IFP Assessing the plausibility of a mathematical approach's being useful

IFF Identifying fallacies and misuse of mathematical concepts

Implicit in the ten-dimensional outcomes tree is equipping learners at a much earlier age with a wider toolkit. This involves the intelligent application of calculator and computer use. I think that actually in the modern world, the intellectual powerhouse in math is how we apply the calculator and computer in a way in which that process is really useful. The sort of creativity, the edginess, is in figuring out how to apply our tool set, this much larger tool set than most people are taught at school. The tool set should be the total tool set we can apply with what we know, with competence, including the entire computer tool set. How can we take that creatively and use what we know to solve problems that we have? What is interesting about the creative process is the fuzzier the problems get, the more creativity we often need to figure out what we do with the math to get an answer from it.

In terms of moving toward more complex problem setting by learners, where they are asked what can be done with a given situation, students need as wide a toolset as possible. If they do not know the breadth of the tool set, they are going to struggle with trying to figure out what tool to use for the job because they will not know what the tools are. The moment the problem gets more sophisticated, learners will have lost the strategy for doing it because the strategy that they developed for the simpler problem is not applicable to the harder problem. If we give a harder problem to start, along with some basic assistance, students are enabled to understand how to build the strategy to allow them to do the hard problem and then the stuff becomes less scary. They develop mathematical confidence and ultimately creative confidence. We are stripping that confidence out because what we are giving learners is the equivalent of toy stuff, and then suddenly they get into the real world and it isn't a toy any more. The problem is that if we give learners too narrow a range of tools, then they're completely at sea because it is increasingly more difficult for them to visualize problem solving and problem setting as it is perceived as very difficult, if not possible.

We should be getting students used to the fact that real-world problems are a lot messier, being more diverse and complicated. After a time of getting it and applying wider and more sophisticated tool sets, strategies for walking through this messiness emerge, leading to increased creative confidence. What we really want to do is to have a tool set including these processes that allows us to express our creativity. Consider this example: in the real world of business and website data, a common question is "How can we make this website better?" In a sense, that is a problem and it is quite open. Where do we start and what do we do to address this problem? One of the applicable tools that we could apply in this context is to consider the top five or ten questions we could ask about the situation. These types of strategies for a toolkit should be implicitly derived as we go through education. We could be much more explicit about these kinds of questions that could help to scaffold learners through varying contexts of problems to things they can do themselves.

When you start solving problems you've set, you can start to surface those five or ten techniques. This enables engagement in more sophisticated problems and learner-originated problems that exemplify creative practice, ultimately leading to creative development.

REFERENCES
computerbasedmath.org. *Computer-Based-Math.org*. In Lets Get On with Fixing Math Together. Retrieved January 11, 2016, from computerbasedmath.org.

5

Assessment as Creative Development

ROBERT KELLY

Foundations for Assessment as Creative Development

Appropriate application of assessment strategies is essential for enabling creative development and the design of educational environments conducive to creative development as learners grow toward an intrinsically motivated disposition of innovation and invention. As creative development is highly idiosyncratic, any assessment regimen designed for creative development must inherently accommodate diverse individual growth and creative development trajectories of learners.

Assessment of learners is often the most likely point of communication interface between teachers and parents and educators and learners, as well as educators and administrators. It is also most likely how many parents and students measure academic success. Ultimately, assessment of learners can also be a large contributing factor in the development of learners' self-perception of their social and cultural valuation. With these deep-rooted implications, it is no wonder that assessment in education can be a hot-button topic. Assessment and creative development must be carefully considered in learning environment design to be implicitly developmental in nature while avoiding counter-developmental skew effects. To achieve this, assessment should be part of a larger educational ecology that focuses on creative development.

Assessing anything in the field of creativity in education requires a clear foundational definition of the term *creativity*, as this concept is subject to so many variations in definition and interpretation (Starko, 2010; Treffinger, Young, Selby & Shepardson, 2002). A clear foundational definition will inform the nature of the assessment strategies that make the most sense for the definitional context. These definitional contexts were discussed in detail in chapter 1 (Understanding Creativity, Creative Capacity, and Creative Development). For the concept of creativity in this volume, Lubart's (2000) definition is used to understand creativity as "a sequence of thoughts and actions that leads to novel, adaptive production" (p. 295). This is linked to the term *creative capacity*, which is defined as the level of complexity at which one can engage in creative practice. Creative capacity is informed by the level of demonstrated sophistication in the engagement of creative design practice applied through the eight interrelated creative development strands. Creative capacity refers to a point in developmental time. Creative development has been defined as the growth in creative capacity over time by an individual or group.

The concept of creative development is also informed by demonstrated growth in sophistication through the eight interrelated creative development strands. Creative development refers to creative growth over time. It is very important at this juncture to stress that the concept of creative development in an educational context is viewed through the lens of a learner's individual creative development relative to that learner's previous creative production and practice (Starko, 2010; Sawyer, 2012).

The Creative Development Assessment Design Challenge

The central assessment design challenge is to create comprehensive, appropriate tactics and strategies for creative development assessment that nurture individual and collaborative creative development and avoid instruments, tactics, and strategies that may be developmentally counterintuitive (e.g., the factors limiting creative development discussed in chapter 1). This is the pre-inventive structure for this design challenge.

Keep in mind that creative development assessment is not necessarily intended to be a supplemental approach to traditional education, as the creative development construct is designed around an interrelated ecology of eight developmental strands culturally very different from traditional educational practices. This design challenge is intended for an educator as designer, facilitator, collaborator, and mentor and a developing learner who is an explorer, inquirer, experimenter, innovator, and inventor. This speaks to a primary design consideration of dispositional development that is continual (Costa & Kallick, 2014). This design challenge considers that the learner is developing into an intrinsically motivated primary owner of creative practice through the development of original research, production, and action. Inherent in this process is the development of learner metacognition, where the learner has knowledge and control over their cognitive processes (Armbruster, 1989). Creative development assessment design must enable and maximize growing creative development. This is the central design challenge.

Discovery and interpretation through investigation

As we have discussed in chapter 3 (Engaging in Creative Practice), a great place to start a design challenge is by investigating the field to discover information that is potentially useful for this design task. Once this information has been gathered, it is necessary for us to interpret it though discussion and analysis to better understand its usefulness in the context of the design challenge. In the field of educational assessment, this implies wading through a large number of assessment approaches, along with their corresponding vocabulary, and the infinite ways they could be combined. Summative, formative, and diagnostic assessment, along with assessment of learning, assessment for learning, and assessment as learning are some of the central terms that could inform creative development assessment design (Treffinger et al., 2002; Ontario, 2010; Ontario, 2013; Starko, 2010; Kaufman, Plucker & Baer, 2008; Earl, 2013; Soriano, Bruno-Faria & de Souza-Fleith, 2014; Beghetto, Kaufman & Baer, 2015).

Formative assessment monitors learner performance and progress during educational engagement and is typically ungraded. It is commonly used as a way for educators to see if students are making progress toward an end goal. Educators use formative assessment techniques to monitor learner progress to inform more effective educational strategies while providing feedback or help along the way through collaboration and mentoring. Summative assessments are designed to measure student achievement in a specific learning context at the end of an instruction sequence. These types of assessments evaluate student learning at the end of a project, unit, course, or school year. Summative assessment scores are typically recorded and factored into student academic records in the form of letter grades and scores. These quantifiable scores are often used for comparative analysis in a wide range of educational contexts. Diagnostic assessments assess strengths, weaknesses, and prior knowledge. This type of assessment is often used in the context of detecting basic skill deficits and learner strengths to inform remediation and differentiated instructional strategies.

Assessment of learning, assessment for learning, and assessment as learning are described by WNCP (2006) and later echoed by Ontario (2013) in the following way.

> *Assessment of learning is summative in nature and is used to confirm what students know and can do, to demonstrate whether they have achieved the curriculum outcomes, and, occasionally, to show how they are placed in relation to others. Teachers concentrate on ensuring that they have used assessment to provide accurate and sound statements of students' proficiency, so that the recipients of the information can use the information to make reasonable and defensible decisions.*

> *Assessment for learning is designed to give teachers information to modify and differentiate teaching and learning activities. It acknowledges that individual students learn in idiosyncratic ways, but it also recognizes that there are predictable patterns and pathways that many students follow. It requires careful design on the part of teachers so that they use the resulting information to determine not only what students know, but also to gain insights into how, when, and whether students apply what they know. Teachers can also use this information to streamline and target instruction and resources, and to provide feedback to students to help them advance their learning.*

> *Assessment as learning is a process of developing and supporting metacognition for students. Assessment as learning focuses on the role of the student as the critical connector between assessment and learning. When students are active, engaged, and critical assessors, they make sense of information, relate it to prior knowledge, and use it for new learning. This is the regulatory process in metacognition. It occurs when students monitor their own learning and use the feedback from this monitoring to make adjustments, adaptations, and even major changes in what they understand. It requires that teachers help students develop, practice, and become comfortable with reflection, and with a critical analysis of their own learning. (pp. 13–14)*

Data collection and interpretation

Any assessment approach has to be based on some kind or data or evidence gathering and interpretation. Questions arise around how and what should be collected as evidence, in what contexts the evidence should be interpreted, who should interpret the evidence, and how the interpretation will be communicated. Treffinger et al. (2002) describe four possible routes for data collection: tests, rating scales, behaviour and performance data, and self-reported data.

The first category, tests, is described as a "person's responses to a structured set of tasks or questions, administered under controlled or standardized conditions, through which the person demonstrates his or her ability to think or respond creatively" (p. xii). Kaufman et al. (2008) comment on how the history of testing in the field of creativity assessment is focused on the testing of divergent thinking capacity. They remark that there is ironically little divergence in the history of testing in the field of creativity. Starko (2010) describes several standardized creativity tests based on the processes of divergent thinking. These encompass the Torrance Tests of Creative Thinking (TTCT), Guilford's Structure of Intellect assessments, and the Wallach and Kogan tests, to name a few. The best-known of these psychometric tests are the Torrance Tests of Creative Thinking (TTCT). This family of psychometric tests has grown through several iterations and related manifestations over time. Starko (2010) describes the TTCT as appearing in both figural and visual versions where the test taker is asked to complete a series of open-ended questions. "For example, the verbal test asks . . . to list all questions he or she can think to ask about a certain picture. Other test items require . . . to list possible uses for a product and unusual uses for a common object" (p. 289).

Fundamental assessment questions

A question arises: "Is this kind of testing, a form of summative assessment, necessary in the context of assessing creative development?" To reflect on this, consider my recent experience at an elementary school where the staff was working on a three-year professional development project to grow creative practice among learners while growing the creative capacity of both educators and learners. They proposed using the TTCT at the end of each year of the project as the primary assessment tool to indicate whether progress was being made or not. I recommended against this assessment measure because this particular instrument is not an indicator of comprehensive creative development. Runco (1993) describes the TTCT focus on divergent thinking as "a predictor of original thought, not a criterion for creative ability" (p. 16). One has to consider all eight developmental strands to develop an accurate assessment picture for creative development. Taking any one of Guilford's (1967) characteristics of creativity out of context and testing for each of them is counterintuitive to the concept of creative development. These kinds of assessments and their results can be easily misused as proxy assessments for overall creative capacity and creative development when a much more holistic, comprehensive approach is required. They can also influence and skew educational and assessment design for teaching solely to the characteristics of creativity, such as flexibility, elaboration, fluency, originality, divergent thinking, and convergent thinking. This can be misinterpreted as teaching creativity when the educational focus should be on longitudinal creative development.

Another fundamental question arises: "Is it necessary to test individuals to assess whether they are creative or whether they exhibit the traits of creative people?" A dangerous skew effect that influences responses to this question is a belief by many that if an assessment instrument doesn't result in a quantitative numerical value for comparative analysis, then its validity is questionable. We do not require assessment instruments that provide quantitative numerical values for comparative analysis to conduct valid assessment that supports creative development. To apply summative assessment strategies to discern whether someone is creative or not is educationally irrelevant as the creative potential of both learners and educators is assumed in the context of creative development. To apply summative assessment strategies to test for traits of creative people is limited in scope and lacks the embedded context of a learner engaged at some stage in innovative or inventive practice. This approach also contributes to factors limiting creative development through external application and vertical comparisons when exactly the opposite is required to nurture creative development. The development of learner metacognition is central to growth toward intrinsically motivated invention. These considerations move creative development assessment design away from assessment of learning through summative assessment toward variations of formative assessment through assessment for learning to assessment as learning.

Assessment as Learning and Metacognition

Earl (2013) describes assessment as learning in the following way: "Assessment as learning is a subset of assessment for learning that emphasizes using assessment as a process of developing and supporting metacognition for students" (p. 28). She goes on to add that "Assessment as learning focuses on the role of the student as the critical connector between assessment and their learning. Students, acting as critical thinkers, make sense of information, relate it to prior knowledge, and use it to construct new learning" (p. 28). Costa and Kallick (2014) reflect on the type of assessment strategy needed for dispositional growth and development as requiring "different forms of assessment both from the design of the assessment as well as from the expectations of how the assessment data will inform curriculum, instruction and most important our student's capacity to become more self-evaluative" (p. 99). They add further that it is important to want students to be spectators of their own growth.

It is essential for learners to take ownership of their own growth and development, and thus assessment approaches that enable this to happen and sustain itself in the context of assessment as learning are required. This points to two principal areas of formative assessment—self-formative assessment supported by co-formative assessment. These assessment approaches are characterized by high degrees of student ownership and intense student reflection and documentation within a highly collaborative, dialogic environment in which the emphasis is on learner development not learner measurement. These are cast through the collective lenses of the eight creative development strands.

A framework for assessment as creative development

To establish a framework for assessment as creative development we can establish an assessment prototype by combining Costa and Kallick's (2014) recursive self-assessment feedback spiral and Goldman et al.'s (2012) concept of design practice mindshifts through the eight interrelated creative development strands. This prototype is meant to be a pre-inventive structure from which educators can design and build assessment plans that embrace creative development for their specific educational contexts.

FEEDBACK SPIRAL.

We can begin by adapting Costa and Kallick's (2014) feedback spiral structure specifically to engagement in creative practice. Through this creative practice feedback spiral, learners are continually "self-learning, self-renewing, and self-modifying" (p. 102). The feedback spiral is characterized by seven elements that continuously repeat as the spiral progresses through the stages of the learning experience design for creative development (Stage 1—Explore; Stage 2—Inquire and Experiment; Stage 3—Innovate and Invent). Costa and Kallick's spiral elements play out as follows (pp. 102–103):

Clarify goals and purposes. What is the underlying purpose of what you are doing? What questions need to be explored? What outcomes are expected?

Plan. What actions will be taken to achieve desired outcomes in response to essential questions? How can you move into early prototyping to test ideas? What evidence would you collect to inform prototype development? How will you leave the door open for other unexpected discoveries and possibilities? What process will you put in place that will help you describe what actually happened?

Take action/prototype. Develop ideas into preliminary prototype(s) to test effectiveness of ideas.

Assess prototype. Gather evidence. Analyze prototype effectiveness for refinement or development of new prototypes.

Study, reflect, evaluate. How did the initial prototyping results align with your goals? Who might serve as an expert or supportive resource to coach further prototype development?

Modify actions based on new knowledge. What will be done differently as a result of reflection and integration of new knowledge? How will prototyping development proceed through the stages of refinement?

Revisit goals and purposes through each iteration. Repeat this entire process through each cycle.

This feedback spiral represents the structural assessment spine for creative development where there is continual opportunity for formative co- and self-assessment through learner reflection, documentation, and developmental dialogue within a supportive collaborative environment.

MINDSHIFTS.

Goldman et al. (2012) use the term *mindshifts* to describe potential active shifts that learners make within this feedback spiral. They describe "the learning of design thinking dispositions as an emergent journey—with various levels of sophistication, transformation, application, and integration" (p. 15). They go on to describe four foundational mindshift premises that encompass the eight creative development strands. These include human-centred, collaborative, experimentational, and metacognitive mindshifts.

Empathy is at the core of human centredness where learners transition from an egocentric disposition to one that is sensitive to real-world problems for real-world audiences beyond their personal needs and desires. Learners seek solutions to meet the needs of others. This mindshift to human centredness encompasses collaborative development, self-instigative development, research-investigative development, and generative development. The collaborative mindshift recognizes that collaboration through continual collaborative development is a true enabler of creative practice. It also recognizes the potential design strength of diverse collaborative groups. The experimentational mindshift recognizes that "everything may be considered a prototype. Having an experimental stance changes one's approach to problem solving by allowing one to do, make, and visualize as integral parts of thinking and of the evolving ideas (p. 17). This embraces generative development and experimentational development. The metacognitive mindshift is centred on the development of learners' self-awareness of where they are in the design process and within each of the eight developmental strands relative to the creative challenge at hand. The growth in metacognition is commensurate with development toward intrinsically motivated, self-instigated innovation and invention where the complete ownership of the creative dynamic and its corresponding metacognitive assessment are taken over by the learner.

Metacognitive Approaches to Assessment as Creative Development

There are many strategies and tactics that can be deployed by both the learner and educator to engage the use of the feedback spiral structure as a central framework for the assessment of creative development. With the array of digital tools available to most educators in interconnected environments, the potential exists to create portfolios and rubrics that demonstrate learners' process engagement and development in real time.

The living process portfolio

A foundational assessment component that is perhaps the most effective, efficient, multi-dimensional co-assessment and self-assessment tool is the living process portfolio. The living process portfolio is an electronic-based platform for learner documentation of, and reflection on, the recursive journey through the feedback spiral that includes a capacity for dialogic interaction with experts and peer plussing. It is a virtual inventor's notebook. Inventors traditionally used these notebooks to record ideas, invention processes, experimental tests and results, and observations for documentation purposes, sometimes necessary for getting a patent. In this tradition, the living process portfolio is an organic, perpetually evolving portfolio that can be accessed at any moment for a real-time view of learners' developmental journeys and their developmental interactivity.

The living process portfolio goes far beyond a product-focused, passive collection of longitudinal data. It is a platform where learners record reflections and documentation of engagement through the seven feedback spiral stages. It is ideally interconnected with the process portfolios of peers to create an organic interrelated space connected to educators and expert resources for ongoing plussing, feedback, and feed forward. This gives the process portfolio a very different character, as it becomes a living water sample of engagement and growth in process while bearing witness to real-time dialogic interactivity with resources in the broader resource environment. Educators or outside experts participate in the living process portfolio as collaborators and mentors to fuel process development as opposed to measuring process development. The integration of educators as collaborators or mentors in the student-owned living process portfolios offers an insightful and useful perspective of learners' creative growth and development that one could have regarding an authentic, informed assessment.

The metacognitive rubric

The metacognitive rubric is another foundational formative self-assessment platform that enables metacognitive growth specific to creative development. Constant process, situational awareness is essential to maximize creative potentials. In general, rubrics offer learners a coherent set of criteria for their creative practice. As such, rubrics are descriptive, not evaluative: they describe the levels of sophistication of actions and production learners may reach throughout their engagement in various aspects of the design process (Brookhart, 2013). The metacognitive rubric should be designed so it is learner-centric and not external to learners (as if someone else is observing them). Further to this idea, metacognitive rubrics can be constructed by learners as self-assessment tools for dispositional development. Costa and Kallick (2014) add that "through student's self-authoring of descriptions and indicators of what they will be doing and saying . . . rubrics promote self-managing, self-monitoring, and self-evaluating" (p. 115). The metacognitive rubric is equally valuable as conversational gateways between learners and educators as collaborators and mentors. Co-constructed rubrics may be necessary to help scaffold learners through the stages of learning experience progression (Stage 1—Explore; Stage 2—Inquire and Experiment; Stage 3—Innovate and Invent).

The following tables (Tables 5.1–5.5) provide examples of rubric designs adapted from the d.school (2016) Design Thinking Rubric and from Costa and Kallick (2014). These are basic samples designed to inform learner/mentor conversations and the design of metacognitive rubrics specific to learner contexts. The design challenge is to fashion metacognitive rubrics that are tailored to specific learner contexts that will vary considerably with age/grade level and the creative capacity of the learner.

TABLE 5.1 COLLABORATIVE DEVELOPMENT (EMPATHY) RUBRIC

1.	I am not comfortable getting information from others.
2.	I am starting to get comfortable getting information from a variety of sources, including some that I am not familiar with.
3.	I am beginning to understand the ideas and experiences of others.
4.	I understand others and how they think and work. I am developing the ability to think like others.

TABLE 5.2 RESEARCH/INVESTIGATIVE DEVELOPMENT (RESEARCHING TO DEFINE A PROBLEM) RUBRIC

1.	I can pick out one promising idea or problem after I have explored. I can only do this with guidance.
2.	I can explore several ideas and needs and make them into one design question with some guidance.
3.	I can gather research ideas and information from inside my school and from resources outside my school. I can make them into a design question with little guidance.
4.	I can get feedback from others to develop my design question further without any guidance.

TABLE 5.3 SELF-INSTIGATIVE DEVELOPMENT RUBRIC

1.	Ideas do not come easily to me. I need suggestions from others. I need lots of encouragement to start a project.
2.	I have some difficulty staying engaged in a long project without someone guiding me.
3.	I try to take responsibility for my own motivation but I sometimes need encouragement.
4.	I am motivated to work throughout my project. I do not need anybody to encourage me.

TABLE 5.4 IDEA GENERATION RUBRIC

1.	I can generate and record ideas with others.
2.	I can build off the ideas of others and build some wild ideas.
3.	I can lead a group to explore and generate lots of ideas including simple ideas and wild ideas.
4.	I can use a variety of ways to generate a large number of ideas.

TABLE 5.5 EXPERIMENTATION (PROTOTYPING) RUBRIC

1.	I can make a physical or visual representation of my idea.
2.	I can make a physical or visual representation of my idea that can gather feedback and be improved.
3.	I can use feedback to develop new ideas for developing my prototype.
4.	I can develop my prototype into a more complicated prototype to solve the problem from a variety of approaches.

Strategies to Promote Dialogic Assessment Opportunities

Authentic dialogue among learners, learners and educators, and learners and their broader community is the lifeblood of assessment as learning. Personal contact, deep listening, and third-level listening (attending to all the senses and body language) are the key to authentic assessment. Such dialogue is also the key to collaboration and collaborative creativity. The following are examples of assessment strategies that promote dialogic opportunity.

Co-reflective assessment

This is a dialogic assessment strategy requiring substantial written reflection from learners as a means for insight and dialogue with peers and educators. Educators and learners collaborate to co-develop insight questions that reflect engagement experience in design practice. Learners write substantial reflections on their creative process experience, including their intentions, difficulties, and successes (Kelly, 2012). These written reflections form the basis for conversations to advance creative practice.

Assessment by metaphor

This is a fun strategy to get learners talking about the subtleties and nuances of their creative practice (Kelly, 2012). It is a great strategy to get learners to move from their preoccupation with marks and grades to an interest in talking about their work and all of its complexities. To conduct this assessment, learners present their design work in an interactive forum. The educator and/or fellow students choose metaphors that best approximate their understanding of the intent and underlying meanings and implications of the presented student work. I have used ice cream flavours, pasta shapes, or any number of other things as metaphors of student work. Once familiar with this approach, students have made up their own metaphorical themes to engage in this type of dialogic assessment. These metaphors usually evoke a dialogic response, as learners will discuss the fine nuances of chosen metaphors and whether they are appropriate (e.g., Is cherry pomegranate a reasonable metaphor for someone's work?). Deep discussions about appropriate metaphors can offer educators and learners an opportunity to gain deeper insight into learners' understanding of processes, concepts, and ultimately metacognition.

Other Assessment Strategies and a Caution

As we move forward in designing assessment regimens for creative development, we cannot lose sight of the focus on assessment as learning when counterproductive skew effects creep into the assessment environment. Educators have an array of instruments that can be used in the assessment as learning spirit, but these can quickly change to become counterintuitive summative assessment instruments. The use of checklists, interviews, open-ended questionnaires, performance observations, co-reflective conversations, and any of a myriad of formative assessment instruments should all be designed in the spirit of educators working as developmental facilitators, collaborators, and mentors alongside learners to enable creative development through innovation and invention. This enables the most authentic assessment possible and fuels the inventive momentum of the whole educational environment.

Assessing Educational Environments for Sustained Creative Practice Potential

Assessing educational environments for their potential to enable sustained creative practice gains considerable importance when these environments are in transformative phases, moving from traditional practices to a broader focus on comprehensive creative development. It is importance to optimize comprehensive environmental attributes to maximize the inventive potentials of all participants. To assess educational environments and their potential, we must consider the following:

- The element of time spent engaging in practices specific to creative development
- The creative capacity of the educator(s) responsible for a specific educational environment
- The collective and individual creative capacities of the learners within a specific learning group
- The physical, organizational, and resource availability attributes of a specific educational environment

The following mathematical construct, adapted from Kelly (2012), can be used as a general analytical template to assess the potential of a specific educational setting to enable creative growth and development through sustained creative practice.

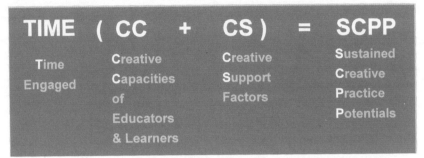

Figure 5.1: Assessing sustained creative practice potential in educational environments

This template can serve as a lens to assess needs and corresponding actions that may enhance the evolution of an educational setting to be more conducive to enabling sustained creative practice. The parts of the equation are explained below.

Time (T) represents the amount of time devoted to creative practice in an educational environment. Zero time spent engaging in creative practice implies a zero value for the whole equation. The greater the amount of time spent engaging in creative practice, the greater the creative practice potentials.

Creative capacity (CC) is an assessment of the level of complexity in which one can engage in creative practice. This includes the creative capacity of the educator and the general creative capacity and individual creative capacities of the learning group. It is important that the creative capacity of the educator be greater than the general creative capacity of the learning group to enable a learning culture conducive to creative development. Assessing creative capacities of educators and learners can sharply focus professional development needs and learning experience design considerations to optimize creative development growth toward Stage 3 (Innovate and Invent) activities.

Creative supports (CS) refers to the resources and environmental supports that are available in the educational environment. This would include administrative support, research resources, organizational structures, and the attributes of the immediate physical space. Creative supports can serve to amplify sustained creative practice, whereas a lack of creative supports can hinder any creative growth.

When all the template components are considered together, a picture emerges that frames the needs and assets of a specific educational environment and its potential to enable sustained creative practice (SCPP). This assessment of the educational environment and its potential can inform how the environment can be further improved to enhance creative practice and creative development.

Educator-Developed Metacognitive Assessment Tools for Creative Development

The following examples are educator-developed metacognitive assessment tools for creative development designed to heighten learner awareness of their developmental progress and to promote dialogue about creative development. These tools were developed by K to 12 educators largely from the Calgary Board of Education and the Calgary Catholic School District in the province of Alberta in western Canada. These educators have all engaged in graduate work in education and represent extensive and diverse professional experience in design thinking and creative practice.

Creative development assessment map

SHANNON CLARE, DANNY COOPER, RHONDA MCCARTHY, AND MYLES OLSEN

This is a flexible assessment tool that students and teachers can use to track their creative development over time. With the Creative Development Assessment Map, participants can plot their level of engagement in each creative development strand on the map. The farther out from centre a learner plots, the stronger their engagement in that strand. This

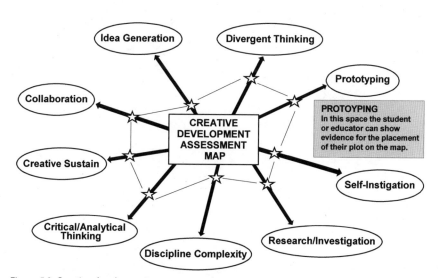

Figure 5.2: Creative development assessment map

can be done in the beginning, middle, or end of a learning task. For each plot on a strand, students or teachers would be asked to support their decision with evidence. The evidence can be anecdotally written on the map or reference can be made to evidence supplied in portfolios, videos, or blogs. This map is an opportunity for metacognitive discussions among learners, educators, and parents. The map can also be a self-assessment tool for individuals or groups of learners. Educators can use the map as a formative tool to see where learners are at and adjust their practice accordingly. The collection of and reflection on several maps over time is a powerful tool to assess longitudinal growth in creative development.

A metacognitive assessment conversation tool

ERIN QUINN

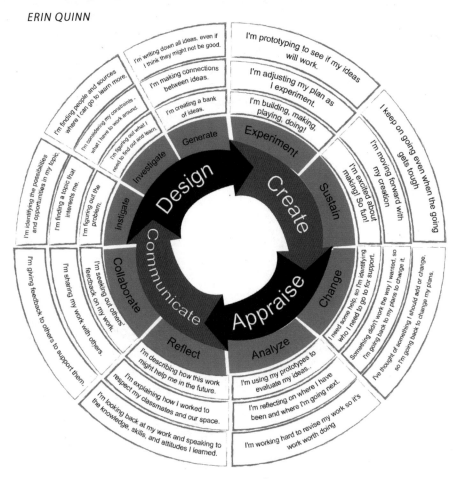

Figure 5.3: Metacognitive assessment conversation tool

THE ROBOTIC HAND.

Heads down, two thirteen-year-old boys crowd around pieces of drinking straws and string. One pulls a string, and the straw bends.

"So, if we attach these strings, what will happen?" Graeme asks.

"The straws should move," Josh answers.

"How do you know that?" I ask.

"Because when you pull one string, it tugs the straw closer. It would make sense if more strings made more straws move."

"Try it!" I say, as I move away. They lower their heads again to carefully tie more knots.

I make notes on the circular chart on my clipboard. Under the headings "I'm prototyping to see if my ideas work" and "I'm reflecting on where I have been and where I'm going next," I jot down the boys' names and some of their conversation about what they were testing through making.

DESIGNING THE EXERCISE AND THE ASSESSMENT.

This project began when three boys finished their Genius Hour project and needed to start a new one. They were sitting together, talking about what they might do next, when one boy happened to look at his hands. He noticed the tendons stretching and contracting as he moved his fingers. He asked an innocuous question that launched their next project: "Could we make a robotic hand?"

Genius Hour, also known as 20% time, allows students to self-identify something they are passionate about learning about and spend 20% of their week on that project. I added a twist to the activity by adding the caveat that students must create something as part of their inquiry. This kind of approach to learning could have ended up looking a bit like a free-for-all, but careful scaffolding of the design process allowed the students to identify something they really cared about learning and doing. An important piece of this open-ended task was the assessment strategy I designed, which was based almost solely on conversation.

I knew I had clear outcomes to assess because the Genius Hour exercise addressed clear curricular outcomes from Career and Technology Foundations (CTF), a program of studies that takes students through the design process in reference to one (or more) of twenty-eight possible occupational areas. I planned to assess these outcomes through their Genius Hour projects but, more importantly, I wanted to help my students become practiced and confident in speaking about their own creativity to further their own creative development. To do that, we needed to talk. So talk we did.

I knew I needed an assessment tool that would enable the students and I to engage in this conversation about assessment and focus their thinking and conversation. A rubric would not be sufficient for this purpose. To me, poorly designed rubrics would close the conversation rather than opening it. Drawing from my knowledge of the strands of creative development and the CTF program of studies, I created a circular assessment tool that focused the students on the four central processes of CTF, as well as some of the key creative skills they would be developing. I tested this prototype by trying it with the students.

DISCUSSING THE ROBOTIC HAND.

This brings us back to the students with their straw-and-string prototype of a robotic hand. As they tested their ideas to see if they would work, I sat alongside them and asked them to make their thinking visible. At one point, I left them to try out their next iteration, and when I came back to see how they were doing, we had a conversation.

"Did it work?" I ask.

"Yeah." Josh grins up and me, and tugs the central string to get all four "fingers" to clench into a fist. I hold my hand out, and the prototype hand gives me a high five.

"What's next?" I ask.

"Now we have to figure out the robotics."

"How will you do that?"

"We're going to go online and search robotics that make things move."

I show the boys the circular assessment wheel and ask them where they might position themselves within it. Graeme points to the yellow Design section, and the box that says, "I'm identifying possibilities and opportunities in my topic."

"Why that one?" I ask.

"Because we need to learn more before we can move forward. We have to figure out which robotics system will be the best one. And learn how to use it. Maybe we can ask Mr. Thompson," he replied, referring to another teacher who has expertise in robotics.

This conversation clearly demonstrates that the students know what they need to learn next to progress their design, and they know how to find it. I never would have known this had we not had this conversation.

Through this conversation, my students actually provided themselves with the feedback they needed to take their next steps. They understood what worked, what went wrong, and what they needed to find out next. They had taken steps toward developing their metacognition.

It took me nearly ten years of teaching to realize how powerful conversation is as an assessment strategy. I would argue it is more effective than rubrics, checklists, or "I CAN" statements. When you engage students in a conversation about their learning, you can understand more deeply what they know and are able to do than you ever could otherwise. Formative feedback is inherent in the conversational approach to assessment.

Extending and deepening play for assessment

STEPHANIE BARTLETT

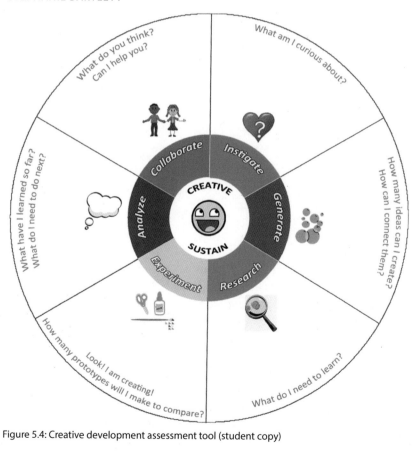

Figure 5.4: Creative development assessment tool (student copy)

At the age of five, George and Angus were engineers and designers. Wearing hard hats and tool belts, they stood talking in the corner of a noisy French Immersion kindergarten class in a public K to 12 school. On this particular day, they were building a tower in the block centre. I approached them and asked if they would like to draw the plans for their building on the whiteboards installed on the wall. Handing them each a marker was the equivalent of handing them a magic wand because that is what happened from an educator's point of view: magic. Their eyes lit up, they looked at each other excitedly, and they started to draw, talking all the while.

"I'll draw this rectangle over here."

"This is me. I'm working with my friends."

"I'll draw me over here. With the wires."

"This one is taller than yours."

"Let me draw another one over here."

With wide strokes and brightly coloured markers, the boys drew an elaborate electrical plant, complete with themselves and others included as workers. And then they shouted, "Let's build it!" as they hurried to gather blocks and build the structure. The boys glanced over from time to time at their drawing as they built and rebuilt their idea.

As an educator, this moment with George and Angus was rich with opportunity, and it became the right scenario to explain how I use the assessment tool for creative development that I designed. When I began to embed creativity in my teaching practice a few years ago, I realized that I needed a way to document and follow the creative development of each child. The assessment tool prototype that I designed helped me to stay focused while observing students during their activity time.

As the boys began to draw, I made notes on the students' individual creativity assessment wheel and also on my skills checklist, so that I could document creative development and their mathematical understandings at the same time. As I observed George and Angus, I noted what behaviours they were exhibiting. Not only was I able to keep track of the anecdotal comments and the date when the students worked in a certain phase of creative exploration, but I could also easily spot the strengths and the gaps of each particular student at a glance. My understanding of both children's creative development helped me to deepen their play through suggestions of materials, ideas, writing, research, and more.

This personalized approach models to all students that their opinions are valued and that the possibilities are as endless as their imaginations.

Now in my classroom, and consistently for the past three years, I am careful to showcase examples such as the work of these engineers so that the class can learn from each other. We model the different strands and use an enlarged copy of the assessment tool as a foundation for our conversations. This way, we deepen our understanding of the vocabulary of creative development. Assessing creativity becomes natural when students engage in original work. At first thought, this seems like an insurmountable step when teaching kindergarten. To the contrary, I have found that encouraging the mindset of creativity and design thinking by teaching the strands of creative development leads to an intensely personalized program that is engaging for both educator and learners.

Interactive creative development assessment tools

KEITH CHRISTENSEN

THE LEARNING EXPERIENCE OWNERSHIP FOR CREATIVE DEVELOPMENT SLIDER TOOL.

As a student moves from Stage 1 (Explore) through Stage 2 (Inquire and Experiment) and then into Stage 3 (Innovate and Invent), the degree of the learning experience ownership shifts completely to the student. The Learning Experience Ownership for Creative Development Slider Tool is a laser-cut and 3D-printed metacognitive assessment tool that can promote dialogue between the learner and educator regarding the degree of student ownership at a particular point in a learning experience. The top slider represents the maximum proportion of student autonomy in any specific learning experience design. This reflects the intent of the learning experience design from the educator's perspective in that some experiences are meant to be purely explorative or co-owned, while others may be intended for learners to assume complete ownership. The bottom slider represents the stage or degree of learning experience ownership reached by the student. The diagonal section running vertically through the stages shows the proportion of student ownership reflecting learner investment, autonomy, and creative sustain. The greater the learning experience design allows for more student ownership, the greater the potential for learners to reach the stage of complete ownership of innovation and invention. The sliders can be moved to the appropriate level for any given task or learning experience.

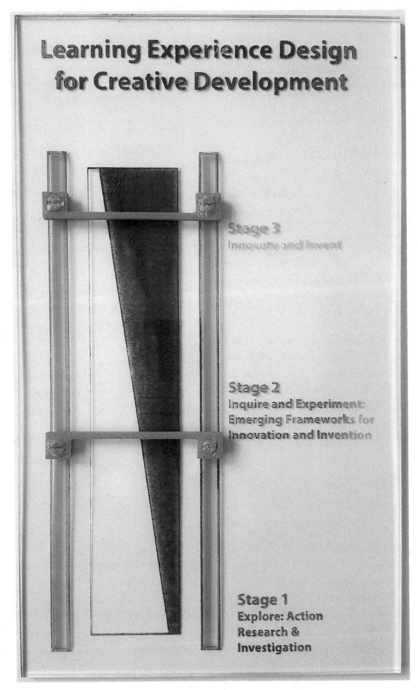

Figure 5.5: Learning experience ownership for creative development slider tool

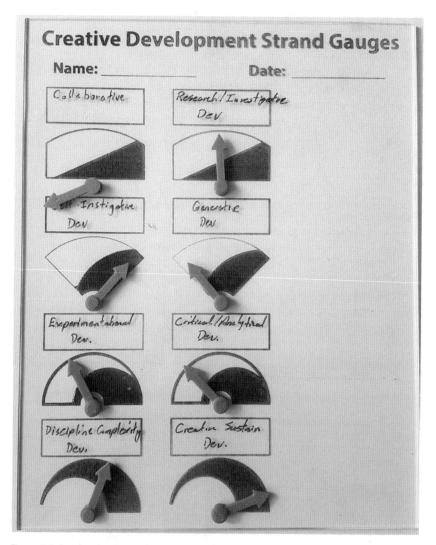

Figure 5.6: Creative development strand gauge tool

THE CREATIVE DEVELOPMENT STRAND GAUGE TOOL.

The Creative Development Strand Gauge Tool is a laser-cut and 3D-printed tool with adjustable needles. This tool is intended to be a conversation starter between students and teachers in regard to a student's current capacity in any one of the eight creative development strands. After gaining a solid understanding of the creative development strands and reflecting on recent work, a learner would adjust the gauges to reflect his/her understanding of his/her current level of capacity in that area. The learner would then discuss with the teacher each gauge setting. Both educator and learner are also able to write notes on the surface of this tool. Together the learners and teachers could adjust the gauges until a consensus is reached on the current level in each creative development strand. The physical adjustability of the tool and its lack of numbers are meant to be nonthreatening ways to engage in meaningful discussions in order to improve a metacognitive understanding of the learner's current creative development capacities as well as inform steps for further growth.

REFERENCES

Armbruster, B. M. (1989). Metacognition in creativity. In J. A. Glover, R. R. Ronning, & C. R. Reynolds (Eds.), *Handbook of creativity* (pp. 177–182). New York: Springer. http://dx.doi.org/10.1007/978-1-4757-5356-1_10

Brookhart, S. M. (2013). *How to create and use rubrics.* Alexandria: ASCD.

Beghetto, R. A., Kaufman, J. C., & Baer, J. (2015). *Teaching for creativity in the common core classroom.* New York: Teachers College Press.

Costa, A. L., & Kallick, B. (2014). *Dispositions: Reframing teaching and learning.* Thousand Oaks: Corwin Press.

d.school (2006). Design thinking rubric. Retrieved from BetterLesson.com.

Earl, L. M. (2013). *Assessment as learning.* Thousand Oaks: Corwin Press.

Goldman, S., & Carroll, M. P., Kabayadondo. Z., Cavagnaro, L. B., Royalty, A. W., Roth, B., Kwek, S. W., and Kim. J. (2012). Assessing d.learning: Capturing the journey of becoming a design thinker. In Plattner, H., Meinel, C. & Leifer, L. (Eds.). *Design thinking research: Measuring performance in context.* New York: Springer. http://dx.doi.org/10.1007/978-3-642-31991-4_2

Guilford, J. P. (1967). *The nature of human intelligence.* New York: McGraw-Hill.

Kaufman, J. C., Plucker, J. A., & Baer, J. (2008). *Essentials of creativity assessment.* Hoboken: John Wiley and Sons.

Kelly, R. (2012). *Educating for creativity: A global conversation.* Edmonton: Brush Education.

Lubart, T. L. (2000). Models of creative process: Past, present and future. *Creativity Research Journal,* 13(3–4), 295–308.

Ontario Ministry of Education. (2010). *Growing success: Assessment, evaluation and reporting in Ontario schools.* Toronto: Government of Ontario.

Ontario Ministry of Education. (2013). *Learning for all: A guide to effective assessment and instruction for all students.* Toronto: Government of Ontario.

Runco, M. A. (1993). Divergent thinking, creativity, and giftedness. *Creativity Research Journal,* 14, 427–438.

Starko, A. J. (2010). *Creativity in the classroom.* (4th Ed.) New York: Routledge. (original work published 1995).

Soriano, E. M. L. Bruno-Faria, M., & de Souza-Fleith, D. (2014). *Theory and practice of creativity measurement.* Waco: Prufrock Press.

Sawyer, R. K. (2012). *Explaining creativity: The science of human innovation.* New York: Oxford University Press.

Treffinger, Grover C. Young, Grover C., Selby, Edwin C., & Shepardson, C. (2002). *Assessing creativity: A guide for educators.* Storr: National Research Center on the Gifted and Talented.

WNCP (2006). Rethinking classroom assessment with purpose in mind. Western and Northern Canadian Protocol for Collaboration in Education. Retrieved from www.wncp.ca.

6

Creative Development in Teacher Education, in the Field, and Beyond

PART 1—CREATIVE DEVELOPMENT AND DESIGN THINKING IN TEACHER EDUCATION

ROBERT KELLY

Creative Development and Design Thinking in Teacher Education

Teacher education has to undergo fundamental changes to enable educational cultures of collaborative creativity. Many large-scale teacher education programs are thwarted in accomplishing this, as the skew effects of the machine organizational structure inevitably limit them despite their best transformational efforts. The surrounding social/economic culture and its ultra-connectivity are changing rapidly. At the same time, educator roles within a culture of collaborative creativity have become more diverse and complex. The repetitive model of training developing educators in dated field models is counterintuitive. Teacher education must move seamlessly through theoretical, applied, and action research to immerse educators in training that moves them from a consumption-intense perspective to a disposition of design. This goes beyond offering traditional courses, lectures, and workshops about creativity, design, and makerspaces in which participants are placed largely in the role of consumers of information; it moves into a space of first-hand longitudinal creative engagement as research.

These considerations have informed the design and development of the Creative Development in Educational Practice and the Design Thinking for Innovation graduate programs. These programs have been developed over the past fourteen years in faculties of education at four universities in western Canada, principally at the University of Calgary. The programs, despite being interrelated, are differentiated by each having a unique emphasis. The Creative Development program focuses on longitudinal engagement in creative practice and the increase of creative capacity of each participant through first-hand action and applied research, and engagement in and documentation of longitudinal, creative practice. The Design Thinking for Innovation program applies design thinking and design practice to specific creative problem-solving contexts of social innovation, the physical design of educational space, and educational design across the professional teaching spectrum relevant to each participant's educational practice. Program participants are supported in highly collaborative and interactive environments. A fundamental understanding here is that the creative capacity of the educator must be greater than the general creative capacity of learners in their trust.

Designing for Creative Development and Design Thinking in Teacher Education

There has to be an educational growth and development space where each educator can engage in longer-term creative practice and contextual creative problem solving around a personal passion area to experience recurrent rounds of collaborative idea generation and prototyping. This first-hand research is essential in providing an authentic research base to enable the creative development of learners. Despite being housed in traditional four-course structures over ten-month periods, these programs are treated as continuing programs in which all participants engage in longitudinal creative development throughout the program period. This is absolutely necessary to garner any kind of inventive momentum to provide an adequate research base. These programs are informed by the following rationale (Kelly, 2012):

1. Developing the creative capacity and design practice functionality of an educator is optimally accomplished through long-term engagement in creative production that is emotionally and intellectually relevant to the participant.

2. All educators and students at every level of education in every discipline should be creating original work. Original work in this context is described as new or novel adaptive production relevant to the previous personal production of each educator and learner (Starko, 2010).

3. Creative development and design practice applies to all discipline areas.
4. A positive, collaborative educational environment is essential in enabling creative development and design practice.
5. Creative practice applies to interpretation and learning experience design of mandated curriculum as well as the production of original work beyond curriculum content.
6. Creative development and design practice is based on eight interwoven developmental strands: collaborative development, self-instigative development, research/investigative development, generative development, prototyping/experimentational development, discipline complexity development, critical/analytical thinking development, and creative sustain development.

Program Structure

The cornerstone of the Creative Development program is the overarching Personal Creative Development Project (PCDP). The PCDP is launched out of the first course (Creative Development: An Introduction) at the beginning of the program and lands in the fourth course (Instructional Design and Assessment for Creative Development) ten months later at the end of the program. The PCDP is the primary platform for longitudinal, first-hand research and engagement in creative practice. It ultimately leads to a growth in creative capacity while providing an intimate understanding of sustained creative practice that can be applied to teaching practice. In this project, creative work is deliberately focused on personal themes outside students' educational practice to enable a fresh lens on creative growth that is not impeded by biases or entrenched habits from a typical work routine (Kelly, 2012). Any field is fair game for these creative development projects. They range from writing plays or books of fiction, non-fiction or poetry, to starting businesses, to launching initiatives of social or entrepreneurial innovation. The first course in this program launches this project after establishing a trusting, collaborative environment fuelled by contemporary creativity and creative development theory and vocabulary and small-scale, collaborative, creative design challenges.

The second course (Creativity in Communication) expands collaborative and independent creative experience to the field of communication with a focus on creative writing. This also fuels the PCDPs of many participants who focus on creating original written work. The third course (Creative Development across the Disciplines) expands understanding of creative development into the maths, sciences, humanities, and arts, as well as economic and social innovation. This course further fuels the PCDPs while providing teaching practice ideas in these areas. The fourth and final course (Learning Experience Design and Assessment for Creative Development) sees the completion, presentation, and research analysis of the Personal Creative Development Projects. This research is applied to the educational practice of each participant through the creation of learning experience design strategies and assessment regimens to systematically enable longitudinal, creative development of all learners across disciplines.

The Design Thinking for Innovation program follows a similar trajectory with a sharp focus on contextual creative problem solving though the application of design thinking. It starts with the establishment of fundamental design thinking principles in discipline-neutral contexts through engagement in a series of collaborative design challenges that grow in complexity. It then goes through three interrelated design lenses: social innovation and human-centred design; spatial relationships and the design of educational space; and educational design throughout the program as participants accumulate design portfolios in each context. The program moves from establishing design fundamental basics at the start to engaging in more sophisticated applications to real-world contexts.

Creative Development and Design Thinking Program Design Considerations

The growth and development of the Creative Development and Design Thinking programs over a series of prototypes embodies the very creative and design dynamics that the programs are about. They are each living, evolving prototypes, constantly redesigned and adjusted as new issues and problems arise as the programs unfold through a diverse range of participants over time. The following are some of the design considerations and response strategies that influenced the evolving design of both programs.

Transitioning into a learning culture of open collaboration

Sharing ideas and giving ideas does not come easily for many as traditional educational cultures are often characterized by a preoccupation with competition, privacy, and ownership of ideas. This is counterintuitive to a collaborative culture of creativity in which participants are required to openly give and accept ideas in a positive, highly social environment. The transition into this way of doing brings considerable anxiety to participants until they get used to it and learn to trust that it will eventually bear considerable creative fruit.

The program design response to this is to create a statusless class environment (Sweeney, 2004). This involves creating a learning culture in which all ideas are unconditionally accepted and added to. Once a positive, statusless culture is established, the collaborative idea generation and prototyping of ideas flourishes.

Transitioning from extrinsic to intrinsic motivation

Students who come into postsecondary educational environments often expect traditional, instructor-generated assignment structures involving research reading and reporting. This type of structure inherently relies on extrinsic motivation, as it is largely instructor-driven. Transitioning participants into the initiation and execution of personally meaningful, intrinsically motivated, long-term, creative explorations is a considerable program challenge. The program design response to this challenge is to invest considerable time in metaphorical self-inventories to discover participants' personal passion areas. An accompanying response is to also work on giving participants permission to engage in these passion areas where they initially did not perceive themselves as being able to create. This goes as far as enabling participants to give themselves permission to create where they had never imagined or been enabled before.

Learning to create a pre-inventive structure to start creative practice

A primary learning challenge for participants in the Creative Development and Design Thinking programs is learning how to create pre-inventive structures that describe their creative intentions in a manner that enables them to move their work forward. A pre-inventive structure is basically a design brief that describes the goals and parameters of a potential creative exploration (Finke, Ward, & Smith, 1992). A good pre-inventive structure allows enough room for exploration and play while providing enough structure and focus to prevent creative efforts from floundering from the paradox of choice. The character of the pre-inventive structure will vary from student to student, depending on their individual level of creative development (Kelly, 2012). The program design response to this is to walk educators through increasingly more complex, collaborative design challenges as a group to demonstrate how an effective pre-inventive structure is created before they move on to create their own.

Managing assessment anxiety

Assessment anxiety seems to be ever present in most classes. Adults in postsecondary teacher education programs are not immune to this experience. Many participants fear being compared with others or fear being measured by instructors. This negative disposition is certainly not conducive to the development of a highly collaborative, creative culture in a statusless environment. If these fears are not dealt with from the onset, inventive momentum of any kind will be difficult. The primary program strategy to counter this is to move the conversation away from a discussion about grades toward a dialogue about the creative work they are engaged in. Specific tactics involve using co-reflective assessment where specific, insightful developmental questions are co-developed with students, leading to cooperative, highly dialogic assessments that focus on the development of students' work. Assessment in this context is nurturing and non-threatening and is an integral part of the collaborative, creative educational environment.

Maintaining inventive momentum in the virtual space between physical classes and meeting times

Sustained creative practice requires a lot of stimuli to maintain inventive momentum. This is the fuel that sustains creative practice when students are in an environment where there is constant bombardment by new ideas. In an intense, social environment of scheduled class time, this is easy to accomplish with class-based generative experiences and the invaluable casual conversations among participants that occur over lunch, coffee, and other short spaces between scheduled coursework. When weeks or months pass between physical meetings, the challenge arises of maintaining a high-stimuli, inventive environment in virtual space among group participants. The primary program tactic used in response to this challenge is to place everyone in virtual group discussion boards where they constantly post their ideas and prototyping examples for plussing. This is a positive, open, constantly changing, generative environment that approximates the living process portfolio concept. Another tactic is to conduct all interactions using communication vehicles such as Skype, where faces can be viewed. This strategy enables a deeper form of listening, making it easier to maintain the social/emotional connection among group members established during physical class meetings. Regardless of the virtual space strategies, periodic physical meeting times are essential to reboot this process as the phenomenon of diminished returns presents itself in extended virtual time spaces.

Educator Stories of Action/Applied Research for Personal Creative Development

The following are two vignettes from educators who engaged in longitudinal personal creative development in the Creative Development graduate program as a form of applied/action research. They represent two very different personal creative journeys, but both corroborate the notion that this kind of research should be built into the fabric and experience of teacher education to enable a deeper understanding of an educational culture of collaborative creativity. The first vignette is from Vera Her who is a math/science educator with a background in music education, while the second piece is from Sandra Becker, who is an experienced classroom educator engaged in doctoral studies in education with a focus on makerspaces as creative learning environments.

The senior's choir

VERA HER

HOW I DECIDED TO START A SENIOR'S CHOIR.

My initial idea was to create a CD of songs of my own kind of compilation. It was actually through the idea-generating sessions that we had in class that perpetuated it to grow. A classmate mentioned something about starting a group, kind of rock group or band with seniors playing in it. It piqued my interest because I was interested in music. I had taught music before (choir) at the elementary and middle school levels. So through the idea-generation sessions, it really was a collaborative decision of where I came up with a whole idea of starting a senior's choir. What really drew me to that particular idea was the connection of music. I enjoy music, I love music, and that initial in the program start of figuring out who we are and what our passions are was very important. It helped to lead me to come to that conclusion and decide on attempting to create a senior's choir as a personal creative development project.

GETTING STARTED.

There was a seniors' home right near my school. I made contact with the recreation manager there. She mentioned how they'd never done anything like that before. They always have choirs come to the seniors' home but never have they had them actually engaged the seniors to perform. It was very certainly a new and novel idea from the perspective that I had never done this before and neither had the seniors at this home experienced anything like this either. So I knew that it was a seniors' home that was open to having music. But other than that, I had never taught seniors or worked with seniors in music except for interacting with my grandmother but never in a group setting.

INITIAL QUESTIONS AND ANXIETY.

I had a lot of fears at the beginning. I didn't even know if this was going to work. Would this group of seniors even be able to sing? I was concerned about stereotypical about seniors that as they get older they can be ornery and not very participatory and that they have their own set ways. I worried that it might be really difficult to keep them as a group and have them even be cordial to one another if they were very set in their own ways. I was quite nervous as to how this would work or if there would be a lot of backlash or disapproval. I know as humans we're not really prone to accepting change and a new approach thing in a positive way, so I did have a lot of fears in beginning.

MY FIRST MEETING AND MY FIRST BUMPS.

My initial meeting with them was with ten ladies. I quickly found out that my speech, the way I talk to them, needed to change because I kept using the word *guys* and there was one senior lady who became very upset with me. She reminded me: "We are not guys, we are women, you need to stop saying that." I felt like I wasn't starting off on a good foot. I had to really change my speech to think twice as to how I was communicating certain things. I also had to learn to speak much louder. A lot of times they couldn't hear what I was saying, and I didn't want to overcompensate. I had to learn very quickly. Then when we started to sing, I was a little too ambitious. I was doing a lot of typical choir things and a lot of them just couldn't keep up. Some of them left as a result, and then I had to think about planning in a way that would keep them attending.

GATHERING MOMENTUM.

I began to ask more questions. I set up an opinion box for feedback to incorporate ideas that they had to offer. Eventually we built relationships and people just came to sing or to listen. Now every time I come

Figure 6.1 Accompanying the senior's choir

in, I don't know why, but they clap. There is also a lady now who just joined who plays the piano. She will start and warm up with them. This has grown for them to develop in their own ways. At first many lacked confidence and they would apologize and they're at their preliminary singing attempts. Now there's almost little to no apologizing. They sing quite well. I even recorded them one time just so that they could hear themselves, and they were very surprised because they thought we sound decent!

I am into my third year of working with this choir. After my first year as part of my studies, they thought I wasn't coming back. So they were surprised that I said I would be returning. Over their break, they would continue to sing on their own. They got their family members involved so it just snowballed into something much bigger. They have relationships with one another because not all of them knew each other. Our repertoire is growing as well, and we're becoming more ambitious now. In the beginning, I think I started too strong and as I had to take more time to build their confidence. Now they're way more confident and they're recruiting others, I don't even need to be recruiting anyone any more.

REFLECTIONS.

My biggest surprise in engaging on this journey was how self-sustaining something can be when you find something that you are passionate about. Like it's almost little to no effort on my part at this point. It is no longer work, it is something that is natural in some sense where it continues to sustain itself and I didn't think that was possible. I always felt it was through your efforts that things are sustainable but it's really finding that passion and establishing something that is relational that is keeping it going. I don't think I would have ever dreamed of this particular scenario if I hadn't stepped out of my comfort zone. This choir project wasn't necessarily easy. I had to do something outside of my own repertoire and schedule, and I had a lot of fear of failure. I learned how to take risks and if it fails to not worry about my reputation whatever the case may be.

I am trying a lot more creative ways of approaching ways to help students learn and study rather than the traditional ways. I am encouraging my students to just try everything and anything. There is nothing that's stupid or useless and not to think so much about the outcome but the journey. I had to learn this through my own first-hand experience.

Writing my first play

SANDRA BECKER

Writing is a form of expression I have always felt connected to, and for the last few years, I have yearned to write a play. I have no idea where this yearning came from, but in choosing a personal creative project as part of extended action research, it seemed the only option. I had to do it. From an action research standpoint, I wondered, "What are the implications both educational and affective, of a personally instigated, sustained, long-term creative project?"

My play centres around the metaphor of baseball, and for a long time, I had the title in my mind. It is called *Extra Innings*, and the two characters in the play are twin brothers in their late seventies. They have not spoken in over fifty years, and throughout the course of the play, their histories and family issues unfold. Where did I get the idea for this play? My mother had uncles, twin brothers, one who stayed on the farm and the other who moved to California, but neither of them ever married. Both my father and my father-in-law were avid baseball fans. Somehow I thought of meshing these two things together to inform the characters in this prospective play.

WHERE TO START.

One of my colleagues in the Creative Practice graduate program was a drama teacher, and she recommended I begin by reading lots of plays, so that is how I got started. I felt a fair bit of angst because I really knew nothing about playwriting. Compared to other forms of writing that I have tried, the characters came to life quite quickly. In fact, in the beginning, they seemed to write themselves. The play is set in Swift Current, Saskatchewan, at the Canadian Little League Championships. A wayward brother is returning after fifty years to watch his great-nephew play for the hometown team. I structured the play in a series of nine scenes to mimic the innings of a baseball game. But a month or two into the process, I came to a complete halt. Though the dialogue between the brothers flowed easily, the play lacked interest and tension. Frankly, it was boring. I needed an idea, event, or conflict that would engage and surprise the audience in a way they had not anticipated, and I couldn't think of a thing.

REGAINING MOMENTUM.

With a deadline looming, and a couple of weeks of procrastination (as a teacher, it is difficult to ask for help), I sent a desperate message to my Creative Practice colleagues and got a flurry of responses, similar to "What if you did this?" From their plussing, I was able to continue and the play took a direction that was completely unexpected, even for me. After I had written a draft of thirty pages, I contacted a former student, who is now an actor and director, to ask if he would do a reading with me. Joe's comments were insightful, and he was tough but gentle. He kindly told me that what I had was an outline, and he suggested where I needed to develop the story. He also asked if he could be the first to direct my play. Wrapping up our Creative Practice cohort, we were invited to share our projects. Knowing there was not time for the entire play, I selected a scene and asked two colleagues with drama and acting experience to play the brothers. They did a wonderful job bringing the brothers to life, and I had a great deal of positive feedback. Two young teachers in the cohort came to me, gave me a hug and said, "You *have* to get this play produced." Those were encouraging words, and I have to admit, I have become very attached to both characters in the play.

I now have sixty pages and am aiming for eighty to ninety. I am still dealing with issues of staging, pacing, language usage, and character development. When ready, I plan to send this work to a group associated with a local college who critique plays. I confess I am a bit nervous about this. Unlike previous readings, these are people I don't know and who don't know me.

IMPLICATIONS FOR TEACHING PRACTICE.

Reflecting on this journey, what has sustained me in continuing this creative work? I think importantly, I was able to choose a mode of expression that I feel confident enough in to take risks. I have given myself extensive amounts of time to complete different stages of this project, but also used deadlines, whether internal or external, to force evolution. But I believe critical to my personal progress was not only my acceptance of plussing in a supportive, collaborative community, but actually seeking it out to move my project forward. It was the feedback, positive comments, and honest recommendations that made me believe in the importance of what I was doing. I hope to embed this in my professional practice.

Destinations Unknown . . . Always a Prototype

Traditional teacher education programs must be reconfigured to embody creative development and the disposition of design as central to becoming an enabling educator in an educational culture of collaborative creativity. It is not enough to discuss or briefly sample new educational theory and practice and expect it to be educationally transformative. True educational empowerment will come from empowered and enabled educators and learners who have a solid first-hand research experience basis to inform educational practice and the design of educational environments conducive to creative development. Teacher education programs must live what they talk about. Educators must live what they expect learners to do. The Creative Development in Educational Practice and Design Thinking for Innovation teacher education programs attempt to embody this through continual prototyping, redesign, and refinement. Everything is a prototype and the participants know it. It gives them permission to prototype, experiment, and make mistakes without being in a punitive environment. These programs will evolve into iterations that have not been discovered yet. Engaging in creative practice in pursuit and discovery of outcomes unknown is always so exciting. It is of paramount importance that these programs live and embody what they are about.

PART 2—CREATING CHANGE IN THE FIELD
ROBERT KELLY

Creating Change in the Field

Throughout this volume, we have heard from many educators who are working to create educational change from a variety of perspectives. As their narratives in the Creating Development features attest, these educators are working in diverse contexts to enable creative practice and the growth of creative development of both educators and learners. The Creating Development narratives in this chapter point the way to numerous pathways for change and the evolution of educational practice to enable creative development in reconceptualized educational settings and beyond into regional, national, and global communities.

Creating Development 9

TRANSFORMING MY ELEMENTARY SCHOOL CULTURE: A PRINCIPAL'S STORY.
Creating Development 9 (Transforming My Elementary School Culture: A Principal's Story), with former elementary school principal Charles Schneider, guides us through a journey that many public school administrators and school staffs want to take, and that is to transform the culture of a school to become more creative and innovative. This is not an easy task when dealing with the many factors at play in an elementary public school setting with diverse staff interests. Ultimately, the majority of the staff work together to attempt to answer the fundamental question: "How do we grow the creative capacity of a school staff to enable the potential of a transformative curriculum model in a large, public elementary school?"

Creating Development 10

CHALLENGE CONVENTION.
Gerald Figal's Creating Development 10 (Challenge Convention) questions some of the inherent structures in public education that are automatically accepted as normal because they represent how things have always been done. Koestler (1964) called this the "anesthesia of conditioning." Change does not come easily for many, as I witnessed a few years ago while instructing a fourth-year university studio painting class for the first time. On the first day of class, I noticed that all of the students showed up with a variety of sizes of rectangular, white,

flat-surfaced canvases that they had either made or bought pre-made and primed. My first words were, "Where is it stated that all of your paintings are to be on a rectangular format and on a flat, white surface?" My question was initially met with silence, and then "Why not? This is painting class, isn't it?"

These students were merely acquiescing to the cultural convention that a painting is perceived to typically be on a rectangular-formatted, flat surface. This phenomenon applies to educational practice and school design, where we blindly accept traditional practice and corresponding organizational structures because those are the ways things have always been done. This conditioning precludes incredible potentials for change through innovation that may better serve student-learning needs by enabling the growth and development of educational environments conducive to collaborative, creative development. Creating Development 10 is an invitation to challenge convention.

Creating Development 11

SCALING CREATIVE DEVELOPMENT FROM DISTRICT TO NATION.
Jean Hendrickson's Creating Development 11 (Scaling Creative Development from District to Nation) addresses the need to develop the capacity and methods to scale educational practice conducive to creative development beyond the walls of a school to a more pervasive transformative reach across districts, states, provinces and nations. As Director Emeritus of Oklahoma A+ Schools, Jean Hendrickson explores how the scalability of the A+ model can serve as an exemplar for scaling creative development across increasingly larger geographic jurisdictions.

Creating Development 12

INVENTING AND CREATING A NEW SCHOOL.
Creating Development 12 (Inventing and Creating a New School) focuses on pioneering initiatives by educators to invent and innovate by creating new educational spaces and new ways of doing that enable an educational culture of collaborative creativity. Matthew Wunder, CEO of Da Vinci charter schools in Los Angeles, California, is one example of a pioneer in this area. Da Vinci Schools are free, college-preparatory, public charter schools open to all students in California. They are authorized by the Wiseburn Unified School District. They consist of Da Vinci Innovation Academy (K to 8), Da Vinci Communications High School, Da Vinci Design High School, Da Vinci Science High

School, and Da Vinci Extension. Da Vinci Schools combine a project-based, college-preparatory curriculum with real-world active learning, internships, and early college classes ensuring that students acquire the twenty-first-century skills needed for today's workplace. Da Vinci students "learn by doing"—a philosophy called *edu-creation*, or education you create—through hands-on, interdisciplinary projects that address real-world problems and challenges, transforming students from passive receivers of information into enthusiastic learners, thinkers, and problem solvers who assume greater responsibility for their learning. Students work cooperatively in technology-rich classrooms where they are encouraged to ask questions, explore, investigate, collaborate, manage resources, strategize, solve problems, and decide how they will achieve their goals. Matthew Wunder describes the impetus for starting the Da Vinci Schools:

> *I was a middle school principal in a traditional Los Angeles–area district named Wiseburn Unified School District. Our students were falling off an academic cliff and going into a feeder high school district that was under-performing. I was given the opportunity by a superintendent to explore this crazy notion called charter schools. Wiseburn was a K to 8 district and they wanted another alternative from an underperforming and unsafe high school district because Wiseburn was a K to 8 district. I think any organization that is going to be successful has to be willing to fail. And as we like to say, fail forward fast. How you do that is to have your bosses create a safe place where you're allowed to make mistakes as long as those mistakes aren't harming students. We had this crazy idea of let's start our own charter school, but we didn't know what it would be.*

> *Our vision is ultimately to end poverty. Education is the very best way of doing that. If schools are supposed to teach you what you're supposed to know when you get out of school, then aligning to real-world readiness is key. The world is changing so dramatically and the world our children will inherit is something we can't even predict. With this in mind, creativity is one of the most valuable and employable skill sets one can have. We want a school that's real-world ready. We are blessed to be right in the aerospace capital of the world where there is lots of opportunity for our students to connect with real-world initiatives. I think some of these things informed our desire to create high schools that focused on project-based learning with real-world connections.*

> *We want to solve problems efficiently and effectively. One big part of it is to strip out fear by creating an environment where students know it's okay to fail and that it is actually part of the creative process. Also*

networks and lateral connections are so critical. Equally critical is moving from a school-centric point of view as most schools are really designed to be efficient for adults, to a learner-centric perspective. (personal communication, January 12, 2016)

Matthew Wunder is one of many pioneering in educational practice that is conducive to a culture of creative development. Creating Development 12 features a conversation with Andy Smallman, cofounder of Puget Sound Community School (PSCS) in Seattle, Washington. PSCS is a private school for grades six to twelve that enables and empowers students to engage in individual and collaborative, creative practise. The stories of educational inventors and innovators such as Matthew Wunder in Los Angeles, Andy Smallman in Seattle, or Gever Tulley and his Tinkering and Brightworks Schools in the San Francisco area are all invitations for educators to embody a disposition of design by creating and inventing new educational spaces and new ways of educational doing.

Epilogue

THE WAY FORWARD: IMPLICATIONS FOR GLOBAL EDUCATION AND ITS TRANSFORMATION.

Creating Development 12 (Inventing and Creating a New School) is followed by an Epilogue (The Way Forward: Implications for Global Education and Its Transformation) by Dennis Cheek. Dennis is a cofounder and executive director of the National Creativity Network, and conceiver and co-chair of Global Creativity United. He points to the way ahead from a global perspective with an invitation to actively embrace creative practice and creative development.

REFERENCES
Finke, R. A., Ward, T. B., & Smith, S. M. (1992). *Creative cognition: Theory, research and applications*. Cambridge: MIT Press.

Kelly, R. (2012). *Educating for creativity: A global conversation*. Edmonton: Brush Education.

Koestler, A. (1964). *The act of creation*. London: Pan Books.

Starko, A. J. (2010). *Creativity in the classroom*. (4th Ed.) New York: Routledge. (original work published 1995).

Sweeney, J. (2004). *Innovation at the speed of laughter*. Minneapolis: Aerialist Press.

Transforming My Elementary School Culture: A Principal's Story

CHARLES SCHNEIDER

Charles Schneider is a former school principal now working as an educational consultant and coach in the Lower Mainland of British Columbia in western Canada.

Bringing Creative Development into a School Culture

The Question: How do we grow the creative capacity of an entire school staff to enable the potential of a transformative curriculum model in a large, public elementary school?

In 2012, the British Columbia Ministry of Education announced its Education Plan. Through it, the ministry seeks to transform the province's curriculum, calling for "A more flexible curriculum that prescribes less and enables more, for both teachers and students and a system focused on the core competencies, skills and knowledge that students need to succeed in the 21st century."

The ministry emphasized the need to "give teachers more time and flexibility to allow students to explore their interests and passions, with a view to enabling innovation." Since then, new curriculum documents were developed, and implementation has begun.

Gone are the long lists of learning outcomes to be addressed. In their place are "big ideas," a small set of "core competencies," "content" for each subject area, and an emphasis on "cross-curricular connections" rooted in practical applications.

Abandoning the learning outcomes checklists can be both liberating and scary for educators. We might fear losing control, missing critical outcomes at crucial times, and being too flexible in our instructional approach, perhaps to our students' detriment.

In reviewing the ministry's plan, we were faced with several key questions. How do we implement such a transformative curriculum model? How do we build a culture of creativity, exploration, and experimentation in a public school of more than five hundred students and thirty teachers? How do we become comfortable with daily co-planning with teaching colleagues and students, with collaborative design thinking and problem solving, and a steady diet of unknown outcomes?

First Steps

The first, most important step was to acknowledge that significant change brings discomfort, and even fear. When asked to step into the unknown, we feel unprepared and lack confidence to face the challenges. To address this perceived lack of creative capacity, we offered the teachers of École Élémentaire Casorso Elementary School an opportunity to engage in a personal Creative Development Project (CDP). We believed that as each of us built our capacity in this area, we would feel more competent and therefore confident to take on facilitating, collaborating, and mentoring roles rather than the traditional instructing role with our students. We would be more able to entrust them with the responsibility of co-determining their learning paths with us. In order for us to truly grow through our projects, our work would have to challenge us both intellectually and emotionally. Despite the effort, we were hopeful that our increased creative capacity would potentially help us when we ran into difficulty implementing the new curriculum, inventing new paths for learning and empowering learners as they grew their own creative capacity.

Our Creative Development Project

We designed our Creative Development Project (CDP) to unfold over a two-year period. The whole first year was to be devoted to personal projects, and in the following year, we would try to apply what we learned to the implementation of the new curriculum.

In a spring staff meeting, teachers were introduced to the idea of the CDP and invited to join. At that meeting, everyone was asked to create a personal metaphor, and through a "snowball" activity, the metaphors were shared anonymously. Eighteen of our thirty teachers and one administrator from another school accepted our invitation, joining our vice-principal and me as we addressed our first task: to come up with at least five possible ideas for our own individual, personal, creative development projects.

SETTING THE FOUNDATION

Our group met at the end of August on two of the three designated teacher professional development days, once in September, and then again on our October administrative day. In these sessions, we practised creating, sharing, and building on each other's ideas for innovations, creativity, and our personal projects. We agreed that we needed a flat, non-hierarchical structure within our group. We established the practice of only building on and not critiquing others' ideas (without praising them too much, either). In addition to coming up with multiple project ideas, we agreed to not settle quickly on any one idea. We also committed to sharing with each other in writing our project ideas and designs in addition to providing written, constructive feedback for one another. Finally, we agreed to meet off campus monthly to share our progress and support each other in our project work.

Many of us struggled to come up with multiple project ideas. Some of us never became comfortable with the idea of doing a project simply for ourselves, totally unrelated to our work at school. We were additionally challenged to fit our project work into our busy lives. Despite these and other impediments, most of us established our projects by the October deadline we set for ourselves and began attending our monthly sharing meetings.

DOING THE WORK

Our November, December, and January sharing meetings were well attended. Some of us were really rolling, and our feedback to those individuals was more a celebration of their successes than the contributions we initially intended to offer. For others, the projects were not progressing or even begun as hoped. In these cases, we were reminded that generating more ideas was important and that eventually something would stick. Regardless of their varying degrees of progress, group members were generally open about their projects and were excited for and supportive of each other. We had fun hearing about colleagues' projects: jewellery making, an online vintage accessories boutique, a book of children's wisdom, extended-family memoires, and landscape design and implementation, to name a few.

As our CDP progressed into the next calendar year, attendance at the January through April sharing meetings declined. Busy lives and family commitments were at least partly to blame. So, too, was the fatigue that accompanied our individual projects as well as staying connected in our collaborative network. Written feedback dwindled to practically nothing.

CHANGES IN DIRECTION

A few projects evolved in unanticipated directions. One person, who had never felt comfortable with pursuing her project entirely for herself, worked with her students to co-write engaging songs that had strong curricular links. Another group member abandoned her seniors' home design project and began a very successful series of visits to a neighbouring seniors' residence with her students.

A third participant started writing a book with her students, made significant progress, then decided it was not developing as she wanted. A few months later, she began designing and making clothing, and is now totally engaged. As we approached the one-year mark in our CDP, more than half of our group was working on projects other than those with which they started! Not only was this not a problem, it helped to reinvigorate those individuals and the group as a whole.

CROSS-POLLINATION

While our personal CDP work evolved, regular schoolwork and projects were simultaneously occurring. Teachers and parents collaborated with our vice-principal to create an outdoor learning space. Our teachers also worked with administration and district staff to develop a school-based writing continuum for all of our students. This project ultimately involved all staff and students in the school. Teachers on the committee scheduled co-teaching sessions with colleagues, introducing a variety of small- and large-group instructional strategies to them and their students.

As part of the writing continuum project, the committee sought student input for a writing prompt that would appeal to all students, kindergarten to grade six. When that was established, committee members, aided by a parent with a graphic design background, created a "magic portal" in a room off the back of the school library. The student-generated prompt and the portal inspired the students to produce wonderfully creative writing that would be used as exemplars in the continuum. Students and staff were enthralled with this project.

Numerous staff members have commented that they believe the excitement and passion engendered by our CDP greatly benefited our work in the above curricular and other projects. The unplanned, simultaneous timing of these projects served as a reminder that the schedule established for the CDP, neatly dividing the personal side of the CDP into the first year and the curricular side into the second, did not really reflect the true, unpredictable nature of creativity. We cannot put it in a box and then take it out at just the right time to play with it. The ongoing development of creative capacity will inevitably permeate everything that we are doing.

CREATIVITY AND THE NEW CURRICULUM

Another unexpected development in the CDP arose in year two when the time came to formally focus our efforts on implementing the new curriculum. The CDP was always open to any staff member, and as we reconvened in the new school year, several teachers who had chosen not to engage in the first year of creativity projects joined us. These conversations were unfortunately delayed by the labour dispute between our teachers' union and the provincial government. In fact, we missed out entirely on the designated professional development days at the end of August and welcomed students back to school for the first time three weeks into the regular year. This made for a difficult start to the year for all, adversely affecting our CDP and many other efforts.

Despite this stumbling block, teachers engaged in the curriculum implementation discussions enthusiastically. They explored a variety of ideas for collaborative planning and integration of subjects (i.e., cross-curricular connections). Ultimately, the majority of our teachers settled on a single initiative to get their feet wet. We engaged an English professor from a local college to lead our teachers and their students in workshops to write and present performance poetry.

Implementation of the new curriculum continues in other ways. Members of our original CDP group, again joined by other teaching colleagues, are implementing a collaborative approach to math instruction, emphasizing student independence and student-driven applications of their math skills and concepts. Other teachers are using the instructional strategies they learned through the CDP and writing continuum project to benefit student creativity in language arts and other subject areas.

In Their Words

Our teachers clearly see a link between the work they did in their personal projects for the CDP and their evolving professional practice. The statements below, provided by a sampling of CDP participants, illustrate this point.

> *Perhaps I would have stumbled across a lot of the ideas and information I have found anyway, but I find myself less hesitant and more enthusiastic about what I am discovering with this creative project always in the back of my mind.*
>
> *New Teacher*

> *The creative project gave me a kind of structure. Perhaps more importantly it gave me a community. We didn't exactly collaborate because we each did our own project. We supported and celebrated each other's work. This project has, I feel, expanded my creative capacity and stamina . . . I feel it's made me more confident. That confidence has seeped into my professional practice, helping me be more authentic, less of a perfectionist, more of a risk taker, more flexible, more fun, quite frankly . . . It's also made me even more determined to help students explore what interests them . . . Collegial friendships feel more robust and more resilient. Collaborative projects since have felt a bit bolder, a bit more daring. Also, sensitive or challenging topics have been easier to broach.*
>
> *Teacher-Librarian*

> *The structures I used in writing my children's book were explored with the students. These strategies helped the students create their stories . . . The idea of plussing is one that sticks with me. It is common practice*

that staff members are still using years after it was introduced. It has allowed the staff to trust each other in collaboration.

Vice-Principal

Working with my colleagues in a different context (other than teaching) was a fun, shared learning experience. Hearing everyone talk about their passions inspired me to pursue mine . . . [it] affected the way I taught subjects, from fine arts to writing. It allowed me to view it as a process, rather than a criterion that had to be met. This transformation was emphasized even more in my practice because I was focusing on creating a space that was much more student-led. For the school as a whole, I think that any shared learning journey is positive—it reinvigorated my colleagues and created some cohesion.

Masters Degree Candidate

What I really took away from this project is "ideas are a dime a dozen" and it's really what you create with those ideas, whether they're yours or not, that define creativity. This had a profound impact on students who had difficulty coming up with their own ideas for writing. Once students realized it was okay and were even encouraged to take another's idea to create something of their own, the process of creating came with more enjoyment, ease, and desire to continue. This is a strategy that I continue to employ with my students across the curricula, not just writing.

Experienced Teacher

I grew watching my colleagues. I was inspired by their creative projects and their "nothing's going to stop me" attitude . . . It was as if someone had freed a part of them from the birdcage . . . I believe that the single most profound impact was on the school's school-wide write project, in which a portal was created for students to "enter" to unleash their creative composition. I do not know which came first, the Creative Development Project or the portal with the Instructional Leadership Team, but my gut tells me the writing project went way beyond what we would normally see because teachers were in an environment where creativity was valued.

Experienced Teacher/French Coordinator

Lessons Learned

Our teachers are definitely more confident in their creative capacity as they continue to implement the new curriculum. Along the way, we learned a great deal about what works and what does not. We saw that our interests and abilities took us in myriad unanticipated directions, and that it was best to follow them.

We learned not to get too attached to a particular timeline. Creative opportunities, interruptions, and other issues came up. Each required our attention, but we never lost sight of our ultimate goal.

We held true to our collaborative foundations: a flat hierarchy; plussing each others' projects and ideas rather than evaluating them; not settling on the first idea but exploring multiple iterations; and finally, choice in all matters.

We saw that going off campus, sharing food and refreshments, and making the whole process as much fun as possible really helped everyone to persist. Throughout, we practised for each other what we wanted for our students: genuine appreciation of each person's ideas and contributions, and support for each other to develop individual passions, strengths, and innovations.

Our teachers repeatedly told me how important it was to them that our vice-principal and I engaged in individual projects and the sharing sessions with them. We felt the same excitement, uncertainty, frustrations, changes of direction, and fatigue. These experiences helped me to understand our teachers' perspectives and showed clearly that nobody was above doing the hard work. It certainly contributed to a statusless creative culture.

On a personal level, I learned much more than I expected through the CDP. As a principal, I was usually in the support role, and having the tables turned, being more personally dependent on our teachers in the context of the project, was both a challenging and enriching experience for me. Sharing the project journey with the teachers while working with them at the same level of creativity was one of the happiest and most fulfilling endeavours of my working life.

And Now . . .

As with any transformative process pursued by a large group of people, each person was and continues to be at a different stage of development in terms of implementing our new curriculum and collectively growing creative capacity. Happily, the staff of École Élémentaire Casorso Elementary School is engaged in that pursuit creatively, collaboratively, and purposefully.

REFERENCES
British Columbia Ministry of Education. (2012). Education Plan. Retrieved from bcedplan.ca.

CREATING DEVELOPMENT 10

Challenge Convention

GERALD FIJAL

Gerald Fijal is former secondary school educator who has held several administrative positions with secondary schools, metro school jurisdictions, and the government in Alberta, Canada.

The fact that high schools are trapped in conventional practice was never more evident to me than when I was in the last principalship of my career. I was appointed as principal to the high school that I graduated from thirty-two years previously. I came to this school as principal with several prior experiences working in settings where conventional practice was challenged by groups of innovative educators.

I spent the bulk of my first year at this school observing practice and engaging in conversations. One of my first observations was that the time-table that was being used to manage the school was virtually identical to the timetable that had managed the school when I was a student there. Bells rung as I had remembered them; students moved throughout the hallways in an efficient and polite pace; teachers welcomed students at their doors and began their instruction with the chatter and day's organization that was so familiar to me from decades past. The school was orderly, quiet, purposeful, and predictable. And the results were respectable. This was a dream school for a principal—it literally ran itself as it had been doing for decades.

Another powerful observation over this first year was comparing curricular and extracurricular activities. And, more to the point, how classes such as fine arts were able to blend the line between curricular and extracurricular to the benefit of student engagement. In short, this school came to life when teachers and students worked together outside the structures and routines of the classroom. The school had a solid core of dedicated teachers who were deeply invested in the passions and interests of the students in areas that were relevant to them: marching band, show choir, robotics, athletics, and automotives. With these programs, the relationships between the students and teachers shifted significantly to shared agency in learning. In these activities, students and teachers were both engaged.

I ended that first year by sharing my observations with the staff, as well as a question: "How could we take what we know about the way that students and teachers work together in our extracurricular pursuits and use this knowledge to transform our practice in the classroom?" It seemed like a reasonable and obvious question. Unfortunately, it did not lead to the enthusiastic response that I had hoped for. The question was generally perceived as a threat to proven practice that kept the school safe, predictable, and comfortable.

I left the school in the middle of my second year to lead a province-wide high school redesign initiative. This province-wide initiative was based on challenging the organizational structures through the removal of the Carnegie Unit—a linking of time to credit. The purpose of the initiative was to determine whether the removal of the time per credit requirement would encourage high school communities to transform their practices in a manner that would lead to more engaged learning for students. At the core of this initiative was the question: "Does the organization and use of time in a high school impact the learning outcomes of students?" Seven years after this work began, results in these high schools are encouraging; much has been gained by the collaborative exploration of alternative conceptions of organization and program delivery that is worthy of our attention.

One outcome of the removal of the time per credit requirement is that it has shifted the culture of schools in significant ways. Given the foundational aspect of the credit attainment system to all facets of high school practice, the linking of time with credit is deeply embedded in the assumptions that teachers and students of high school bring to their daily existence, resulting in risking the value of learning being reduced to the accumulation of credits.

Credit attainment becomes the tangible outcome of high school education and in linking this attainment with time spent on a learning task, the entire endeavour of high school learning is quickly reduced to a balance sheet of goals neatly measured through the accumulation of grades and credits. There is no need for students to seek intellectually engaging experiences if grade and credit accumulation can serve as a tangible proxy of success in learning. Removing the time per credit requirement for high schools involved in the redesign initiative has created a significant interruption to the assumptions that lie at the core of a consumption-intense high school practice. For some, it has served as a threat to established practices and control. For others, this work has opened a new territory of professional judgement where time is seen as a bountiful resource to be used to engage in meaningful and relevant learning.

Over time, several common mindsets and strategies have emerged in the creative work of high school practitioners involved in the redesign efforts. These mindsets and strategies have evolved as an integrated set, building on each other to move school communities forward to more creative practice.

Teachers as Designers of Learning

The delinking of time and credit has led to a broad-ranging discourse among high school practitioners that revolves around this question: "If learning in school is not measured by the amount of time spent on tasks, then how am I to plan for student learning?" Planning for learning for many teachers had been an exercise done with a textbook and a calendar. It was assumed that the tasks would take care of the discipline knowledge and that hard work and compliance to deadlines would ensure student learning. Removing the Carnegie Unit has led to a fresh look at the nature of the mandated program outcomes and has led to conversations about the major ideas that are at the core of the disciplines. Teachers are more inclined to consider how experts live within a discipline and consider this as a starting point for designing learning activities that expose students to the disciplines in real-world contexts.

Student Direction

A shift in a mindset about the role of teacher as designer of learning has been accompanied by a second shift in a mindset about the role of student as an independent, capable learner. While the desire to create environments where students develop a strong work and study ethic is not abandoned, it is expanded to include explicit approaches to appeal to students' intrinsic desire to know how to live in the world within a discipline. Compliance is no longer the standard for exemplary student behaviour; it is replaced with independence, research orientation, collaboration, curiosity, creativity, and innovation. This shift in thinking about learning behaviours beyond compliance has led teachers to create learning environments that display a significant shift in power structures. Steps have been taken to encourage students to take control of their learning and how much time they spend on various tasks, and also to offer more choice in who they learn with and how they learn.

Variable Time for Students and Teachers

A school cannot manage the spaces, material, and human resources for large numbers of students by simply handing time over to students. Some scheduling practices have emerged that have mitigated the timetabling challenges presented by a large student population. At the heart of these practices is the notion that time is a resource that is best managed by teachers and students who are most advantaged by its use. The following practices demonstrate this notion of variable time for students and teachers:

- **Flex Time:** One very common strategy employed by schools is reducing the number of minutes in each instructional block and using these minutes to create a Flex Block. The Flex Block is time for students to direct their learning. In such blocks of time, all teachers are available to students for drop-in tutorial support or to engage in remedial or student-driven creative activities that might be planned by teachers or requested by students.
- **Cohort Scheduling:** Some schools have divided students into smaller subgroups within the school and assigned this cohort of students to a team of teachers to manage a portion of the student programming. Commonly, the student cohorts are comprised of 150 to 200 students who are assigned to a team of five to eight teachers. The school schedules a large block of time, usually an entire afternoon or morning each day of the week, to the cohort, and then it is up to the team of teachers to plan for, organize, and manage the programming for these students.
- **Team Teaching:** Similar to cohort scheduling, team teaching is the coming together of two or more teachers to manage the programming for a group of students over an extended period of time. The difference between team teaching and cohort scheduling is that team teaching arrangements generally emerge between teaching colleagues versus an intentional scheduling approach by the school. Team teaching arrangements often emerge due to shared interest or pedagogical approaches but always end up in two or more teachers working with a larger group of students in a back-to-back period scenario. In this scenario, teachers have an extended period to manage the learning for themselves and their students.
- **Looping:** A common strategy used in elementary schools in which teachers are assigned to teach a group of students over multiple years has emerged as a common practice on a smaller scale in high schools through redesign work. At the high school level, looping usually occurs in a single-subject discipline. A teacher who might work with the same group of students over an entire year to teach both the grades eleven and twelve chemistry programs is an example of looping. In this arrangement, the teacher has a longer period of time to manage several outcomes from two connected programs, allowing the teacher to design learning activities that might span outcomes from both years of programming.

Schools that have explored the use of the above strategies have discovered that teachers and students build stronger relationships as a result of the extended time they have with each other and that teachers and students have more flexibility to use time as they might need it to explore ideas at a deeper level. These strategies also develop stronger collaborative approaches between teachers as they are managing time with students along with one or more colleagues. These collaborations have led to more creative practices and risk taking.

Multi-Disciplinary Projects

As teachers consider the nature of learning as well as the nature of their disciplines, the lines between traditional subject areas begin to blur. The removal of the time requirement has led teachers and schools to question the validity of continued separation of subject disciplines as discrete objects of study. As schools explore alternative scheduling models where groups of teachers are responsible for planning the programming for larger numbers of students over a variety of subject areas, there is an increase in project-based approaches that cross several discipline lines. The end result has been the design of learning environments that are more relevant to the way that disciplines live in the world and the way that experts practise their disciplines in the company of their peers.

Expanding Learning Beyond the School

While the strategies and mindsets discussed thus far are based on learning that is bounded by the resources and expertise that resides in the school, redesign conversations have led to a concerted effort to look beyond school resources to engage students in meaningful and relevant learning. As flexible approaches to the use of time have allowed students to engage in the foundational aspects of learning in a discipline at a pace that is commensurate with their needs, schools are more inclined to consider time away from the school as fertile ground to engage with experts and seize opportunities to access resources that may not be present in the school. Cooperative education opportunities, internships, exploratory programs, and dual credit opportunities, as well as engaging with experts in their fields of endeavour, are beginning to expand. As students engage in these real-life learning opportunities, they return to the school with renewed enthusiasm for the foundational learning that is best made available to them in traditional classroom settings.

Scaling Creative Development from District to Nation

JEAN HENDRICKSON

Jean Hendrickson is director emeritus for Oklahoma A+ Schools and an educational consultant. She is a writer, speaker, and practitioner of building systematic, sustainable, and innovative practices into the lives of communities through their schools.

How do we move education beyond the pockets of successful, creative practice that are found in numerous locations around the planet and take the best approaches with the most promising outcomes to scale? Why has it been such a challenge to sustain effective efforts when now, more than ever, the world is collectively crying for creative solutions to its momentous problems?

Everyone, from business leaders to educators, is calling for a more creative, innovative, and effective way to meet the world's challenges. Especially in schools, this space has become crowded with potential providers of the solution to the lack of creative development in classrooms. There is a mad rush to find a way to generate creativity in schools, even while standardized tests and their accompanying standardization still reign supreme as the chief indicators of success. There is a need to break away from cookie-cutter, one-size-fits-all approaches to school that have led to a narrowing of the curriculum and a culling of enriching, creative, arts-based experiences, particularly for the most needy of America's children who can most benefit from them (Catterall, 2012). One of education's fiercest critics and friends, Sir Ken Robinson (2015), continually reminds us that "we're all born with immense natural talents, but by the time we've been through education far too many of us have lost touch with them" (p. xviii).

It stands to reason that if there were a silver bullet, someone would have found, patented, and sold it. That not being the case, it is clear that a single strategy (e.g., more arts integration!) will not move the world toward transformation. The answers are more complex. It is important that we learn to use the tools, strategies, and discoveries that have launched existing programs into successful-yet-isolated examples and apply them more broadly.

The A+ Schools movement (www.nationalaplusschools.org) in the United States can serve as an example of an initiative that began in a single place—North Carolina—and has been scaled to include statewide networks in Oklahoma, Arkansas, and Louisiana, with a new program launching in Cape Town, South Africa, in 2016, and other colleagues in Kansas, South Dakota, Michigan, and Bern, Switzerland. Beginning with twenty-five schools in 1995, the effort now hosts more than 160 schools across the country. Built on the premise that every child is entitled to a rich, full, creative education, the A+ Schools network depends upon a school-by-school, systematic approach to building out the ideal school in every community, everywhere, around the world. This requires a very creative mindset that takes into account the cultural context and resources within each community while still holding the school accountable for providing the full suite of experiences that the model supports.

Officials in Oklahoma A+ Schools (OKA+) note that the demand for more creative, effective, and forward-thinking classrooms is not tied to a geographic location, income level, or cultural group. Rather, school communities need connectivity with other diverse school communities, as is found in the OKA+ network and across the growing national network. Literally around the world, societies are seeking a better way to do school, a system that takes into account what Thomas Friedman calls "our hyperconnected" world. There is a demand for a collaborative setting more consistent with the rest of the world, rather than the antiquated industrial model of the past that is now difficult to find anywhere in the United States except in its schools.

Some helpful things have been learned about scaling out effective, creative organizations that can provide a way forward for others.

Connect What We Do to What Society Wants and Needs

It is vital to understand how what we do is valuable to the society in which we live. Look for and document the ways that the needs of the society are being effectively addressed by the work; there is simply no substitute for having an attractive and effective approach that is clearly articulated.

The Importance of Data

To be sustainable and scalable requires more than a good marketing approach. Within the A+ Schools example, a valuable set of information has been provided by data to support its claims, along with significant and ongoing research into implementation and practices. This important data has been used to do several things, including:

- Providing evidence of effectiveness to potential and current stakeholders and funders;
- Providing ongoing information to the practitioners on what is and is not effective;
- Allowing for collaborations and conversations across the increasingly diverse and growing network.

Ongoing research and attention to related literature have been features of the model throughout its development, creating a laboratory for testing the practices against the outcomes. The commitment to ongoing research has fed a collaborative environment in which partners and practitioners understand their value and contributions to the process, thereby continually lifting up the initiative and affirming the role of researcher in everyone.

Use the Same Building Blocks to Scale and Sustain Initiatives

Next, remember to use the same building blocks for scaling an initiative as those used within the initiative. The key features for unleashing students' creative development encompass imagination, ownership, and identity, freed from the limiters of preconceived notions, extrinsic motivation, and many other factors that have been described previously in this volume. Those same features are critical to successful scaling of a larger initiative. We can examine those features at play in the National A+ Schools Consortium (NASC) by understanding that while the individual networks within the consortium adhere to the same set of eight commitments known as the A+ Essentials, the cultural context and the organizational infrastructure is different in each location. North Carolina's office is found within North Carolina's Arts Council. Oklahoma's initiative is a department at the University of Central Oklahoma. Both Arkansas and Louisiana run their programs through private family foundations. And Cape Town, South Africa's initiative is a collaboration between Standard Bank and the Cape Craft and Design Institute.

Understand the Roles of Cultural Context and Community

It is clear that the cultural contexts are quite different in each of the above examples. In fact, acknowledging, celebrating, and harnessing the power of culture is an important ingredient of successful implementation and sustainability.

The innate desire for expression and for grounding that expression in cultural context is present in all societies. When initiating and then maintaining a school initiative, one of the main reasons such initiatives fail is their inability to take into account and to value the communities within which the schools reside. Too often, a predetermined set of conditions and standards arrive, fully developed, along with a short-term series of workshops so that the teachers "learn" what to do and what not to do. As has been clearly shown previously in this work, such an extrinsic approach is hardly the way to sustain a creative environment. Further, by failing to acknowledge and celebrate the rich cultural context that uniquely surrounds each school, multiple opportunities for self-expression and true learning are lost.

Connect to a Larger Network

The ability to share steps, successes, and failures with knowledgeable, committed peers is important for growth. Collaborations, think tanks, and free-work days at places like Google attest to the power of the collective. There is a danger, however, in groups that become too homogenous in their membership, effectively reintroducing the limiters and barriers to creative development that we are trying to curtail. So, how does a dynamic and growing network manage to improve and grow without losing the central identity that brought it together in the first place? The A+ Schools success suggests the following:

- Commit to a common set of conditions. Be they the eight A+ Essentials or some other common set of goals, it is important to develop and hold each other accountable for the common language that guides the conversations and helps sustain and sharpen the expectations within the group.
- Recognize diversity within the network. For the example of the National A+ Schools Consortium (NASC), the differences in the locations and challenges faced brings fresh perspectives and ways of thinking to the table. This effectively ensures a new set of topics and approaches with each gathering.
- Commit to regular and defined meeting times and places. And with this commitment, it is important to revisit John Naisbitt's 1982 bestseller *Megatrends* and understand the importance of high tech/high touch for effective gatherings. NASC holds meetings with the leaders of each organization on a quarterly basis, with two meetings a year in person and two online. The group rotates the responsibility of leading the gatherings, and the agendas are collaboratively developed, guided by a set of guidelines that define the group's goals, how it is governed, and how it admits new members and maintains common commitments.

This notion of co-creation is simple and yet challenging to implement. Sam Chaltain (2010), in his book *American Schools*, reminds us that in organizations, the challenge "is striking that balance between individual freedom and group structure: Freedom for all to express their opinions, balanced by a shared framework of rules and expectations that clarify what the community values and what it will and will not accept" (p. 59).

Build and Sustain a Community of Learners

The role of ongoing professional development is critical in successful scaling of promising initiatives. In the A+ Schools example, this training is carried out through regular and expected site visits with feedback to and from the schools themselves. Customized professional development then occurs with representatives from the A+ Schools network, including staff members and, importantly, through practitioner-trainers known as A+ Fellows.

This group of contracted providers represent fellow teachers, artists, and other school-based personnel who are performing their respective professions at a high level. They are not only accomplished practitioners; they also understand the unique characteristics of adult learners. They engage in regular opportunities to further hone their own facilitation skills by voluntarily participating in ongoing development within the A+ Schools model, learning and practising the set of commitments that make up the foundational pieces of the work. As such, they have high credibility and esteem within the educational community, and particularly within the school faculties for whom they provide services.

Each school receives an initial five-day institute to become grounded in the philosophy and methodology. Subsequently, each school receives at least two on-site professional development sessions each year on topics that are collaboratively determined to be of highest need for each campus. While these sessions are occurring, the facilitator scans the participants to discover good candidates to recruit to the Fellows' cadre. Thus begins an apprenticeship model within the Fellows' ranks that is mirrored in the school's growth process as well. Over a period of three years, schools move from initial implementation to fully demonstrating the tenets and methodology.

This method of growing our own ensures cultural and societal relevance while maintaining the central commitments to the model. Through this process, the model continues to grow, sustain, and evolve. The professional development experiences support adult learning by fostering creative personal realization and well-being, as well as by building the basis for communication and connections that are relevant to the teachers and to their students. The culture of continuous learning is nurtured in a safe environment where teachers from different disciplines, grade levels, school communities and life experiences are led through training by exemplary practitioners who are using the techniques that the participants are expected to acquire.

The Journey Ahead

To successfully scale out initiatives that provide ongoing professional development within a culture of creativity and innovation, it is important that each person acknowledge his or her unique role in the process. By deliberately adopting what Carol Dweck (2006) calls a *growth mindset* instead of a *fixed mindset*, we can systematically contribute to an encouraging environment that embraces challenges, persists in the face of setbacks, and finds lessons and inspiration in the success of others.

We want to address the need for education that keeps students engaged (and therefore in school), prepares them for success in college, careers, and communities, and weaves creative, student-centred learning into the fabric of each school. We must systematically equip teachers by building capacity to teach in an integrated, collaborative environment, to make use of meaningful connections across curriculum, to provide daily arts instruction to support learning, inspire student-generated work, and use instructional strategies that encourage systematic creative development. This is the type of school environment that can make best use of scaled and sustained creative development strategies. It is also the type of school that we want for our own children and for the world's children.

REFERENCES
Catterall, J. (2012). *The arts and achievement in at-risk youth, research report #55*. Washington, DC: National Endowment for the Arts.

Chaltain, S. (2010). *American schools*. Lanham, MD: Rowman & Littlefield Publishing Group.

Dweck, C. (2006). *Mindset: The new psychology of success*. New York: Ballentine Books.

Naisbitt, J. (1982). *Megatrends*. New York: Warner Books.

Robinson, K. (2015). *Creative schools: The grassroots revolution that's transforming education*. New York: Viking Penguin.

Inventing and Creating a New School

A CONVERSATION WITH ANDY SMALLMAN, EDITED BY ROBERT KELLY

Andy Smallman is cofounder and director of Puget Sound Community School in Seattle, Washington. PSCS is an independent school in the Seattle Chinatown-International District for students in grades six to twelve. Andy, along with his wife Melinda Shaw, started the school in 1994.

What Informed My Decision to Create a New School?

I grew up in an educational system that I feel didn't really serve me. I graduated from high school, and I was one of those kids who could coast through school fairly easily and get decent grades because it came easily to me, but it was a waste of time. I did not really feel that education was doing anything to help me know who I was, and it seemed counterproductive in some way. Most people did not really have any idea at the point of graduating from high school what they wanted to do, so they went on to college because that is just what you did next. I chose not to do that because why would I want to go spend four more years doing something that did not make any sense to me? That was kind of one of the first pillars to it.

Over the next few years, I discovered that I really wanted to work with children and I had the idea that being a teacher was the way to do it. I found Evergreen State College in Washington State where I went and got my undergraduate degree. It was there that I started seeing student-engaged education or student-involved education. I had this question in my first year: "Why could I not do this when I was thirteen?" So over the course of the next several years, I finished my undergraduate degree, pursued getting a teaching certificate and a master's degree, and in that process of getting my master's degree, I was hired to fill a position at a private elementary school outside Seattle. This was at a time when I was studying a lot of humanistic education. I was studying this idea of free schools, as I was interested in the idea of self-actualization. I tried to combine all of those ideas into a basic concept. I did that to some level of success at this private elementary school, but soon realized that to continue it in the way I wanted to was not going to really allow me to go as far as I wanted to go to develop this work.

I had worked there for three years and had a group of parents who appreciated the way I worked with their children. They had asked me where to send these students when they outgrew this elementary school. My answer was that there was no place except maybe homeschooling. Melinda, my wife, had been working as an administrator at a small college, and we discussed this issue and said: "Why don't we make a go of this? What if we were to propose an idea that was basically built around the way we want to live?" We wanted to have jobs that really meant something to us and that made us feel like we were making a difference. We were starting to raise a family and we had this idea that it would be nice to grow a school that would be something that we would feel is appropriate to send our own children. I pitched an idea to a group of about ten parents in December 1993 that was basically the outline of what would become Puget Sound Community School. I informed the inquiring parents that if we had five families commit by the end of February 1994, Melinda and I would give notice at our jobs and commit all of our resources to starting the school. We ended up getting those five families, and when we started PSCS in September 1994, we had ten and then added an eleventh family a month later and here we are now twenty-one-plus years later.

What Informs Puget Sound Community School?

The premise that I had when I started the school was that the best expert for an individual is the individual himself or herself. The idea being that students know themselves better than anyone else, but they need some tools to develop access to some of that awareness. I believe that everybody is born with a purpose and a sense of self, and that a big part of education is to help them find the language and tools to access that self-awareness. How do we help people become self-aware? My belief is that part of how we do that is to create an environment that's supportive and nurturing so people are naturally willing to take chances and to take risks. "Act with courage" is how we phrase it here. One way that I try to explain that concept to people is to consider what good parents do for their babies and toddlers. They create safe spaces and then they let their children explore. They may introduce certain things into the environment, but they more or less give their little children, babies, and toddlers a lot of freedom within a structured environment. That is what we try to do here: create a loving and nurturing space that has some criteria around it in terms of presence and that sort of thing. We have to develop a sense of self-awareness so we know what we want, what our passions are, and what we want to pursue, as opposed to just being and doing what someone tells us to do or getting on some sort of bandwagon that says this is what we should do or what we're supposed to do.

How Does This Get Done?

We start with the environment that really says to each child, "You are okay with who you are now. You do not have to be someone else, be who you are." We find different ways to celebrate that. We have a morning meeting in which individual appreciations are shared. We make time for people to really talk; we call it "toot your own horn" where we get to say things that we are interested in and doing. That's part of the environment that helps nurture this thing. There are regular advising sessions, so each of the students has one-on-one time with a member of the staff. A major purpose of these meetings is for the staff member to develop, to help the student know what they are interested in doing and help us learn how we can support them in doing that. And so that happens. Then again, we cannot assume any of these things, but we are always offering ideas and soliciting input from students, "What do you want to do? Here are some things we think you might be interested in. Here are things that I love to do." We bring people in from the community, and I tell them the one criterion I want them to honour when they come here is just to love what they do. What I want that to demonstrate is role modelling of someone pursuing something that they are interested in and encouraging students to be doing that as well. From that, we then create these different structures that help develop the curriculum, which is how the activities get scheduled and decided through a very elaborate process that is fully collaborative between the students and staff.

How Are Students Enabled to Develop Original Work?

The overarching idea here is for students to know themselves—to know themselves in community. We want students to think about how they do the things that are interesting and important to them while supporting others doing the same thing, even when some of those activities might not be interesting to me. It may seem like these are conflicting ideas, but in our environment, they are all part of the same thing. When students first apply, we have them create something original as part of their application. We are not interested in standardized tests. We are not interested in hearing what teachers in other settings have said about potential PSCS students. We want to know who they are and what interests them. They start by applying with a project of original work when they enter this school. So at the point of application, if they are an eighth grader, or roughly around age thirteen, we want them to complete a project, something that helps them say who they are and that can be shared. It is nothing elaborate, it is not difficult to do, we just want students to get in the mindset that here we want them to show things that they like doing. Anything could be a project, really. A recent example is from an eighth grade project from a student who was really interested in baking and who happened to have dyslexia. For him, it was something that he had grown up with that had defined him, so he made a series of cakes that demonstrated some of the challenges that he has had with reading. He then presented those in a community setting, which was pretty spectacular. In tenth grade, we ask students to collaborate with somebody else, so we encourage students to work together to create something that can be shared. The twelfth grade or senior project is the culmination of the learner's experience here and involves sharing something that they are passionately interested in. I describe the senior project as something students are going to do anyway because they just can't not do it. An ideal senior project is something that they are going to be doing because they are driven to do it.

On Teacher Training

My own teacher training experience was a nine-month program where we would end with both Washington and California state teaching certificates and with the majority of the work being hands-on in schools and in classrooms, as opposed to more theoretical study and teacher training. When we did our classroom work as a class group, we were adults working with adults and we would meet in places like the attic of an old house. And so it was; the feeling again is different, and that is part of what I mean by environment. When one goes into a traditional teacher-training class, they often experience a more sterile environment, sitting there and listening to someone talk a lot about theory and classroom management. When we start spending so much time training teachers on classroom management, we are missing the point. What typically is being taught is how to deal with the environment that has artificially been created. If we can create an environment that is more natural to humans, then we do not have to manage the behaviour, and then we do not have to spend so much time dealing with these issues. It typically takes two years to get a teaching certificate because so much time is spent training people to do things to help condition young people to not do what they are naturally inclined to do. When we combine all of that, it becomes a serpent that feeds itself in a way.

To be a teacher is to be fully human. I describe it as high character. I think that a lot of what the world and life does to us, be it schools or even society overall, is to cause us to compare ourselves to other standards outside ourselves. What I want when I hire teachers for PSCS is something I describe as "I want your numerator to align with your denominator." What we are constantly doing is trying to align our numerator with somebody else's denominator; we are constantly comparing ourselves to someone else. I hire people who have their numerators and denominators aligned. When we extend the mathematics metaphor, anything over itself in math, so obviously five over five or ten over ten, a hundred over a hundred, is all equal to one. It is all whole. It is one whole. How do we make a human being whole? Align their numerator and their denominator. If we do that, we have a natural teacher, a person who in that state is naturally going to do things that attract other human beings to them because of their alignment of being true to themselves. That is not rocket science; that is just allowing people to be people.

Most schools, when they hire, are hiring for a position that gets posted for a specific role or discipline. I would characterize it this way: it begins by drawing a circle like a target, with the outer ring being the position that is being posted, a grade seven science teacher, for example. The position is posted saying there is an opening for a science teacher with whatever criteria, etcetera, etcetera. Then the next ring, as we move toward the middle of the circle, might be more specific to the applicant's individualized experience. Then as we progress deeper and deeper toward the centre of the circle, the inner part of the person is revealed. The centre of the circle is the least important part considered for the position. So hiring is typically done from the outside in, with outside considerations taking precedence over the centre of the circle. My approach to this is the opposite. PSCS hires from the inside out. We are interested first in the core of the human being, then interested in what they might bring to the school. If their centre pieces are solid, the collaborative nature that happens among the teaching staff has incredible potential. You can't imagine what they'll create. Again, it is about creating the elements that are natural to letting human beings fully be who they are, and then everything else falls into place.

The Way Forward:
Implications for Global Education
and Its Transformation

DENNIS CHEEK

Dennis Cheek is a co-founder and executive director of the National Creativity Network, conceiver and co-chair of Global Creativity United (an informal global alliance of nine organizations spanning 160 nations), and Visiting Professor of Entrepreneurship and Innovation at IÉSEG School of Management in France. He has held leadership roles at the Ewing Marion Kauffman Foundation, John Templeton Foundation, state education departments of New York and Rhode Island, and Science Applications International Corporation (SAIC). Dennis has worked with thirty-two public and fifteen private institutions of higher education across nine nations on three continents, including service as a college trustee, advisor to the president of the United States, and teacher in three bachelor's, eleven master's, and five doctoral programs. He holds five degrees in biology, education, history, and theology, including a PhD from Pennsylvania State University and a PhD from Durham University. He has authored, edited, or contributed to over 800 publications.

A large number of academics, researchers, and educators have focused their curiosity, teaching, and intellectual skills to take up the difficult challenge of formulating theories of creative development that can inform and undergird teaching and learning efforts across age groups, cultures, disciplines, and contexts (Sefton-Green et. al, 2012). Is the framework for creative development described in this volume, using vivid examples from the practices of the author and others, correct? The simple answer is "We do not (yet) know." How should teachers, school administrators, policy makers, and other stakeholders (preeminently learners and their loved ones) respond to this dilemma? Let me offer an answer that draws upon the insights and exploits of three well-known, highly creative persons, two of whom I have been privileged to work with and the remaining one perhaps the best-known scientist of all time. Their lives and achievements serve as vivid examples that intersect all eight interrelated creative development strands described within this volume.

Albert Einstein's brilliant insights into the natural world were built upon an uncanny ability to engage in prolonged thought experiments whose very execution required consciously changing the ground on which the observer stood. By shifting perspectives, Einstein was able to discern matters that had eluded other investigators—some of whom undoubtedly possessed written qualifications, mathematical skills, and other talents superior to his own. As cited in Calaprice (2005), Einstein invoked concepts that had not been thought about before by asking what seemed to be innocent but exceedingly odd questions like "What if one were to run after a beam of light? What if one were riding on the beam? If one were to run fast enough, would it no longer move at all?" (p. 214). His profound and startling counterintuitive insights, backed up by a lot of difficult mathematics, have fuelled revolutions in our scientific and technical understanding across many domains of the sciences and engineering. His ideas spawned entirely new theories, questions, methods, measurements, and devices that show no sign of diminishing as we explore our universe and other possible universes in this new century and millennium.

The late Sir John Marks Templeton, one of the most successful and famous financial investors of all time, was born in a very small town in eastern Tennessee in the United States. Sir John was also knighted by the Queen of England for his additional outstanding work in philanthropy. He adopted as one of his core mottos the phrase "How little we know, how eager to learn." (Templeton, 2000, p. 12). This motto and others he used to guide his decisions and life derived from an even deeper insight. Human beings, he believed, collectively know less than one percent of what there is to know about god. Templeton hoped that, over the next two centuries, such knowledge would multiply a hundredfold, even while suspecting it would still hardly exceed one percent compared to what could be known. This core insight can be equally applied to describe the current state of human knowledge across various areas of human endeavour, including astronomy, biology, chemistry, economics, education, history, linguistics, mathematics, neuroscience, medicine, and psychology. This fundamental starting point of a cultivated humility in the face of reality enabled Sir John to ignore widely held, expert financial opinions and maintain a highly successful contrarian view toward investing (whether in financial markets or in philanthropy). It also enabled him to question virtually everything and to cultivate a lifelong and zestful thirst for himself and for the three foundations he created as part of his legacy to explore the vast terrain of the ninety-nine percent or more that is still to be known. A humble approach became a path to untold riches—both intellectual and financial—and wider human flourishing.

Born in Central Sulawesi, part of the vast archipelago nation of Indonesia, and fatherless by the age of twelve, Ciputra by Indonesian tradition goes by only one name. He graduated from Bandung Institute of Technology in Indonesia with a degree in architecture and went on to become one of Southeast Asia's best-known real estate developers and philanthropists. Ciputra is famous for his uncanny ability to look over a vast expanse of undeveloped or underdeveloped land and visualize thriving communities of businesses, homes, schools, universities, hospitals, parks, resorts, shopping facilities, and roads, which frequently equal or exceed over one-fifth to one-quarter of an entire city. His philanthropic vision is to cultivate four million additional entrepreneurs across his beloved country. They will create new businesses and millions of additional jobs needed to provide good livelihoods, foster educational and social opportunities, and improve quality of life within the fourth most populous nation on Earth.

So to return to our earlier question, what are the takeaways from these three world-class personages as applied to the concept of creative development described in this volume? Here are several to consider:

1. We can safely assume that ninety-nine percent of what there is to be known about creativity still lies ahead of us, including how best to cultivate and enhance it. Philosophers who have puzzled over the word *creativity* are themselves a bit bewitched and befuddled as to what it really means (e.g., two recent explorations by Martin (2016) and Singer (2011)). Creativity researchers (as distinguished from philosophers) are equally divided about various aspects of creativity (compare recent research summaries by Carayannis et. al, 2013; Kaufman & Sternberg, 2010; Runco, 2014; Runco & Pritzker, 2011; Sawyer, 2012; and Shalley, Hitt, & Zhou, 2016). These experts have cumulatively devoted hundreds of academic lifetimes to studying these matters, yet unassailable clarity of understanding and unanimity of opinion still elude us. Sir John's one-percent rule leaves us lots of room to vigorously apply this volume's framework for creative development in learning settings worldwide to expand our tacit knowledge and experience of creative development, while simultaneously encouraging and expanding human creativity in concert with learners everywhere.

2. From our earliest days on this planet, we all spend considerable waking hours in formal learning institutions we call "schools." Informal learning settings include museums and other cultural institutions, zoos and aquaria, and recreational facilities. But we should also consider religious institutions, neighbourhoods, families (both nuclear and extended), and other social groups. We learn an extraordinary amount in these informal settings that influences us throughout our lives. Virtually all humans before they even learn to walk are already observing and testing, curiously exploring, and coming to terms physically, mentally, socially, and emotionally with many new relationships, interactions, sights, sounds (including languages), smells, and objects in a dazzling array that we rarely stop to fully consider. Our imagination, creativity, and ability to innovate are already on full display. In this sense, we can find much in the creative development framework described in this book that genuinely builds on that which already exists in all of us. The issue then reduces to a straightforward question of whether these innate abilities can be further cultivated, enhanced, expanded, improved, reconfigured, consciously invoked, and critically examined. The author and thousands of people who think deeply about these matters, including our three distinguished exemplars, reply with a resounding "ABSOLUTELY!" This means that even if some of the details within this volume ultimately turn out to be not quite correct, there is little harm and likely considerable good to be gained by deploying the described creative development framework in our own sphere of influence both as learners ourselves and as people who regularly (formally or informally) teach others. These are physical and mental tools for improvement. Like any tool, they take practise to learn how, when, where, why, who, and for how long to use them in various contexts. This book provides helpful tools, a conceptual vocabulary, general guidelines, and real-world examples. Highly proficient tool users become that way through continued use, metacognitive awareness, insights that develop over time and (often only) through wide and deep experience, and, of course, persevering through failure. Even master carpenters still mismeasure or miscut wood, hit their fingers, bend nails, or miss studs from time to time. Failures, properly understood, are guideposts on the path to future success.

3. Changing our perspective on ourselves is perhaps most critical to the venture before us. Each of the three people I briefly called to your attention could have turned out so differently if they had

stayed within the presumed larger narrative into which they were born. No one, not even their parents and siblings, knew the extent of the latent and powerful creative potential lurking within them. Schools, homes, communities, and work environments, all exist as by-products of the activities of countless human beings who entered this world before us. Demographers generally believe that about 120 billion people preceded us. Virtually everything around us has been shaped and reshaped by those who have come before us (unless you are currently sitting in a very remote jungle, a small island in the Pacific, or shivering in Antarctica—and even in these places, you are still being indirectly affected in various ways by what humans before you have done). Einstein, Templeton, and Ciputra remind us of the simple fact that the future is never fully determined by the past. We can, do, and will make a difference—large or small—in the wider world as a result of our being here. What we choose to do, become, and leave behind as a legacy remains to be created. Schools and other institutions are serendipitous by-products of histories, people, issues, ideas, and circumstances from the past that continue in varying ways into the present human moment. None of them is entirely impervious to change, but all change starts somewhere (including those changes that brought us to the present). We can be potent agents of change beginning within the small arenas over which we have almost total control. Every teacher, for example, knows that when they close the door to their classroom (no matter what the grade level or the environment), what happens next in that space is known only to them and those whom they are among at that moment, in that place, at that particular time. This is an opportunity to begin taking the first steps in a journey toward unleashing in both controlled and uncontrolled ways the innate aptitudes, dispositions, and talents that we, and those with us, already possess. It is also an opportunity for further acquiring, improving, expanding, and exercising those same aptitudes, dispositions, and talents to co-create a different future than that which has come before. This volume equips us with a creative development toolkit, but we must be the ones to adapt it—seeking powerful results within our particular contexts.

4. All three of the signature individuals I discussed made their mark on the world and influenced much larger systems than those over which they had direct control. Educators, administrators, parents, policy makers, or students (of any age) have the potential to not just effect change among the few, but also to scale it to the

many. If you are a principal, school superintendent, or working at a state, provincial, or national level, you already know the small group of social network influencers you need to enlist for just such an effort. Dan Hunter of Hunter and Higgs LLC in Boston, Massachusetts, for example, has thus far successfully convinced the state legislatures of Oklahoma and Massachusetts to create and pass legislation that governors have signed, legislation that requires the state education departments to lead a process to create and implement a creativity index for schools. Working on the theory that what gets measured, gets done in schools, Hunter's singular effort has resulted in two states in quite different regions of the United States requiring schools to annually report to the public what they are doing to proactively improve the imagination, creativity, and innovation of their students. It is for just such a mandate that *Creative Development: Transforming Education through Design Thinking, Innovation, and Invention* can be applied at scale to realize the vision of our National Creativity Network for "a vibrant and flourishing North America where imagination, creativity, and innovation are routinely valued, skillfully applied, and continuously expanded." But of course, why stop at North America? This is where you come in, wherever you find yourself on planet Earth. So get out there and keep imagining, creating, and innovating for yourself and with others toward a brighter, more productive future! (And let everyone know how your journey goes.)

REFERENCES

Calaprice, A. (Ed.). (2005). *The new quotable Einstein*. Princeton, NJ: Princeton University Press.

Carayannis, E. G., Dubina, I., Seel, N., Campbell, D., & Uzunidis, D. (Eds.) (2013). *Encyclopedia of creativity, invention, innovation, and entrepreneurship*. New York: Springer Academic, four volumes. http://dx.doi.org/10.1007/978-1-4614-3858-8

Kaufman, J. C. & Sternberg, R. J. (Eds.). (2010). *The Cambridge handbook of creativity*. New York: Cambridge University Press. http://dx.doi.org/10.1017/CBO9780511763205

Martin, L. (2016). *Creativity: A critical realist perspective*. New York: Routledge.

Runco, M. A. (2014). *Creativity: Theories and themes: Research, development, and practice* (2nd ed.). Waltham, MA: Academic Press, 2e.

Runco, M. A., & Pritzker, S. R. (Eds.) (2011). *Encyclopedia of creativity*, vols. 1–2 (2nd ed.). New York: Academic Press/Elsevier.

Sawyer, R.K. (2012). *Explaining creativity: The science of human innovations* (2nd ed.). New York: Oxford University Press.

Sefton-Green, J., Thomson, P., Jones, K., & Bresler, L. (Eds.). (2012). *The Routledge international handbook of creative learning*. New York: Routledge.

Shalley, C., Hitt, M. A., & Zhou, J. (Eds.). (2016). *The Oxford handbook of creativity, innovation, and entrepreneurship*. New York: Oxford University Press.

Singer, I. (2011). *Modes of creativity: Philosophical perspectives*. Cambridge, MA: The MIT Press.

Templeton, S. J. (2000). *Possibilities of over one hundredfold more spiritual information: The humble approach in theology and science*. Philadelphia: Templeton Foundation Press.

Flying into the Unknown

ROBERT KELLY

Creative Development: Transforming Education through Design Thinking, Innovation, and Invention is filled with invitations to embark on a transformative journey to fundamentally change educational practice and embrace an educational culture of collaborative creativity. This goes beyond thinking outside a box, as creativity involves original action and production. It involves a fundamental belief in the infinite creative potentials and interrelatedness of everyone. It involves a fundamental belief in the power of collaborative creativity to effect perpetual, positive change. It points to a fundamental shift to empowering educators and learners to create a culture of hope, imagination, exploration, experimentation, and invention. Gone will be the fear of outcomes unknown, as they become welcome spaces and opportunities for innovation and invention for positive change. The journey will be exciting and enjoyable.

Finally, thank you for engaging on this journey of exploration on Air Creative Development, the only airline where destinations are unknown. If flying into the unknown is your home, then welcome home.

Glossary

adhocracy: a flattened, amorphous organizational structure designed to enable fluid innovation and creative practice

atelier: an interdisciplinary studio space introduced into the Reggio Emilia preschools by Loris Malaguzzi

assessment anxiety: the fear of appearing less competent in front of peers because of overt comparison due to assessment

assessment by metaphor: an example of formative assessment to encourage dialogic assessment whereby a metaphor is applied to a learning outcome to stimulate discussion and feedback on student initiatives

assessment of learning: summative in nature; used to confirm what students know and can do to demonstrate whether they have achieved the curriculum outcomes and, occasionally, to show how they are ranked in relation to others (WNCP, 2006; Ontario, 2013)

assessment for learning: typically formative in nature; designed to give teachers information to modify and differentiate teaching and learning activities, acknowledging that individual students learn in idiosyncratic ways (WNCP, 2006; Ontario, 2013)

assessment as learning: a process of developing and supporting metacognition for students focusing on the role of the student as the critical connector between assessment and learning; involves students monitoring their own learning and using the feedback from this monitoring to make adjustments, adaptations, and even major changes in what they understand (WNCP, 2006; Ontario, 2013).

big-C creativity: creativity that has considerable impact in a field or discipline

brainstorming: the production of ideas or problem resolutions through group conversation and interaction

collaborative development: one of eight interrelated creative development strands involving the development of the capacity to engage in social, shared creative production through the exchange of ideas exemplified by generative, flexible, and elaborative thinking

connectivity: the capacity for interconnection between systems, processes, or concepts

convergent thinking: the process of narrowing down a list of alternatives to select those with the greatest potential for problem resolution through comparative analysis

co-operative/reflective assessment: a type of co-reflective formative assessment characterized by writing-intense dialogic assessment in which key developmental and process questions are developed between the student and educator specific to a creative exploration and are answered by both as points of discussion

creative confidence: the positive feeling derived from validation received through taking risks and recognizing that all ideas that one creates have value; a term associated with design thinking practice at Stanford's d.school

creative development: the growth of one's creative capacity from adaptive/intuitive creativity to encompass the ability to engage in increasingly complex sustained creative practice

creative sustain development: one of eight interrelated creative development strands involving the capacity to engage in recurrent iterations of idea generation and form experimentation with increasing complexity over extended periods of time

creativity: the sequence of thoughts and actions that leads to a novel, adaptive production (Lubart, 2000)

critical thinking: the ability to explore a problem, question, or situation; integrate all the available information about it; arrive at a solution or hypothesis; and justify one's position (Warnick & Inch, 1994)

critical/analytical thinking development: one of eight interrelated creative development strands involving the application of critical-thinking skills to compare and assess potential solutions to a problem

design process: the methods and processes for investigating problems, acquiring information, analyzing knowledge, developing alternatives, and prototyping in the design and planning fields across a wide range of disciplines; also contextual creative problem solving; defined by IDEO as the stages of discovery, interpretation, ideation, experimentation, and evolution

diagnostic assessment: a type of assessment often used in the context of detecting basic skill deficits and learner strengths to inform remediation and differentiated instructional strategies

dialogic assessment: a form of assessment based on dialogue between the student and the educator as mentor or coach that is focused on the development of student work

discipline complexity development: one of eight creative development strands involving the growth in understanding of the content, processes, and complexities of a discipline

disposition: the tendency to act in a certain manner under given circumstances, or when something is dispositional in nature, there is an increased likelihood that effective actions will be taken when confronted with problematic situations (Costa & Kallick, 2014)

dissociation: an emotional detachment from the learning environment

divergent thinking: the expansive development of alternative resolutions through idea generation and form experimentation

divergent-convergent pulse: in idea generation, a series of repeated divergent-convergent phases in which numerous ideas are generated and then a small number are chosen as promising solutions

early closure: the tendency to close the idea generation process early; usually the result of conditioning developed when most learning experience outcomes are known

elaboration: the ability to add complexities to existing forms

enterprise: a disposition or initiative that reflects the tackling of difficult or complex problems in new ways

entrepreneurship: the pursuit of opportunity beyond resources controlled; involving a mindset to imagine new ways to solve problems and create value (Eisenmann, 2013)

experimentational development: one of eight interrelated creative development strands involving a growth of the capacity to consistently test out ideas as potential solutions to set problems in the medium of the field or discipline where the creative production occurs

extrinsic motivation: motivation for task engagement and task completion that is external to the student

feedback spiral: a recursive, cyclical process designed for learners and educators to constantly gather data that is analyzed and interpreted for self-learning and self-modifying actions

flexibility: the ability to abandon old ways and adapt to a new way of thinking

fluency: the capacity to effortlessly generate ideas and alternatives in creative practice

formative assessment: a range of formal and informal assessment procedures that typically involves qualitative feedback (rather than scores) to enhance student development in process engagement and performance

fourth sector business: a business approach that integrates social and environmental aims, often embodying features like fair compensation, environmental responsibility, community service, and contribution of profits to the common good

generative development: one of eight interrelated creative development strands involving a growth of the capacity to continuously generate ideas as potential solutions to problems

historiometrics: a quantitative method of statistical analysis of an individual's accomplishments that places one's creative practice on a vertical scale of importance relative to the fields where the practice occurred

hypercompetitiveness: a cultural phenomenon in which there is an overemphasis on being at the top of vertical comparison hierarchies

hyperconsumption: a cultural phenomenon in which a disproportionate focus is placed on the accumulation of commodities, information, wealth, etcetera

idea mapping: a graphical method of tracking the intersection of ideas with other stimuli to observe the development of new idea combinations and the creation of new ideas

ideation: a purposeful stage for the generation of ideas and alternatives

ideation waves: the compounding of an idea as it goes through successive hybridizations by combining with new ideas and continually creating new iterations

illumination: a time of convergence when thoughts come together for potential solutions

imagination: a special feature or form of human thought characterized by the ability of an individual to reproduce images or concepts originally derived from basic senses but now reflected in one's consciousness as memories, fantasies, and future plans

incubation: an active subconscious stage where ideas are reorganized and elaborated upon

innovation: an application of creative thinking in which an idea is introduced and applied to a situation that benefits the job, process, or organization, or the development of a product where this occurs

innovative creativity: a form of sustained creative practice involving the redesign or modification of an existing form, product, or system; usually associated with business and industry

interdisciplinary: creative practice across more than one discipline

interpretive creativity: a form of sustained creative practice involving the redesign, modification, evolution, or interpretation of existing work or forms often associated with the arts

intrinsic motivation: the drive to engage in a learning experience or creative exploration that comes from within an individual through substantial personal interest

intuitive/adaptive creativity: the creative acts that are part of everyday living

invention: the application of creativity that leads to the development of something new across any number of fields or disciplines

inventive creativity: a form of sustained creative practice involving the creation of original work across disciplines

inventive momentum: a strong, creative dynamic that develops in high-stimuli, highly generative, and experimentational environments

inventive structure: the defined parameters of a creative exploration that emerges after considerable idea generation and experimentation

learning creatively: the development of novel responses or solutions to curriculum content problems or dilemmas largely through creative problem solving

learning to create: the creation of personally meaningful original work through sustained creative practice that goes well beyond the demands of traditional curriculum content

little-c creativity: the creativity that every human being engages in on a daily basis

machine bureaucracy: a management structure with a high degree of formalization and specialization in which decisions are largely made at the top level and organization output is largely focused on standardization

makerspace: an interdisciplinary studio space that is a collaborative work area for tinkering, design, and invention

metacognition: thinking about and understanding one's own cognitive processes

metaphorical thinking: a mental process in which comparisons are made between qualities of objects that are usually considered in separate classifications, enabling new constructs to be formed and comfort with ambiguity

mindshift: a move from designing for ego-centric purposes to broader human-centred goals

originality: a creative response that is novel, remote, and statistically unusual, or a departure from previous responses relative to an individual's previous creative output or relative to a field or discipline

outcomes known: a learning experience characterized by the restating and retelling of known responses

outcomes unknown: a learning experience characterized by explorations that are set in motion without exact knowledge of the form of the final outcome

passion: an intense emotional connection to engaged creative production

plussing: in collaborative idea generation, the act of accepting any idea and adding to it

pre-inventive structure: the loosely defined parameters for a creative exploration within a field or discipline that are wide enough to enable further play and exploration but defined enough to prevent floundering from lack of focus

preparation: the notion of initial problem setting or dealing with a discordance that requires some sort of resolution for which the outcome is unknown

principle of infinite potentials: the belief that any idea has the potential for an infinite number of combinations and recombinations with other ideas, and a corresponding belief that as the creator of ideas, anyone has infinite potentials specific to ideation and ultimately to creative production

principle of interrelatedness: a foundational belief that every organic and inorganic entity is connected, requiring a heightened state of empathy to enable collaborative, creative problem solving

principle of perpetual change: a foundational understanding that education should enable participants to adapt to perpetual change and to create positive, perpetual change

prototyping: a preliminary design form to test out problem-resolution concepts to enable design refinement

redefinition: the capacity to give up traditional interpretations and invent new ones

research/investigative development: one of eight interrelated creative development strands involving growth in the capacity to bring discipline knowledge and stimuli to sustained creative practice through a disposition that is relentless in collecting data from any source

self-instigative development: one of eight interrelated creative development strands involving growth in the capacity to engage in an intrinsically motivated, creative exploration that is intellectually and emotionally meaningful and relevant

skew effects: engrained behavioural patterns or organizational predispositions that undermine transformative initiatives

statusless environment: a learning environment that suppresses vertical hierarchies for the purpose of providing a safe, collaborative space for participants to be vulnerable in the sharing of ideas while precluding harsh judgement

STEM: an acronym for the disciplines of science, technology, engineering, and mathematics, often used in the context of improving science and technology development in education; STEM becomes STEAM when A for art and design is added to the acronym

summative assessment: a form of assessment that demonstrates the extent of a learner's success in meeting the assessment criteria used to gauge the intended learning outcomes of a module or program, and which contributes to a quantifiable final grade

sustained creativity: the capacity to engage in successive iterations of idea generation and experimentation in creative practice over time

tinkering: exploratory and experimental repair, making, and inventing in a wide range of media

unschooling: a purely democratic form of schooling in which learning decisions lie almost completely with the student

verification: the point in the creative process at which thoughts are given form to test whether they actually work as solutions

REFERENCES

Costa, A. L., & Kallick, B. (2014). Dispositions: Reframing teaching and learning. Thousand Oaks: Corwin Press.

Eisenmann, T. R. (2013). *Entrepreneurship: A working definition*. Harvard Business Review. Retrieved from hbr.org.

Lubart, T. I. (2000). Models of creative process: Past, present and future. Creativity Research Journal, 13 (3–4), 295–308.

Ontario Ministry of Education. (2013). Learning for all: A guide to effective assessment and instruction for all students. Toronto: Government of Ontario.

Warnick, B., & Inch, E. (1994). Critical thinking and communication (2nd ed.). New York: MacMillan.

WNCP (2006). Rethinking classroom assessment with purpose in mind. Western and Northern Canadian Protocol for Collaboration in Education. Retrieved from www.wncp.ca.

About the Author

Educator, author, and artist Robert Kelly is an associate professor at the University of Calgary in western Canada. His research is focused on bringing the concept of creative development into the mainstream of educational practice from early childhood to post-secondary education. This work has involved the design and coordination of the transformative Creative Development in Educational Practice and Design Thinking for Innovation graduate programs in the Werklund School of Education. His current work is focused on transforming educational culture through reconceptualizing schooling and learning experience design around the concepts of creativity and design practice.

Robert has previously edited *Educating for Creativity: A Global Conversation* (2012) and *Creative Expression, Creative Education: Creativity as a Primary Rationale for Education* (2008).

He is currently director of the Alberta Creativity Network, where he collaborates to promote the development of creativity and design practice across the education, health care, culture, and creative economy sectors.

Robert has a passion for teaching and is profiled on the University of Calgary's Great Teachers website. He is also a featured keynote speaker and consultant nationally and internationally in the areas of creative development and design thinking, in which he engages diverse organizations in an enthusiastic journey drawn from his personal and professional creative practice.

Contact: rkelly@ucalgary.ca Website: www.robertkelly.ca